Asmad rūpa sa
svātmanātmani.....
Śivaḥ karotu nijayā
Namaḥ Śaktyā tatātmane
v.1 Śiva Dṛiśti

"Let Shiva, who is myself,
do pranam to His real nature,
to Universal Shiva, by His
own Shakti, for removing
bondage and limitation,
which is Shiva."

Swami Lakshmanjoo
Om Namah Shivaya
Sadgurunatha Maharaj ki jay!

Śivastotrāvalī
of
Utpaladeva

Swami Lakshman Joo
(1907–1991)

Śivastotrāvalī
of
Utpaladeva
A Mystical Hymn of Kashmir

Exposition by
Swami Lakshman Joo

Transcribed and edited by
Ashok Kaul

With musical rendering in a CD by
Manju Sundaram

D.K. Printworld (P) Ltd.
New Delhi

Cataloging in Publication Data — DK
[Courtesy: D.K. Agencies (P) Ltd. <docinfo@dkagencies.com>]

Utpala, fl. 900–950.
[Śivastotrāvalī. English & Sanskrit]
Śivastotrāvalī of Utpaladeva : a mystical hymn of Kashmir / exposition by Swami Lakshman Joo; transcribed and edited by Ashok Kaul.
p. cm.
Text of Śivastotrāvalī in Sanskrit (Devanagari and roman); translation, exposition and introductory matter in English.
Hymns on Śiva (Hindu deity).
Includes index.
ISBN 13: 9788124604670 (Hb)
ISBN 10: 8124604673 (Hb)

1. Siva (Hindu deity) — Prayers and devotions — Early works to 1800. 2. Kashmir Śaivism — Prayers and devotions — Early works to 1800. 3. Hindu hymns, Sanskrit — Early works to 1800. 4. Hindu hymns, Sanskrit — Early works to 1800 — Translations into English. 5. Utpala, fl. 900–950. Śivastotrāvalī. I. Lakshman Joo, Swami, 1907–1991. II. Kaul, Ashok. III. Title.

DDC 294.538 22

ISBN 13: 978-81-246-0467-0 (Hb) ISBN 10: 81-246-0467-3
ISBN 13: 978-81-246-0468-7 (Pb) ISBN 10: 81-246-0468-1
First published in India in 2008

Published and printed by:
D.K. Printworld (P) Ltd.
Regd. Office: 'Sri Kunj', F-52, Bali Nagar
Ramesh Nagar Metro Station
New Delhi-110 015
Phones: (011) 2545-3975; 2546-6019; *Fax*: (011) 2546-5926
E-mail: dkprintworld@vsnl.net
Website: www.dkprintworld.com

प्राक्कथन

साक्षात् शिव-रूप श्री गुरुदेव ईश्वर-स्वरूप जी के कई वर्षों में कहे गये वचनामृत को अक्षरश: लेखबद्ध करना गुरु-कृपा का ही प्रसाद होता है । भगवत्-प्रेरणा से किसी भाग्यशाली शिष्य में इस कार्य की स्फुरणा अनायास हो जाती है और वह विवश हो कर अपनी इच्छा को सफल बनाने में सक्षम हो जाता है ।

काश्मीर शैव-दर्शन के प्रत्यभिज्ञाकार भगवान् उत्पलदेव जी कृत शिवस्तोत्रावली ग्रन्थ से हमारे गुरुदेव अति लगाव रखते थे । वे स्वयं इस ग्रन्थ का यदा-कदा आद्योपांत पाठ किया करते थे और अपने शिष्यों से भी पाठ करवाते थे । कश्मीरी भाषा में इन श्लोकों का रहस्यार्थ मार्मिक रूपतया कहते थे । कभी कभी आंगल-भाषा में भी इन श्लोकों का अर्थ समझाते थे । महाराज जी के मुखारविंद से निकले हुए उन्हीं एक-एक शब्दों का संकलन करके श्री अशोक जी कौल ने, जो स्वामी जी महाराज के परम-भक्त हैं, लेखबद्ध किया और समय आने पर पुस्तक का रूप दे दिया । कई वर्षों से अशोक जी इस कार्य में रत रहे । फल यह हुआ कि गुरुदेव के रस-युक्त आंगल-भाषा में कहे गये वचनामृत साकार बन कर पुस्तक की आकृति में परिणत हो गये ।

अशोक जी कौल सैनिक-विभाग में एक वरिष्ठ पदाधिकारी हैं । बचपन से शैव-संप्रदाय के अनुयायी रहे हैं । आस्तिक विचारों से भूषित होने से हमारे गुरुदेव के व्याख्यानों में रुचि रखते हैं । कई वर्षों से वे अपने समय का सदुपयोग करके इसी कार्य में लग गये । फल यह हुआ कि पुस्तक छप कर सहृदय भक्तों के सम्मुख आ गई । इसे गुरु प्रसाद समझ कर पढ़िये, मनन करिये तथा उत्पलदेव जी के निर्विकल्प हृदय में विचरण करिये । गुरुवर्य ने अपने अनुभव की कसौटी पर परख कर इन श्लोकों में वर्णित रहस्यों को सरल शब्दों में कह कर सोने पर सुहागे का काम किया है ।मैंने इस पुस्तक को आद्योपांत पढ़ा । मन अति हर्षित हुआ । हृदय से अशोक जी को आशीर्वाद देते हुए मैं विराम ले रही हूँ । गुरुदेव इन्हें विमर्श-

परायण बनाये रखें। इनके साथ ही मैं सुश्री बेटिना जी, सरला जी तथा आयुष्मान मृणाल जी को भी आशीर्वाद दे रही हूँ, जिन्होंने इस पुस्तक को संवारने में अशोक जी का हाथ बटाया है।

शिवरात्रि महापर्व
५.३.२००८, फरीदाबाद

गुरु-कृपावगाहिणी
प्रभा देवी

Foreword

It is only with the grace and blessing of Guru Īśvara Svarūpa who was the manifestation of the living Śiva that it was possible to render his oral divine teachings into words in the form of a book. Through godly inspiration some fortunate disciple suddenly has the uncontrollable desire to complete this task and he succeeds to fulfil it.

Our Gurudeva greatly loved the *Śivastotrāvalī* which was composed by the great master of Kashmir Śaiva philosophy Utpaladeva, the author of *Īśvarapratyabhijñā*. Swami Lakshman Joo used to recite this text with great devotion and would urge his disciples to do the same. He would reveal the secret and essence of these verses in Kashmiri and would sometimes teach their meaning in English also. Shri Ashok Kaul who is Swamiji's ardent devotee transcribed each word uttered by the divine master and gave it the form of a book at the appropriate time. Ashokji was absorbed in this work for many years. As a result the essence of the nectar of Swamiji's words taught in English took the form of a book.

Shri Ashok Kaul is a senior officer of the armed forces. He has been a Śaiva devotee since childhood. Being spiritually inspired, he showed interest in Gurudeva's lectures. Having spent several years fruitfully in this task he was able to present this book for the perusal of sincere devotees. Looking upon this book as a gift from Swamiji, one should read it, concentrate on it and reflect upon the mind of Utpaladeva which was beyond mundane mental processes. By testing these verses on the touchstone of his own experience, Gurudeva revealed their secrets in simple words and enhanced their value immensely.

I have read this book from beginning to end and derived great joy from it. As I conclude this foreword may Gurudeva grant Col. Kaul the absorption of awareness. I convey my blessings also to Sarla Kumar, Bettina Bäumer and Mrinal Kaul who have lent a helping hand in producing this book.

Śivarātri 2008 **Prabha Devi**
Faridabad

Preface

THE current volume is based on the transcription of the explanation of *Śivastotrāvalī* by Īśvarasvarūpa Swami Lakshman Joo, the greatest exponent of Kashmir Śaivism of modern times.

Śivastotrāvalī is a collection of hymns dedicated to Lord Śiva by Ācārya Utpaladeva, a great Śaivite master intensely in love with Lord Śiva and earnestly craving to be one with Him. The book comprises 450 verses arranged in twenty chapters. Each verse is soaked in the nectar of his intense devotion for the Lord and extreme craving for God-consciousness. The book represents his direct and uninhibited one-way dialogue with Lord Śiva, projecting his problems, one at a time and seeking His indulgence in getting over these.

Each verse depicts a problem and a request for its resolution. The problem starts in a verse and ends in that verse. The next verse describes yet another problem that he wants to be resolved. He seeks solution of all his problems on the spiritual path, all obstacles on the path to become one with Lord Śiva. He is not worried about the problems that stare him in the face on his worldly path. He is ready to face whatever crises come his way in this world but he wants his spiritual path to be obstacle-free.

Gurudeva's extraordinary reverence for *Śivastotrāvalī* is only too well known. He once said, "Leave me alone in the woods with a *feran*[1] and *Śivastotrāvalī*, I don't need anything."

1. *Feran* is the Kashmiri woollen dress.

Every attempt has been made not to miss out on any detail and to include all the discussion pertaining to a particular verse alongside its meaning and not as separate footnotes. This has been done for ease of understanding and to avoid interruption and distraction. Only explanatory notes have been placed in footnotes.

Every effort has been made to retain the original lucid style, childlike simplicity and the keen sense of humour of Gurudeva. The reader may occasionally find a bit of repetition in the text that has deliberately not been discarded to retain the freshness and the smooth flow of the original text. Those conversant with his unique style would feel as if he is actually talking to them.

At the lotus feet of Gurudeva.

Ashok Kaul

Contents

प्राक्कथन v

— प्रभा देवी

Foreword vii

— *Prabha Devi*

Preface ix

— *Ashok Kaul*

Acknowledgements xiii

— *Editor*

Introduction 1

— *Bettina Bäumer*

1. Bhaktivilāsa Stotra : The Joy of Devotion 19

2. Sarvātmaparibhāvana Stotra : Contemplation of the All-in-All 33

3. Praṇayaprasāda Stotra : Supplication with Reverence 50

4. Surasodbala Stotra : The Strength of Divine Nector 62

5. Svabalanideśana Stotra : Longing for One's Own Strength 81

6. Adhvavisphuraṇa Stotra : Clearing of the Path 98

7. Vidhuravijaya Stotra : Overcoming Separation 103

8. Alaukikodbalana Stotra : The Transcendent Power 110

9. Svātantryavijaya Stotra : The Glory of Freedom 119

10. Avicchedabhaṅga Stotra : Breaking the Continuity 131

11. Autsukyaviśvasita Stotra : Longing for Assurance 144

12. Rahasyanirdeśa Stotra : Revealing the Secret 155

13. Saṁgraha Stotra : In Summing Up 176

14. Jaya Stotra : Hymn of Glorification 188

15. Bhakti Stotra : The Song of Devotion 203

16. Pāśānudbheda Stotra : Breaking the Fetters 213

17. Divyakrīḍābahumāna Stotra : Celebrating the Divine Play 226

18. Āviṣkāra Stotra : Revealing Hymn 246

19. Udyotanābhidhāna Stotra : The Meaning Revealed 258

20. Carvaṇābhidhāna Stotra : Savouring the Meaning 267

Śloka Index (श्लोकानुक्रमणिका) 278

Acknowledgments

I am grateful to Sri Dinanath ji Ganju who recorded Swamiji's lectures and for bringing the tapes to the public domain, and to Prabha Deviji for kindly writing the Preface. Dr. Sarla Kumar has once again checked the transcript with the tapes, and Mrinal Kaul has corrected the proofs of the Sanskrit text and transliteration. Dr. Bettina Bäumer has agreed to contribute an introduction and she has read the entire proofs.

Finally, our thanks are due to Mr Susheel K. Mittal, the publisher, who has taken every care to bring out this book in the best possible quality.

Editor

Introduction

Bettina Bäumer

THE present book is a unique testimony to the living spiritual tradition of non-dualist Śaivism of Kashmir, as it was embodied in its last master, Swami Lakshman Joo. He spent a lifetime with this mystical hymn of Utpaladeva and taught it to his disciples and students at many occasions. His exposition and interpretation reflects his personal experience.

The purpose of this introduction is only to familiarize the reader with the background of the text and its author, in the context of the philosophy of Recognition (*pratyabhijñā*).

The Author

Utpaladeva (dated *circa* the end of the ninth–middle of tenth century) was no doubt one of the greatest philosophers of Kashmir who established the School of Recognition or Pratyabhijñā on a solid and systematic basis. He was a disciple of Somānanda who was really the founder of this philosophy, although he does not use the term *pratyabhijñā* in the technical sense in his *Śivadṛṣṭi*.[1] Therefore the Pratyabhijñā School is rightly associated with Utpaladeva and his fundamental text, the *Īśvarapratyabhijñā Kārikā* (Verses on the Recognition of the Lord), and its great commentaries by Abhinavagupta, the *Vimarśinī* and *Vivṛti Vimarśinī*.[2] That this school attained

1. It occurs only once, in IV.120a without the technical meaning.

2. On the *Vivṛti* by Utpaladeva which is lost in its entirety, only fragments of manuscripts have been found.

recognition far beyond the geographical and historical limits of Kashmir is clear from the fact that it was incorporated by Mādhava in his *Sarvadarśanasaṁgraha* in the fourteenth century in south India. His philosophical work includes also the *Siddhitrayī*, namely the *Ajaḍapramātṛsiddhi*, the *Īśvarasiddhi*, and the *Sambandhasiddhi*, where he establishes proof for the existence of the Lord and the nature of Consciousness.

But who was this Utpaladeva about whom Abhinavagupta, his grand-disciple, has spoken with such great veneration and respect? Unlike Abhinavagupta who gives many autobiographical details in the long colophons of some of his works, the case is different with Utpaladeva. We only know that he was the son of Udayākara,[3] and his mother's name was Vāgīśvarī, and she is called a *yoginī*. Hence he must have been endowed with divine qualities right from his birth. His family lived in Srinagar, north of Hariparvat, the seat of Śārikādevī. Utpaladeva was married, his son Vibhramākara was also his disciple.[4] This is the scant information about his life.

The Śivastotrāvalī

Even if we do not know much about his biography, we do have an important source about his spiritual life where he reveals himself as a mystic in very personal terms: that is his *Śivastotrāvalī* or a collection of his hymns to Śiva. This text is one of the greatest mystical documents not only of Śaivism, not only of Indian spirituality, but of mysticism in general. We know that many Indian philosophers have also composed devotional hymns, thus complementing their more dry argumentative philosophical texts. But few of them have

3. Cf.*Īśvarapratyabhijñā Kārikā*, IV.4.3 (colophon).

4. Cf. *Śivadṛṣṭi Vṛtti*, p. 2.

attained the spontaneity, the uninhibited outburst of mystical experience, the intensity of feeling, and the immediate touch of personal experience as the *Śivastotrāvalī* (to talk only of Sanskrit literature, for we do have mystical songs in the vernacular languages in the Sant literature, in the same tradition the *Vākh* or Sayings of Lallā or Lal Dêd).

Kṣemarāja, in the introduction to his *Vivṛti* commentary, explains the composition of the *Stotrāvalī*. He calls Utpaladeva, the author of *Īśvarapratyabhijñā*, his *parameṣṭhī guru* (i.e. *paramaguru* of Abhinavagupta), and describes him as one "who has always had the direct realization of the Great Lord as his own Self" (*satata-sākṣātkṛta-svātma-maheśvaraḥ*). From the same introduction we learn, what must have been current knowledge in the tradition at his time, that Utpala composed the *Saṁgrahastotra*, *Jayastotra* and *Bhaktistotra* (thirteenth, fourteenth and fifteenth Stotra) at the request of his disciples who were desirous of attaining the same state. He calls these *āhnikastutisūktāni*, "Hymns of praise divided in chapters," lit. to be recited in a day (*āhnika*, as also the chapters of the *Tantrāloka*). The remaining hymns consist of independent verses (*muktaka*) which his disciples Śrī Rāma and Ādityarāja arranged in some order, and Śrī Viśvāvartta put into the sequence of twenty *stotra*s, giving them titles of his own. He states that this is also the reason why the *Saṁgrahastotra* (and the other two composed by Utpaladeva in their transmitted form) have enjoyed traditionally the greatest fame and popularity. This is true even in the living tradition up to the twentieth century, where in the Ishvar Ashram in Srinagar, Swami Lakshman Joo used to teach these *stotra*s and make his disciples recite them regularly.

Since most of these verses were the spontaneous outpouring of their author in states of ecstasy and devotional emotion, they do not follow any logical order or, with a few exceptions, a single theme. The irregularity of metres within a *stotra*, or even irregular metres,[5] show that his concern was not poetry (of which he was perfectly capable), but the spontaneous expression of his inner experience, which could not be bound even by the exigencies of Sanskrit metre.

Speaking of the living tradition, the *Stotrāvalī* or *Utpala Stotrāvalī*, as it is often called, also in manuscripts, is one of the most popular texts among Kashmiri Śaivites, who recite at least one *stotra* daily and who know many verses by heart. The collective recitation on festive occasions is impressive, and one can see many devotees with tears in their eyes as they are moved by the text they are reciting. This popularity is also testified by the number of manuscripts preserved, maybe more than any other important text of the school. The continuity of the tradition and the importance of the text can also be seen in a verse by the south-Indian disciple of Abhinavagupta, the ascetic Madhurāja (eleventh century), who praises the work in the following verse:

> Though there are over thousands of
> streams of beautiful verses,
> none at all compares to that
> celestial river, the *Stotrāvalī*.
> As soon as it passes through the *tīrtha* of the ear
> it purifies the soul of man,
> and flows on to the throat,
> where lies the city of Lord Śrīkaṇṭha.[6]
>
> — transl. Rhodes Bailly, p. 25

---

5. E.g. *Stotra*, 7. 4-5.

6. *Śāstra-parāmarśa of Madhurāja-yogin*, v. 8 cited in K.C. Pandey, *Abhinavagupta: A Historical and Philosophical Study*, Varanasi (Chowkhamba Sanskrit Series Office), 2nd ed. 1963, p. 765. The Sanskrit text reads:

→

No attempt has been made so far to relate the philosophical texts of Utpaladeva to his mystical and devotional hymns. The reason is the generally accepted dichotomy between philosophy and devotion, and mysticism is considered too emotional to be mixed with technical philosophy. Should this dichotomy be mistaken in most cases, it is even more so in the case of non-dualist Kashmir Śaivism where all the great exponents were mystics as well as philosophers who were speaking from direct experience and providing philosophical arguments to establish their position. R. Torella writes in his introduction to the *Īśvarapratyabhijñā Kārikā* of "the extraordinary intensity of his hymns" and says further:

> In a sense Utpaladeva inaugurates what was to become a salient feature of the whole Trika in Abhinavagupta's synthesis: namely the tendency not to constitute a monolithic doctrine and a world of religious experience to oppose en bloc everything that does not coincide with it (as in the *ekāntin* trends) but to distinguish planes, that are hierarchically ordered but in which the "higher" does not automatically cancel the "lower" (as Somānanda had already said, Śiva is everywhere, even in differentiation, pain and hell). This is the perspective of the *paramādvaita*, such an elevated viewpoint that it does not fear what is different from itself, is not put in a critical position by it, is not forced to make a choice. If we take the *Īśvara Siddhi*, then we find a still different face. Were it not for its certain attribution, we would never suspect that the refined Naiyāyika speaking here is the same person as the Śaiva theologian in the *ĪPK* or the *bhakta* of the *Śivastotrāvalī*.[7]

→ *santyeva sūktisaritaḥ paritaḥ sahasrāḥ*
stotrāvalī surasarit sādṛśī na kācit ।
yā karṇatīrthamastiśayya punāti puṁsaḥ
śrīkaṇṭhanāthanagarī-mupakaṇṭhayanti ॥

7. R. Torella. *The Īśvarapratyabhijñā Kārikā* . . . ., Introduction, p. xxi.

The personal confession which Utpaladeva makes in the very first verse of the *Kārikās*, in the place of the usual *maṅgalaśloka*, immediately relates this work to his experience:

> Having somehow attained the state of servant of the Lord and desiring the good of the whole of mankind, I shall make possible the awakening of the recognition of the Lord — by giving it logical justification — which brings about the achievement of all perfection.[8]

His typical understatement *kathaṁcit* is commented in his own *Vṛtti* by *parameśvaraprasādāt*, "by grace of the Supreme Lord," and this is precisely the starting point of the entire philosophy. The various aspects of this very grace will be expressed in his *Stotrāvalī*. But what is important in this statement is that he does not consider the grace received as his personal achievement, rather he is impelled to share it with others, with all humankind. His motivation to compose this text — as also Abhinavagupta's in several of his works — is precisely to uplift mankind, in some sense comparable to the Mahāyāna Buddhist *bodhisattva* ideal. Then also the expression "servanthood of the Lord" (*maheśvarasya dāsyam*) should not suggest a dualistic interpretation. As we see in the *Stotrāvalī*, the language of humility and of *bhakti* is not contradictory to the non-dualism of *pratyabhijñā*.

According to Śaiva theology, grace (*anugraha*, but also *śaktipāta*) is the last and final of Śiva's five great acts (*pañcakṛtya*: *sṛṣṭi, sthiti, saṁhāra, tirodhāna, anugraha*). It is the condition for liberation. But how is it to be defined? One of the most well-known and oft-quoted verses of the *Śivastotrāvalī* is found in the *Saṁgrahastotra* (13):

8. *kathaṁcidāsādya maheśvarasya dāsyaṁ janasyāpyupakāram icchan* ।
samastasaṁpatsamavāptihetuṁ tatpratyabhijñāmupapādayāmi ॥
— *ĪPK* I.1.1.

śaktipātasamaye vicāraṇam. . .

At the time of bestowing grace
You should have considered (whether I am worthy of it),
but you never do this.
What has befallen me now
That you delay in revealing your glory? — 13.11

Abhinavagupta quotes this verse in his *Tantrāloka* to bring home the point that grace is always independent, difficult to attain, and that the Lord does not show any partiality in bestowing it.[9]

All this is related to the beginning of the *Īśvarapratyabhijñā Kārikā* : *kathaṁcidāsādya. . . .* And it is important to the philosophy of *pratyabhijñā*, because the actual moment or event of recognizing the Lord who is but one's own essential nature cannot be the outcome of either effort or reasoning, but it comes in a flash (*pratibhā*).

Utpala says in one verse of the *Śivastotrāvalī* how both, philosophy and devotion, are necessarily interdependent:

yadyathāsthitapadārthadarśanam
yuṣmadarcanamahotsavaśca yaḥ ।

yugmametaditaretarāśrayam
bhaktiśāliṣu sadā vijṛmbhate ॥

The realization of things as they really are
and the great festival of your worship —
both are mutually dependent
and they always blossom in those
who are filled with devotion. — 13.7

The language of the *Stotrāvalī* should not mislead us by taking it literally and hence dualistically. Throughout the text, terms

9. *karhicit prāptaśabdābhyāmanapekṣitvamūcivān, durlabhatvam-arāgitvaṁ śaktipātavidhau vibhoḥ* । — *TA*, 13.291.

like *mahotsava*, great festival, *pūjā* or *arcā*, do not refer to external worship or celebration, but rather to the bliss of mystical union. Now, "seeing things as they really are" implies a mind free from *vikalpas*. *Vikalpa* is often translated as "thought-construct" or "mental construct," it is a thought which is bound up in dichotomies and imagination. "The main characteristic of *vikalpa* is that of projecting the object outside the I, of knowing it in terms of separation: this."[10] In his *Kārikās* Utpala says:

> The reflective awareness of "I," which is the very essence of light, is not a mental construct (*vikalpaḥ*), although it is informed by the word. For a *vikalpa* is an act of ascertainment (*viniścayaḥ*) presenting a duality (*dvayākṣepī*). — I.6.1 (transl. Torella).

The task of both philosophy as well as spirituality consists in perceiving reality free from any *vikalpa*.

> With the dissolution of mental constructs by one-pointed awareness one attains gradually the state of the Lord.
>
> — *ĪPK* IV.11.[11]

In the *Stotrāvalī* this thesis takes the form of a prayer:

> O Lord, may the chain of the darkness
> of false perceptions be dissolved,
> may unrestrained freedom arise in my heart.
> When I am drowned in the *rasa* of the bliss
> of the Lord,
> may his image made of Consciousness
> appear to me! — 7.3

This ecstatic prayer clarifies that only on the dissolution of

10. R. Torella, op. cit., p. 128 note 4. See notes 3 and 4 for a detailed description of *vikalpa*.

11. On *vikalpa* see also *ĪPK*, I.2.1-2 and *Vṛtti*.

dichotomizing thought-constructs (*vikalpa*) can there be real freedom — and the tradition is not characterized as *svātantryavāda* by chance, because freedom or absolute autonomy is central to it. Again, on dissolving the obscuring influence of *vikalpa*s and thereby plunging in a sea of bliss, what is revealed to the devotee is not any external Divine image, but the image consisting of pure Consciousness (*cinmayī-mūrtiḥ*).

One can be said to perceive the world in its real form only if one apprehends it unobscured by intervening *vikalpa*s:

yo 'vikalpamidamarthamaṇḍalaṁ
paśyatīśa nikhilaṁbhavadvapuḥ ।
svātmapakṣaparipūrite jagat
yasya nityasukhinaḥ kuto bhayam ॥

Whoever perceives this whole objective world free from mental constructs as your (i.e. the Lord's) very body, having filled the universe with his own nature he is ever joyful — whence the fear? — 13.16

Kṣemarāja, in his commentary on this verse, explains "your body" as "of the form of Consciousness" (*cid-rūpam*), and the "own nature (*svātmā*)" as "oneness of Consciousness" (*cidaikyena*). And "filling the world with one's own nature" means to perceive it as non-different from oneself (*svābheda* . . .), by removing the obstacle of difference or separation. Such a non-dual apprehension of the world alone can bestow bliss and freedom from fear.

Further, even the distinction between *vikalpa* and *avikalpa* is overcome once the state of *jīvanmukti* is attained. Thus at the end of his *Īśvarapratyabhijñā Kārikā* Utpala says in a much quoted verse:

sarvo mamāyam vibhava ityevam parijānataḥ ।
viśvātmano vikalpānām prasare 'pi maheśatā ॥

He who, having all as his essence, thus knows:
"All this multiform deployment is mine,"
he, even in the flow of mental constructs,
attains the state of Maheśa. — IV.12, (transl. Torella)

While using philosophical terms, the mystic poet can go beyond argumentation, as when he speaks of being and non-being (*sat-asat*).

sadasattvena bhāvānāṁ yuktā yā dvitayī gatiḥ ।
tamullaṅghya tṛtīyasmai namaścitrāya śambhave ॥

Homage to the wonderful Śambhu
Who, transcending the two courses
of things existent or non-existent
constitutes the third state. — 3.1

And similarly:

The existent is certainly different from the non-existent,
and the non-existent from the existent.
O Lord! You are neither existent nor non-existent,
but you have the nature of both,
the existent and non-existent. — 3.18

Transcendence and immanence are two aspects of the experience of the Absolute (cf. also 9.20). The nature of the Lord is also described in terms of the *Pratyabhijñā* philosophy:

In this unconscious world
you are the form of consciousness.
Among the knowable, you are the knower;
Among the limited, you are the all-pervasive:
You are the highest of all. — 3.20

The question may be raised how the Lord, being the real "I" and pure Consciousness, can be at the same time the "thou" of the longing of the devotee. In other terms, *bhakti* seems to contradict *advaita*. One answer will be that *advaita* can only be experienced due to an intense *bhakti*, and this being a dynamic process, it contains so many stages and phases. It is in these different experiences of the *bhakta* or mystic that the philosophy of *pratyabhijñā* comes alive.

> Entering you, my own being,
> the fathomless, the undifferentiated,
> the one without a second,
> devouring all sense of (subject and) object,
> O Lord of Umā,
> Ever may I worship and sing praises of you.
> — 13.20 (transl. Bailly)

The *bhakta* remains conscious that in all manifestations the Lord is nothing but pure Consciousness:

> May you be glorified, O Essence of Consciousness,
> the essential nature assuming many forms
> as Agni, the Moon, the Sun, Brahmā, Viṣṇu,
> the mobile and the immobile. — 2.1 (transl. after Bailly)

The author plays on the words *svarūpa* and *bahurūpa*, because the one does not exclude the other. That Śiva is the one and true "I," the ultimate subject, does not exclude the objective awareness:

> Glorified are your devotees
> who are not separated from you
> even when they experience, through the senses,
> subjects and objects. — 16.27

This verse and Kṣemarāja's commentary remind us of a famous verse of the *Vijñāna Bhairava* (though surprisingly Kṣemarāja does not quote it here), saying that "the consciousness of object and subject is common to all living beings, but the difference in the case of *yogīs* is that they are attentively aware of this relationship" (verse 106, *sambandhe sāvadhānatā*).

This implies that the spirituality of *pratyabhijñā* does not exclude any experience, subjective or objective, but views them all in the light of the Divine:

> Every moment, let me perceive clearly
> each and every object of the world
> in an unlimited way
> as You alone, my Lord,
> of universal form. — 12.19

And again

> Why does my mind not view
> the various objects of my desire
> as not different from the limbs of your body?
> In so doing, it would not lose its nature and
> my highest desire would also be realized.
> — 12.20 (transl. Bailly)

This is not a concession to the manifold desires of the human being, but it is an expression of the very philosophy which views Reality under two aspects:

Prakāśa, pure light of Consciousness, and *vimarśa*, reflection of that very light, which makes multiplicity possible. It is precisely this relationship of *prakāśa* (identified with Śiva) and *vimarṣa* (identified with Śakti) that constitutes the dynamism of the metaphysics as well as spirituality of *pratyabhijñā*. In his *Kārikās* Utpaladeva states:

> ***Kārikā***: The multitude of things cannot but shine resting on the self of the Lord, otherwise that act of reflective awareness which is volition could not be produced.

> ***Vṛtti***: As in the self of the Lord, whose essence is consciousness, so also in the objective realities themselves there is a shining without differentiation. . . .
>
> ***Kārikā***: The essential nature of light is reflective awareness (*vimarśam*); otherwise light, though "coloured" by objects, would be similar to an insentient reality, such as crystal and so on.
>
> ***Vṛtti***: Reflective awareness constitutes the primary essence of light. In the absence of this reflective awareness, light, though objects make it assume different forms, would merely be "limpid," but not sentient, since there is no "savouring" (*camatkṛtiḥ*).
>
> — *Īśvarapratyabhijñā Kārikā*, I.5.10-11 (transl. R. Torella)

Camatkṛti (*camatkāra*) is a keyword establishing an inseparable link between philosophy, aesthetics and mystical experience. It implies the sense of "savouring," "wonder," "bliss," "surprise." In the words of Torella, it "refers to the wonder and astonishment that accompanies the return of reality to its original 'virgin' state, the transfiguration that this type of experience operates on reality in freeing it from the veils of the I and of the mine."

Utpaladeva, the mystic, expresses this sense of wonder in various ways. Relating the experience of beauty with devotion he exclaims:

> That which bestows on all objects of beauty
> the sense of giving wonder at the mere touch —
> by that very principle do those endowed with
> unwavering devotion worship your form.
>
> — 13.14 (transl. after Bailly)

Besides *camatkṛti* the keyword is here *sparśa*, touch, which implies a mystical meaning among all the sense perceptions.

One of the most dense verses of the *Stotrāvalī* expresses all in one, the wonder of experiencing self-recognition flowing from the fullness of devotion:

> Tasting the wonder of inner devotion
> With my eyes closed,
> May I worship even the blades of grass thus:
> "homage to Śiva, my own self!" — 5.15

Here the mystic experiences the oneness of his own self with Śiva and at the same time with the whole of reality, even down to the blades of grass.

This brings us to the central doctrine of the *Pratyabhijñā*, the one and ultimate "I" — *aham*, which Utpaladeva unfolds in detailed argumentation in his *Kārikās* and *Vṛtti*, arguing also against the Buddhist Vijñānavādin and the Vedāntin. "Utpaladeva's constant preoccupation is to show . . . the need for a single, dynamic subject that unifies and animates the discontinuity of reality and constitutes the substratum of every limited subject, as well as of every form and activity of everyday life.

This I or Consciousness is, on the religious plane, Śiva. In his highest form, the supreme divine personality is solely "I" — consisting of consciousness and beatitude — in whom all the principles are contained. . . ." — R. Torella, op. cit., p. xxix.

In the *Stotrāvalī* it is only the *bhakta* who experiences the supreme and true "I" (cf. 13.4).

However, this recognition of one's true nature (*svarūpa*) is not always realized and hence it becomes the object of intense prayer, as many verses of the *Stotrāvalī* express it:

> When shall that moment come,

when all of a sudden I recognize you,
the Lord, the Fearless, Exalted, Perfect One,
the One without cause, who has concealed himself —
and in so doing make you ashamed? — 9.6

The style of these prayers shows the great intimacy between the *bhakta* and his Lord, as we find it often in devotional poetry. He also explains why the invocation "O Śiva" is still possible even if there is complete identity:

There is no affliction for your devotees
Nor any worry,
for their own self is identical with you.
Even then, in the external state
the indescribable word "O Śiva" is on their lips.
— 20.15 (transl. after Bailly)

The constant theme of the relationship between *bhakti* and *advaita* reflects the living experience of the mystic:

Where not even a trace of otherness exists,
where self-luminosity is everywhere manifest,
there, in your city, let me reside
forever as your worshipper
— 13.9 (transl. Bailly)

The only condition for achieving this state of non-duality is the removal of obstacles, which may be only a tiny spot of impurity (cf. 13.2):

Therefore, with the consciousness
of the true essence of things
that emanates from the removal of
the obstacles to the nectar of your non-duality,
make me worthy, O Lord of the Gods,
of the worship of your feet. — 13.5 (transl. Bailly)

in the language of the *Stotrāvalī* is often expressed in terms of intoxication with the divine nectar. This theme of *amṛta,* nectar or ambrosia, is running throughout the text — it is the joyful essence of love and devotion, *bhakti-rasa,* which the poet wishes to drink to the full, so as to be united with the Lord and intoxicated with his bliss. Here, the double connotation of *rasa* as the essence of aesthetic experience, and the mystical intoxication is implicit. Since all things are an expression of Śiva's pervasive nature, enjoying them is nothing but a participation in the Divine Body.

The emphasis on *bhakti,* repeated again and again, expresses the supremacy of love over dry knowledge and over *yoga* (cf. 1.16-18). It can be boring only for those who have not tasted that "nectar." On the other hand, the outcome of this non-dual realization or recognition is the overcoming of all opposites. First of all, the Lord himself is the *coincidentia oppositorum* (coincidence of opposites):

> Homage to that wondrous Śambhu,
> the Deluding One
> who is yet pure and clear;
> the Hidden One
> who has yet revealed himself;
> the Subtle One
> whose form yet takes the form
> of the whole universe.
>
> — 2.12 (transl. Bailly)

All the opposites continue to exist for the devotee without distracting him from the reality:

> Whether in disharmony or in harmony,
> whether weeping or laughing,
> whether distracted or in deep thought,
> may I be filled with devotion, O Lord. — 16.8

All dualities are at the same time affirmed, negated and overcome. This applies even to the sacred scriptures which are thus relativized:

> Glory be to the one who is opposed to the Vedas and
> Āgamas,
> who has propounded the Vedas and Āgamas,
> who is the true essence of the Vedas and Āgamas,
> to the Lord, the mysterious One. — 2.7

Even in relation to *saṁsāra* there is an overcoming of opposites:

> Glory be to Śambhu, the sole cause of the world,
> who is the one opposed to the world,
> who takes worldly form
> and who transcends the world. — 2.8

The same principle applies also to the religious traditions which are thus relativized:

> Glory to you O Śarva
> Who are essence of the 'righthanded' path,
> Who are the goal of the 'lefthanded' path,
> Who belong to all the traditions
> And yet to no tradition at all. — 2.19

At the end of the *Īśvarapratyabhijñā Kārikā* Utpaladeva calls this the "new easy path" (IV.16) which he has propounded with logical argumentation (*yukti*). The goal which is rendered possible or awakened by argumentation is the same as the goal of *bhakti*. It would be interesting to take into account Kṣemarāja's commentary on the *Stotrāvalī* because he gives a philosophical interpretation. But one could say, just as the philosophy of Recognition underlies the *bhakti* mysticism, so the mystical experience of *bhakti* underlies philosophy. For even when Utpaladeva addresses Śiva in very personal and even mythical terms, ultimately he always means "the essence of

Consciousness" (*cinmaya*, etc.). Invoking Śiva by his names means nothing but addressing the very power of *mantra*:

> May you be glorified, O Mahādeva,
> O Rudra, Śaṅkara, Maheśvara,
> O Śiva, Embodiment of the *Mantra*. — 2.4

And Kṣemarāja explains *mantramūrti* as *pūrnāhantāparāmarśamayatvāt*, i.e. he is the embodiment of *mantra* because he is the essence of reflective awareness of the full I-Consciousness.

Let me conclude with a last verse from Utpaladeva in which he describes the extraordinary nature of this path:

> Where even suffering is transformed into joy,
> Where even poison becomes nectar,
> Where the world itself becomes liberation:
> That is verily the path of Śaṅkara. — 20.12

References

Editions and Translations of Utpaladeva's Works Quoted

Ācārya Utpaladeva Viracitā Śivastotrāvalī (*mūlamātra*), Īśvarasvarūpa Svāmī Lakṣmana Jū *dvārā saṁśodhita saṁskaraṇa ke ādhār par*, Srinagar: Kashmir, Īśvara Āśrama Trust, 1997.

The Īśvarapratyabhijñā Kārikā of Utpaladeva with the Author's *Vṛtti*. Critical edition and annotated translation, by Raffaele Torella, Delhi: Motilal Banarsidass, 2002 (1st edn., Roma, 1994). (abbr. ĪPK)

Śaiva Devotional Songs of Kashmir: A Translation and Study of Utpaladeva's Śivastotrāvalī, Constantina Rhodes Bailly, Delhi: Sri Satguru Publications, 1990 (1st edn., SUNY Press, 1987).

Siddhitrayī of Rājānaka Utpaladeva, ed. Pandit Madhusudan Kaul Sastri, Srinagar: Kashmir Series of Texts and Studies, no. XXXIV, 1921.

Śivastotrāvalī of Utpaladeva, Sanskrit text with Introduction, English tr. and Glossary, N.K. Kotru, Delhi: Motilal Banarsidass, 1985.

The Śivastotrāvalī of Utpaladevācārya with the Sanskrit Commentary of Kṣemarāja, ed. with Hindi Commentary by Rājānaka Lakṣmaṇa, Varanasi: Chowkhamba Sanskrit Series Office, 1964 (reprint 2008).

1

भक्तिविलासाख्यं प्रथमं स्तोत्रम्

Bhaktivilāsa Stotra

The Joy of Devotion

न ध्यायतो न जपतः स्याद्यस्याविधिपूर्वकम् ।
एवमेव शिवाभासस्तं नुमो भक्तिशालिनम् ॥१॥

na dhyāyato na japataḥ syād yasyāvidhipūrvakam ।
evam eva śivābhāsas taṁ numo bhaktiśālinam ॥1॥

I BOW to that devotee who is glorified with the devotion of Lord Śiva and to whom the appearance of Lord Śiva takes place without conducting meditation or recitation of any kind. He does not recite any *mantra* for Lord Śiva and he does not meditate. Without meditation, without recitation he attains this state where he is in oneness with Lord Śiva. I bow to that devotee. I don't bow to that devotee who meditates and then achieves or who recites and then achieves. That devotee is far away from the one who achieves Lord Śiva without doing anything.

आत्मा मम भवद्भक्तिसुधापानयुवाऽपि सन् ।
लोकयात्रारजोरागात्पलितैरिव धूसरः ॥२॥

ātmā mama bhavadbhaktisudhāpānayuvā 'pi san ।
lokayātrārajorāgāt palitair iva dhūsaraḥ ॥2॥

In fact, I am always young by tasting the nectar of Thy devotion but in the field of worldly activities I feel I am old. Internally

I am always young because of tasting the nectar of Thy devotion, though externally I may appear to be too old because of too much of exertion and attachment to the worldly activities. Internally I am still young and energetic although I may appear old and exhausted by virtue of being in contact with the worldly people and worldly activities.

लब्धत्वत्संपदां भक्तिमतां त्वत्पुरवासिनाम् ।
सञ्चारो लोकमार्गेऽपि स्यात्तयैव विजृम्भया ॥३॥

labdhatvatsaṁpadāṁ bhaktimatāṁ
tvatpuravāsinām ।
sañcāro lokamārge 'pi syāt tayaiva vijṛmbhayā ॥3॥

Those who have achieved the wealth of Your devotion and those who are residing in Thy kingdom, for them, activities in the worldly matters become one with the divinity of God-consciousness.

साक्षाद्भवन्मये नाथ सर्वस्मिन् भुवनान्तरे ।
किं न भक्तिमतां क्षेत्रं मन्त्रः क्वैषां न सिद्ध्यति ॥४॥

sakṣādbhavanmaye nātha sarvasmin bhuvanāntare ।
kiṁ na bhaktimatāṁ kṣetraṁ mantraḥ kvaiṣāṁ na
siddhyati ॥4॥

O Lord, those people for whom this whole universe has become one with Your presence, who feel Thy presence in each and every particle of the worldly field, those are Thy real devotees. For them which place is not a shrine? Shrine is also a shrine but bathroom is also a shrine for them; muddy place is also a shrine for them, a clean place is also a shrine. For them, everywhere there is possibility to attain God-consciousness. In the struggling state of this universe also they can attain God-consciousness. Not only in a temple do they attain God-consciousness but in the outward worldly state also they attain God-consciousness; for them there is no difference.

जयन्ति भक्तिपीयूषरसासववरोन्मदाः ।
अद्वितीया अपि सदा त्वद्द्वितीया अपि प्रभो ॥५॥

jayanti bhaktipīyūṣarasāsavavaronmadāḥ ।
advitīyā api sadā tvad dvitīyā api prabho ॥5॥

O Master, those persons who have become mad by taking the nectarised liquor of Thy devotion, are glorified. They are always divine. (It is liquor because it maddens but it is nectarised as it is filled with God-consciousness.) Where lies the madness in them? Madness because they always boast of being the only ones glorified in this universe and they always crave for attaining the nearness to their Master. At times they say "I am divine" and at times they say "I am nothing"; this is the madness they possess. Those mad devotees of Thee are always glorified.

अनन्तानन्दसिन्धोस्ते नाथ तत्त्वं विदन्ति ते ।
तादृशा एव ये सान्द्रभक्त्यानन्दरसाप्लुताः ॥६॥

anantānandasindhoste nātha tattvaṁ vidanti te ।
tādṛśā eva ye sāndrabhaktyānandarasāplutāḥ ॥6॥

O Master, those people alone experience the reality, the real state of Thy ocean of God-consciousness, who are really soaked in the nectar of the universal God-consciousness. That blissful state of God-consciousness is really an ocean and those people who are soaked properly in that ocean, can alone experience the reality of that ocean. People who are roaming on the shores only don't know the depth and the reality of that ocean. They experience it only superficially.

त्वमेवात्मेश सर्वस्य सर्वश्चात्मनि रागवान् ।
इति स्वभावसिद्धां त्वद्भक्तिं जानञ्जयेज्जनः ॥७॥

tvamevātmeśa sarvasya sarvaścātmani rāgavān ।
iti svabhāvasiddhāṁ tvadbhaktiṁ jānañjayejjanaḥ ॥7॥

O Lord, You are the nature of everybody. Everybody is attached to his own nature, to his own self. (Everyone likes oneself, everyone wants to live, no one wants to be worried etcetera.) Everybody loves himself and that himself in real sense is Your nature. So loving You is achieved automatically by everybody. Everybody loves You because they love themselves. So they love You. So Thy devotion is achieved by everybody, every individual. But there is only one difference: those alone are glorified who know this secret reality, others are not.

नाथ वेद्यक्षये केन न दृश्योऽस्येककः स्थितः ।
वेद्यवेदकसंक्षोभेऽप्यसि भक्तैः सुदर्शनः ॥८॥

nātha vedyakṣaye kena na dṛśyo 'syekakaḥ sthitaḥ ।
vedyavedakasaṁkṣobhe 'pyasi bhaktaiḥ sudarśanaḥ ॥8॥

O my Master, it is a fact that You are achieved only when one shuns all outward worldly activities. But what greatness is there in achieving You that way? Greatness lies in those devotees who achieve You, who experience You in every action of the universe, in all the activities of their daily life. They alone know and experience You in the real sense. In the agitation of objective and subjective world they experience the nature of God-consciousness and that too very easily without adopting any means. To achieve You after adoption of means, *sādhanā*, *prāṇāyāma*, meditation, *yoga*, etcetera is all humbug. Those who achieve You in the very actions of this universe very easily and without doing anything in particular, they really achieve You.

अनन्तानन्दसरसी देवी प्रियतमा यथा ।
अवियुक्तास्ति ते तद्वदेका त्वद्भक्तिरस्तु मे ॥९॥

anantānandasarasī devī priyatamā yathā ।
aviyuktāsti te tadvadekā tvadbhaktirastu me ॥9 ॥

You have Your Śakti, Your wife Pārvatī, and You are fond of Pārvatī because Pārvatī is glorified with unlimited joy and bliss. I too have adopted one woman for You to possess and that is my devotion for You. My devotion is not accepted by You as much as You accept Pārvatī in nearness. My devotion remains away from Your presence. This is my problem.

I want this lady, my devotion for You, to remain one with You, remain wedded to You. I want to devote to You in continuity without any break so that You embrace my devotion, You accept my devotion, and You would be fond of my devotion. You have no fondness for my devotion. I devote my time for You but You ignore that; I love You but You don't care. Pārvatī loves You very little but You care too much for that. So this is my problem. I want similar conduct to be adopted with this lady, my devotion.

सर्व एव भवल्लाभहेतुर्भक्तिमतां विभो ।
संविन्मार्गोऽयमाह्लाददुःखमोहैस्त्रिधा स्थितः ॥१० ॥

sarva eva bhavallābhaheturbhaktimatāṁ vibho ।
saṁvinmārgo 'yamāhlādaduḥkhamohaistridhā sthitaḥ ॥10 ॥

O Lord, the threefold path existing in this universe directs Your devotees to God-consciousness. It may be joy, it may be sadness or it may be sluggishness, it all directs Thy devotees to God-consciousness.

This universal path is threefold. First is the joyful path, filled with joy like when one wants to devote to the Lord. The second is the path filled with sadness; opposite to joy this is full of struggle, exhaustion and is tiring like the construction of a house, repair of motor car, etcetera. The third one is the path filled with sluggishness like when one wants to lie in the bed the whole day. This is the threefold (*sāttvika, rājasika* and *tāmasika*) path of this universe.

भवद्भक्त्यमृतास्वादाद्बोधस्य स्यात्परापि या ।
दशा सा मां प्रति स्वामिन्नासवस्येव शुक्तता ॥११ ॥

bhavadbhaktyamṛtāsvādādbodhasya syātparāpi yā ।
daśā sā māṁ prati svāminnāsavasyeva śuktatā ॥11 ॥

O Lord, to me leaving aside the tasting of the nectar of Your devotion and possessing the supreme state of the Śaivite knowledge is like the sourness of some wine. Possessing the supreme state of knowledge of God-consciousness without devotion is absolutely dry and dull. It does not interest me at all. I want Your devotion, no matter whether You appear to me or not. I want to cry for You. I want Your devotion and nothing else. I don't want knowledge if it is without devotion.

भवद्भक्तिमहाविद्या येषामभ्यासमागता ।
विद्याविद्योभयस्यापि त एते तत्त्ववेदिनः ॥१२ ॥

bhavadbhaktimahāvidyā yeṣāmabhyāsamāgatā ।
vidyāvidyobhayasyāpi ta ete tattvavedinaḥ ॥12 ॥

Those people, who have already experienced the supreme knowledge of Thy devotion, are only experienced to discriminate between the knowledge and the absence of knowledge and not anybody else. They alone can discriminate between what is the real knowledge and what is not knowledge, what is ignorance.

आमूलाद्वाग्लता सेयं क्रमविस्फारशालिनी ।
त्वद्भक्तिसुधया सिक्ता तद्रसाढ्यफलास्तु मे ॥१३ ॥

āmūlādvāglatā seyaṁ kramavisphāraśālinī ।
tvadbhaktisudhayā siktā tadrasāḍhyaphalāstu me ॥13 ॥

This expansion of the universal state of life is really like a creeper. This vine of sound, the fourfold state of sound (*parā, paśyantī, madhyamā* and *vaikharī*) is expanded in this universe. There is one desire in me: I want this creeper to be watered with the nectar of Thy devotion so that it bears the fruit that will have the taste of Thy devotion. I want to experience only Thy devotion in all the fourfold states of life in this world. This is my only desire.

The fourfold branches of the vine of speech are *parā, paśyantī, madhyamā* and *vaikharī*. *Parā vānī* is the supreme Word, without differentiation; sometimes you are established in *parā* when you are in *samādhi*. Next is *paśyantī* when you are only looking and there is no thought in your mind; sometimes you are established in *paśyantī* when you are about to come out of *samādhi*. Next to *paśyantī* is *madhyamā* when you don't speak with words but speak with mind; when you are only thinking in your mind but not acting with your body. The fourth state of *vaikharī* encompasses the state when you speak with words also, when you are acting with the lips also; this is the inferior state of sound.

शिवो भूत्वा यजेतेति भक्तो भूत्वेति कथ्यते ।
त्वमेव हि वपुः सारं भक्तैरद्वयशोधितम् ॥१४ ॥

śivo bhūtvā yajeteti bhakto bhūtveti kathyate ।
tvameva hi vapuḥ sāraṁ bhaktairadvayaśodhitam ॥14 ॥

In Vedas,[1] in *Śiva Sūtras* and all the sacred books, it is said that you must worship Lord Śiva after becoming Lord Śiva yourself (*Śivo bhūtvā śivaṁ yajeta*). Once you have become Lord Śiva, only then are you capable of worshipping Him. As an individual being, you cannot worship that Universal Being. It is out of question. How can a limited being get contact with

1. Swamiji means the Āgamas.

the Unlimited Being? So you must first become unlimited yourself, then only can you worship the Unlimited Śiva.

But Thy devotees have corrected this ruling. They say that you must be devoted to Lord Śiva then only can you get contact with Him. If you are filled with devotion, *Śiva-bhāva*, the state of Śiva, you are not capable of worshipping Lord Śiva but when you are devotedly devoted to Lord Śiva then you are capable of worshipping Lord Śiva. You can worship Lord Śiva only when you are filled with extreme devotion. They have experienced this and clarified in the real sense as to what is right and what is wrong and from my point of view this is the correct way of understanding.

भक्तानां भवदद्वैतसिद्ध्यै का नोपपत्तयः ।
तदसिद्ध्यै निकृष्टानां कानि नावरणानि वा ॥१५॥

bhaktānāṁ bhavadadvaitasiddhyai kā nopapattayaḥ I
tadasiddhyai nikṛṣṭānāṁ kāni nāvaraṇāni vā II15 II

For Thy devotees there is no fixed or prescribed way to achieve the state of God-consciousness. Even going astray also leads them to God-consciousness. For them what are not the ways, what are not the paths to achieve God-consciousness? They reach God-consciousness from whatever corner they may proceed. They may go to movies or dance; even by doing so they are directed to God-consciousness. Thy devotees never become detached from You, they are always attached to You. In all their worldly activities or even sensual pleasures, they are directed towards God-consciousness. This is the divinity of Thy devotees. They may not meditate at all but they are still carried to God-consciousness.

But on the contrary, for those who are not devotedly devoted to You, there are hindrances and obstacles everywhere. Even if they meditate properly with one-pointedness, they are carried away from God-consciousness.

कदाचित्क्वापि लभ्योऽसि योगेनेतीश वञ्चना ।
अन्यथा सर्वकक्ष्यासु भासि भक्तिमतां कथम् ॥१६ ॥

kadācitkvāpi labhyo 'si yogenetīśa vañcanā ।
anyathā sarvakakṣyāsu bhāsi bhaktimatāṁ katham ॥16 ॥

O Lord, it is a deceit that You are achieved by some particular yogic exercises or particular meditation or You are achieved when a person is sentenced to a cave or some secluded corner without the struggle of the universal activities. Giving up the world and shunning all universal activities will never help one achieve God-consciousness. On the contrary when one is situated in the universe and given to the universal activities, there is a possibility of achieving the state of God-consciousness. So it seems that this universe is not separate from the state of God-consciousness. In fact, this universe is the real manifestation of God-consciousness and the reality of Thy nature. If one shuns the reality of Thy nature, how can one achieve God-consciousness? So it is a deceit when someone goes to a cave shunning all the activities of the universe, all the activities of one's daily life with the hope of achieving God-consciousness. There are such devotees in this universe who have become one with You, existing in the universal activity and I have experienced those devotees.

O Lord, Your existence is found at a particular period or at a particular place (say heart or between the two eyebrows) or by performance of some particular *yoga*, etcetera; such theories are a deceit for the seeker. Actually You are not found that way. If it were true then how would those devotees who are devotedly devoted to You, perceive Your presence in each and every act of life? In worldly actions also they perceive Your presence. So for those *yogī*s who find You only in a particular place or at a particular time or by functioning a particular *yoga*, that is deceit, total hypocrisy. The real way of perceiving You is to perceive You in each and every action of life.

So one should find out the ways and means to achieve God in the universal activity and not by shunning activity. This is Śaivism.

प्रत्याहाराद्यसंस्पृष्टो विशेषोऽस्ति महानयम् ।
योगिभ्यो भक्तिभाजां यद्व्युत्थानेऽपि समाहिताः ॥१७ ॥

pratyāhārādyasaṁspṛṣṭo viśeṣo 'sti mahānayam ।
yogibhyo bhaktibhājāṁ yadvyutthāne 'pi samāhitāḥ ॥17 ॥

There is a great difference between *yogī*s and Your devotees. *Yogī*s find You and realise Your nature through meditation and maintaining *pratyāhāra* (restraining the sense-organs). Otherwise they cannot realize Your nature. But on the contrary, Your devotees perceive You in the outside world of action also. They find You in worldly activities also.

न योगो न तपो नार्चाक्रमः कोऽपि प्रणीयते ।
अमाये शिवमार्गेऽस्मिन् भक्तिरेका प्रशस्यते ॥१८ ॥

na yogo na tapo nārcākramaḥ ko 'pi praṇīyate ।
amāye śivamārge 'smin bhaktirekā praśasyate ॥18 ॥

On this path of Lord Śiva, which is away from all delusion, which is absolutely pure and straight, no *yoga* is needed; no penance is needed, no mode of worship is prescribed. The only need here is that of devotion, pure devotion. If the person is really attached to Lord Śiva, he sure will find Him. If he is not, he may perform *yoga*, penance or worship, he cannot find Him. *Bhakti* is the only means to find Him; passion for God-consciousness is the only requisite.

सर्वतो विलसद्भक्तितेजोध्वस्तावृतेर्मम ।
प्रत्यक्षसर्वभावस्य चिन्तानामापि नश्यतु ॥१९ ॥

sarvato vilasadbhaktitejodhvastāvṛtermama ।
pratyakṣasarvabhāvasya cintānāmāpi naśyatu ॥19 ॥

O Lord, I have in the real sense perceived the real nature of the universe. I have perceived the whole universal objective field because all the ignorance has been removed by the light of Thy devotion. Now there is only one request for You: let the traces of the impressions of duality also go from my mind. The differentiated way of perception like this is mine, that is not mine; this is true, that is untrue; this is right, that is wrong, etcetera, all this should vanish from my mind. Even the traces should not remain. This is my request.

शिव इत्येकशब्दस्य जिह्वाग्रे तिष्ठतः सदा ।
समस्तविषयास्वादो भक्तेष्वेवास्ति कोऽप्यहो ॥२० ॥

śiva ityekaśabdasya jihvāgre tiṣṭhataḥ sadā ।
samastaviṣayāsvādo bhakteṣvevāsti ko 'pyaho ॥20 ॥

This is a great wonder that when you recite only the name of Śiva, when the sound Śiva resides on the tip of your tongue in continuity, you don't only realize the nectar of His name but you also realize the nectar of His touch, His embrace, His fragrance, you realize everything of Lord Śiva. Such is the greatness of His name that by reciting His name you achieve the nectar of not only His name but His touch, embrace, fragrance, everything. You are filled with His real existence. If you utter this word Śiva with its meaning (awareness, *aham-bhāva*), it will lead you there.

शान्तकल्लोलशीताच्छस्वादुभक्तिसुधाम्बुधौ ।
अलौकिकरसास्वादे सुस्थैः को नाम गण्यते ॥२१ ॥

śāntakallolaśītācchasvādubhaktisudhāmbudhau ।
alaukikarasāsvāde susthaiḥ ko nāma gaṇyate ॥21 ॥

Those who are bent upon tasting that unique nectar of that

divine bliss, dive in the ocean of the nectar of Thy devotion which is sweet, which is fresh, which is cool, which is calm and unwavering. They dive their ego in that ocean and are bent upon tasting the nectar of that divine bliss. For them nothing remains to be counted, they don't count anything else. They do not feel the necessity of going anywhere else. Their journey ends there.

मादृशैः किं न चर्व्येत भवद्भक्तिमहौषधिः ।
तादृशी भगवन्यस्या मोक्षाख्योऽनन्तरो रसः ॥२२ ॥

mādṛśaiḥ kiṁ na carvyeta bhavadbhaktimahauṣadhiḥ ।
tādṛśī bhagavanyasyā mokṣākhyo 'nantaro rasaḥ ॥22 ॥

O Lord, those people who are just like me, why should they not taste the nectar of the herb of Your devotion; by tasting that they not only achieve the taste of that devotion, but would also achieve the taste of liberation. They simultaneously become *jīvanamukta* also. *Mokṣa-rasa* is attached to *bhakti-rasa*. As soon as *bhakti-rasa* is achieved, *mokṣa-rasa* is also achieved simultaneously. So why should not those people, who are just like me, also appreciate and own this dose of Your devotion?

ता एव परमर्थ्यन्ते सम्पदः सद्भिरीश याः ।
त्वद्भक्तिरससम्भोगविस्रम्भपरिपोषिकाः ॥२३ ॥

tā eva paramarthyante sampadaḥ sadbhirīśa yāḥ ।
tvadbhaktirasasambhogavisrambhaparipoṣikāḥ ॥23 ॥

O Lord, Thy devotees long only for that wealth which produces and further strengthens the fire of desire to embrace that *bhakti-rasa*, the nectar of Thy devotion in them.

भवद्भक्तिसुधासारस्तैः किमप्युपलक्षितः ।
ये न रागादिपङ्केऽस्मिँल्लिप्यन्ते पतिता अपि ॥२४ ॥

bhavadbhaktisudhāsārastaiḥ kimapyupalakṣitaḥ ।
ye na rāgādipaṅke 'smiṁllipyante patitā api ॥24 ॥

Those devotees of Thee alone have actually pointed out and tasted that sharp driving shower of Thy devotion, who in spite of being in the muddy sphere of this universe, have not got stuck in that mud. Although living and remaining in the muddy sphere of greed, anger, lust, the worldly attachments, etcetera, they don't get smeared by this mud. The worldly activities don't blemish them.

अणिमादिषु मोक्षान्तेष्वङ्गेष्वेव फलाभिधा ।
भवद्भक्तेर्विपक्वाया लताया इव केषुचित् ॥२५॥

aṇimādiṣu mokṣānteṣvaṅgeṣveva phalābhidhā ।
bhavadbhaktervipakvāyā latāyā iva keṣucit ॥25॥

In this universe there is one shining creeper of Thy devotion. When this creeper is in full bloom, when it has bloomed perfectly, it bears all kinds of fruits like great yogic powers (*siddhi*s), the great power of being liberated from the cycle of repeated births and deaths (*mokṣa*), etcetera. That creeper of Thy devotion bears the fruit not only of Thy devotion but that of all powers including the final liberation. But in predominance it bears the fruit of devotion. All other fruits of yogic powers and liberation, etcetera are secondary. Devotion to the Lord is recognized as the predominant fruit of this creeper and not liberation.

The first sign of getting absorbed in God-consciousness is the devotion for the Lord, attachment for the Lord. When you are attached to Lord Śiva, don't think of any other powers. All other powers will follow. The creeper of His devotion should be owned. That is important.

चित्रं निसर्गतो नाथ दुःखबीजमिदं मनः ।
त्वद्भक्तिरससंसिक्तं निःश्रेयसमहाफलम् ॥२६॥

citraṁ nisargato nātha duḥkhabījamidaṁ manaḥ ।
tvadbhaktirasasaṁsiktaṁ
niḥśreyasamahāphalam ॥26॥

O desired Lord; this is also a great wonder to me that in reality, by nature, this mind is the seed of all pain, sadness, sorrow, torture, etcetera. All bad things are borne by this seed. (Mind is always occupied with thinking of numerous things without any purpose.) But this very seed when watered by the *rasa* of Thy devotion bears the fruit of liberation, ultimate liberation, the final liberation. This is the great wonder about this seed.

॥ इति श्रीमदुत्पलदेवाचार्यविरचिते श्रीशिवस्तोत्रावल्यां
भक्तिविलासाख्यं प्रथमं स्तोत्रम् ॥

॥ *iti śrīmadutpaladevācāryaviracite śrīśivastotrāvalyāṁ*
bhaktivilāsākhyaṁ prathamaṁ stotram ॥

2

सर्वात्मपरिभावनाख्यं द्वितीयं स्तोत्रम्

Sarvātmaparibhāvanā Stotra

Contemplation of the All-in-All

Sarvātmaparibhāvanā means you find everything in everything; everything is found in everything else.

अग्नीषोमरविब्रह्मविष्णुस्थावरजङ्गम-
स्वरूप बहुरूपाय नमः संविन्मयाय ते ॥१॥

agnīṣomaravibrahmaviṣṇusthāvarajaṅgama-
svarūpa bahurūpāya namaḥ saṁvinmayāya te ॥1॥

O LORD, You are the fire, You have possessed subjective consciousness; You are the moon, You have possessed objective consciousness; You are the Sun, You have possessed cognitive consciousness. You are subjective, You are objective, and You are cognitive. You are Brahmā the creator; You are Viṣṇu the protector also. You are animate and You are inanimate also. Although You are universal, You are above universal; You are only consciousness. I bow to Thy universal form.

विश्वेन्धनमहाक्षारानुलेपशुचिवर्चसे ।
महानलाय भवते विश्वैकहविषे नमः ॥२॥

viśvendhanamahākṣārānulepaśucivarcase ।
mahānalāya bhavate viśvaikahaviṣe namaḥ ॥2॥

O Lord I bow to that supreme fire of Thy consciousness which is absolutely glorified by pure light by absorbing this universe into nothingness, by burning this universe into ashes. You absorb those ashes in Your self-consciousness and by that Your light is glorified all around. This universe becomes just one offering in that fire of God-consciousness. It is not offered in that fire a second time. In one *svāhā* only it is finished. This universe becomes one *svāhā* in one moment, one offering. I bow to that supreme fire of Lord Śiva.

The author has nominated Lord Śiva as great fire, great abode of fire in which this whole universe has been destroyed and burnt to ashes. Those ashes are the traces of the impressions that remain in your consciousness. When you destroy the whole universe by your way of devotion, still those traces that there was some universe in that previous state, remain.

परमामृतसान्द्राय शीतलाय शिवाग्नये ।
कस्मैचिद्विश्वसंप्लोषविषमाय नमोऽस्तु ते ॥३॥

paramāmṛtasāndrāya śītalāya śivāgnaye |
kasmaicidviśvasaṁploṣaviṣamāya namo 'stu te ||3||

I bow to that supreme fire of God-consciousness, supreme fire of Lord Śiva that is cooled down by the supreme nectar. This is cool fire and cools down the whole system; this fire does not burn. At the same time by burning the differentiated perceptions of the universe, it has become hot and by keeping oneself in the field of that nectarised state of being, it is cool. This fire is thus cool and hot at the same time. I bow to that fire.

महादेवाय रुद्राय शङ्कराय शिवाय ते ।
महेश्वरायापि नमः कस्मैचिन्मन्त्रमूर्तये ॥४॥

mahādevāya rudrāya śaṅkarāya śivāya te |
maheśvarāyāpi namaḥ kasmaicinmantramūrtaye ||4||

I bow to Mahādeva, I bow to Rudra, I bow to Śaṅkara, I bow to Śiva, I bow to Maheśvara, and I bow to that unique being of God-consciousness of Śiva. (This is *sarvātmaparibhāvanā*, everywhere He is found).

> नमो निकृत्तनिःशेषत्रैलोक्यविगलद्वसा-
> वसेकविषमायापि मङ्गलाय शिवाग्नये ॥५॥
>
> *namo nikṛttaniḥśeṣatrailokyavigaladvasā-*
> *vasekaviṣamāyāpi maṅgalāya śivāgnaye* ॥5॥

I bow to that *Śiva-agni*, the fire of Śiva, that is furious and frightening like the fire of *śmaśāna agni* wherein the corpses are burnt; the fire wherein the three worlds namely the world of wakefulness, the world of dreaming state and the world of sound sleep (*bhāva, abhāva* and *atibhāva*) are cut into pieces and thrown into that fire. From the body of the three worlds some marrow oozes out which actually are the traces of the impressions that there once was the state of wakefulness, the dreaming state and the dreamless state. Those traces are also offered in that fire in the end.

When one enters the fourth state of *turīya*, initially those traces of the impression that there once was wakefulness, the dreaming state and the dreamless state, remain in the memory. But at the end, those traces are also offered in that fire and then there is only the blissful state of *turīya*.

Śiva-agni is frightful for those who are given to differentiated perception, who occupy, achieve and maintain differentiated perception. But for those who do not achieve differentiated perception, it gives them joy and happiness. If you achieve one-pointedness and are situated in that oneness of God-consciousness, it will give you joy and happiness, otherwise it is frightening. Those who are given to worldly pleasures don't get satisfied by directing their attention towards God-consciousness; they get a feeling as if they are dying. Initially when you start meditating on God-consciousness, you get a feeling as if you are dying and that you should quit meditation. You should however not get scared of that; you should persist on meditation and only then shall you get joy, the absolute joy in the end.

समस्तलक्षणायोग एव यस्योपलक्षणम्।
तस्मै नमोऽस्तु देवाय कस्मैचिदपि शम्भवे ॥६॥

samastalakṣaṇāyoga eva yasyopalakṣaṇam I
tasmai namo 'stu devāya kasmaicidapi śambhave II6 II

I bow to that unique being of Lord Śiva whose sign of perception is to perceive Him in no way.

When you perceive Him in no way, it means you have actually perceived Him, and if you perceive Him in some particular way, it means you have not perceived Him. Those who have perceived Him have not actually perceived Him; those who have not perceived Him, have perceived Him. Because when He is perceived, it means you are away from Him, you are not digested in that perceived thing. You remain at the stage of perceiver, and the God remains at the stage of perceived, which means that the distinction has not been removed. So you have not perceived Him in the right way. In the right way when you perceive Him, you will perceive Him as if you have not perceived Him. One who actually perceives Him, does not say that he has perceived Him, nor does he say that he has not perceived Him. What does he say then? He just perceives Him and that is all. He perceives Him actually and does not say anything at all. He perceives Him actually and remains in it. This is the way of perceiving the Lord.

वेदागमविरुद्धाय वेदागमविधायिने।
वेदागमसतत्त्वाय गुह्याय स्वामिने नमः ॥७॥

vedāgamaviruddhāya vedāgamavidhāyine |
vedāgamasatattvāya guhyāya svāmine namaḥ ||7 ||

I bow to my Master, who is absolutely against the theory of Vedas and Tantras. I bow to Him who is in favour of Vedas and Tantras. I bow to Him who is actually the essence of Vedas and Tantras. I bow to Him who is always hidden, who is always the secret underlying everything. So He is the essence of Vedas and Tantras, He is against the Vedas and Tantras, and He is the protector of the Vedas and Tantras.

संसारैकनिमित्ताय संसारैकविरोधिने ।
नमः संसाररूपाय निःसंसाराय शम्भवे ॥८ ॥

saṁsāraikanimittāya saṁsāraikavirodhine |
namaḥ saṁsārarūpāya niḥsaṁsārāya śambhave ||8 ||

I bow to that Lord Śiva, who is the only cause of torture of the universe, who is the only opposition to the torture of the universe, who is the reality of this torture and who is above this torture.

I bow to that Lord Śiva who is the only cause of the creation of the universe and who is the only opposition to it (through destruction); whose manifestation this universe is and who himself is above the universe.

Lord Śiva is the only cause of producing the torture of this universe, the wheel of repeated births and deaths. Lord Śiva is the only being who is opposed to this torture. In fact, He has become torture of the universe Himself; He has not manifested the torture of the universe. Actually He is above all this.

(He is everything. Completion does not come in being complete. When you are actually complete, it does not mean that you are complete because the state of incompleteness is lacking there. When you are incomplete also and complete also, then only you are actually complete. This is *sarvātma-paribhāvanā*.)

मूलाय मध्यायाग्राय मूलमध्याग्रमूर्तये ।
क्षीणाग्रमध्यमूलाय नमः पूर्णाय शम्भवे ॥९॥

mūlāya madhyāyāgrāya mūlamadhyāgramūrtaye ।
kṣīṇāgramadhyamūlāya namaḥ pūrṇāya śambhave ॥9॥

I bow to that Lord Śiva who is all-round complete. I bow to that Lord Śiva who is found at the root of everything, I bow to that Lord Śiva who is found at the centre of everything, I bow to that Lord Śiva who is found at the top of everything. He will be found one by one at the root, at the centre and at the top collectively. He will be found simultaneously at the root, at the centre and at the top. Actually He is not found at the root, He is not found at the centre, and He is not found at the top because He is complete. I bow to Lord Śiva that way.

नमः सुकृतसंभारविपाकः सकृदप्यसौ ।
यस्य नामग्रहः तस्मै दुर्लभाय शिवाय ते ॥१०॥

namaḥ sukṛtasaṁbhāravipākaḥ sakṛdapyasau ।
yasya nāmagrahaḥ tasmai durlabhāya śivāya te ॥10॥

I bow to that Lord Śiva the recitation of whose name just once in one's lifetime is indicative of the ripening of all one's virtues. This is the sign of the ripening of all your virtues, when you recite His name just once in your lifetime. But the way to recite is something supreme. It is not through the word of mouth. The recitation of His name is by entering in Supreme God-consciousness. That is the real way of reciting His name. If you recite His name that way only once in your lifetime, everything is solved and at the same time it is the way to achieve Him. Thus apparently He is very easy to attain. But the author says even this way also, He is very difficult to be achieved. Only through a miracle or the grace of your Master can you attain Him.

नमश्चराचराकारपरेतनिचयैः सदा ।
क्रीडते तुभ्यमेकस्मै चिन्मयाय कपालिने ॥११ ॥

namaścarācarākāraparetanicayaiḥ sadā ।
krīḍate tubhyamekasmai cinmayāya kapāline ॥11 ॥

I bow to that Lord Śiva who is the only *cinmaya*, the only conscious Being found in the whole unconscious world. He is found playing in everything whether stationary or moving. Actually this body is absolutely *jaḍa*, dull and dumb without awareness. Awareness is only of that Being. Awareness is playing in each and every body; not only in a moving body but in a stationary body also. In trees, in a blade of grass or in mountains, everywhere He is found playing. Lord Śiva is found playing with all *preta*s who have surrounded Him all around, this whole universe is only the body of *preta*s. I bow to that Lord Śiva who is moving in this universe along with those *preta*s. All these skulls are being carried by Lord Śiva in each and every way of life. He is the only conscious Being in this gathering of *preta*s.[1]

मायाविने विशुद्धाय गुह्याय प्रकटात्मने ।
सूक्ष्माय विश्वरूपाय नमश्चित्राय शम्भवे ॥१२ ॥

māyāvine viśuddhāya guhyāya prakaṭātmane ।
sūkṣmāya viśvarūpāya namaścitrāya śambhave ॥12 ॥

I bow to that wonderful being of Lord Śiva, who is always deceitful, who deceives each and every being and at the same time who is pure and straightforward. Deceitful for those who do not care to see Him; who do not care to observe Him, who do not care to perceive Him through meditation. He is

1. *Preta*s means dead bodies, those ghosts who have no consciousness.

straightforward for those who care to see Him, who are devoted to Him, who pray for Him, who care for Him, who are attached to Him. He is straightforward but at the same time deceitful for those who are worth deceiving. He is always hidden for those who are worthy of that, who deserve His being hidden to them. He is already revealed to the devotees of Lord Śiva. I bow to that Lord Śiva who in spite of being very subtle, is very great to have manifested as this universe and who is everything.

> ब्रह्मेन्द्रविष्णुनिर्व्यूढजगत्संहारकेलये ।
> आश्चर्यकरणीयाय नमस्ते सर्वशक्तये ॥१३॥
>
> *brahmendraviṣṇunirvyūḍhajagatsaṁhārakelaye* ।
> *āścaryakaraṇīyāya namaste sarvaśaktaye* ॥13॥

I bow to Thee O Lord Śiva, who is all powerful; I bow to Thee who always possesses all powers and who does act wonderfully. Brahmā the creator creates this universe and Viṣṇu protects this universe all round. They have actually created and protected this universe with great efforts but You just destroy it at once in just one play of Yours. In one movement of Your act You destroy this whole universe and there is no one to oppose.

> तटेष्वेव परिभ्रान्तैः लब्धास्तास्ता विभूतयः ।
> यस्य तस्मै नमस्तुभ्यमगाधहरसिन्धवे ॥१४॥
>
> *taṭeṣveva paribhrāntaiḥ labdhāstāstā vibhūtayaḥ* ।
> *yasya tasmai namastubhyamagādhaharasindhave* ॥14॥

I bow to Thee who is an unlimited ocean of God-consciousness; I bow to that unlimited ocean of Thy Being, by mere treading on whose shores one achieves those eight great yogic powers.

When the rise of *kuṇḍalinī* takes place, the centre of the rise of *kuṇḍalinī* is actually the state of this ocean, the ocean of

Lord Śiva and the shores of this ocean are the eight great yogic powers, those yogic powers which are achieved half way of this *kuṇḍalinī* rise (in *prāṇa kuṇḍalinī* as well as in *cit kuṇḍalinī*). You can achieve these powers when the *kuṇḍalinī* has not risen in its fullness. That is really what is implied by the shores of this ocean.

Those people who tread on these shores also achieve those powers. They do not dive in that ocean, for when they dive in that ocean, they are gone, their personality and existence is over; they are digested in that, they become one with that. Treading on the shores of this ocean means enjoying your being in the enjoyment of and utilization of those yogic powers. For instance your headache does not go with any medicine and I remove it with my yogic powers, I tread on those shores; I have not dived into that ocean yet. If I have dived into that, then there is no question of curing you; one cannot cure anybody then. How can one cure anybody if one has dived into that ocean and one's personality is over? You can cure only when your personality exists and your personality exists only on the shores; and when you are inside, your being is finished. This ocean is limitless and bottomless.

मायामयजगत्सान्द्रपङ्कमध्याधिवासिने ।
अलेपाय नमः शम्भुशतपत्राय शोभिने ॥१५॥

māyāmayajagatsāndrapaṅkamadhyādhivāsine ।
alepāya namaḥ śambhuśatapatrāya śobhine ॥15॥

I bow to Lord Śiva who is just like a beautiful lotus. He resides in the midst of the dense mud of differentiated universe but He is not even touched by it. Such dense mud of differentiated perception of the universe does not affect Him at all. He is above it just like a lotus. I bow to Him.

मङ्गलाय पवित्राय निधये भूषणात्मने ।
प्रियाय परमार्थाय सर्वोत्कृष्टाय ते नमः ॥१६॥

maṅgalāya pavitrāya nidhaye bhūṣaṇātmane ।
priyāya paramārthāya sarvotkṛṣṭāya te namaḥ ॥16॥

O Lord, I bow to Thee who is always auspicious, who is all-round pure, who is the treasure of the universe, who is the ornament of the universe, who is very dear to me, who is the real essence of the universe, and who is above all.

नमः सततबद्धाय नित्यनिर्मुक्तिभागिने ।
बन्धमोक्षविहीनाय कस्मैचिदपि शम्भवे ॥१७॥

namaḥ satatabaddhāya nityanirmuktibhāgine ।
bandhamokṣavihīnāya kasmaicidapi śambhave ॥17॥

I bow to that unique Lord Śiva, who is always bound to the objective world; who is always absolutely liberated from these bondages and in fact who is above any bondages and liberations. That is why He is supreme and unique.

उपहासैकसारेऽस्मिन्नेतावति जगत्त्रये ।
तुभ्यमेवाद्वितीयाय नमो नित्यसुखासिने ॥१८॥

upahāsaikasāre 'sminnetāvati jagattraye ।
tubhyamevādvitīyāya namo nityasukhāsine ॥18॥

I bow only to Thee O Lord who is the only power possessing eternal body of highest beatitude, the highest bliss in this universe that otherwise in essence has become the root of nothingness. In the end there is nothing, no substance in this world, only mockery and unreality.

दक्षिणाचारसाराय वामाचाराभिलाषिणे ।
सर्वाचाराय शर्वाय निराचाराय ते नमः ॥१९॥

dakṣiṇācārasārāya vāmācārābhilāṣiṇe ।
sarvācārāya śarvāya nirācārāya te namaḥ ॥19॥

O Lord, I bow to Thee who is the essence of *dakṣiṇācāra* (the school of Śaivism which is straightforward ideology where no meat or other forbidden things are permitted, where straightforward processes are explained). Not only this, You proceed to *vāmācāra* also (that way of thinking where nothing is right and nothing is wrong, where those forbidden processes are explained).

You are *sarvācāra*, all processes reside in You. O Lord, in fact, You are *nirācāra*, there is no *ācāra* in You, there is not any established rule of conduct, there is no process at all. In fact You are above all this. I bow to Thee, who possesses all these systems.

(*Sarvācāra* is all *ācāra*s; *that* is the real Trika system. Trika system does not forbid the forbidden things. There is nothing right and nothing wrong in that supreme state of thinking of Trika system.)

यथा तथापि यः पूज्यो यत्रतत्रापि योऽर्चितः ।
योऽपि वा सोऽपि वा योऽसौ देवस्तस्मै नमोऽस्तु ते ॥२० ॥

yathā tathāpi yaḥ pūjyo yatratatrāpi yo 'rcitaḥ ।
yo 'pi vā so 'pi vā yo 'sau devastasmai namo 'stu te ॥20 ॥

I bow to Thee O Lord, who is adored in each and every way of worship and who is worshipped in each and every place, not only in shrines but in places like butchery also in the real sense; who is worshipped not only in shrines, temples, mosques or churches but everywhere. He is worshipped everywhere. I bow to that personality whosoever He may be; He may be Lord Śiva, He may be Brahmā, He may be my friend, I bow to Him. I bow to that Being who is universal.

मुमुक्षुजनसेव्याय सर्वसन्तापहारिणे ।
नमो विततलावण्यवाराय वरदाय ते ॥२१ ॥

mumukṣujanasevyāya sarvasantāpahāriṇe ।
namo vitatalāvaṇyavārāya varadāya te ॥21 ॥

I bow to Thee, the bestower of boons; who bestows boons to Thy devotees and who is the embodiment of infinite beauty. Such infinite beauty and charm is seen only in Lord Śiva who is adored by those who have the desire to be liberated. He is the remover of all pains and sorrows.

सदा निरन्तरानन्दरसनिर्भरिताखिल-
त्रिलोकाय नमस्तुभ्यं स्वामिने नित्यपर्वणे ॥२२॥

sadā nirantarānandarasanirbharitākhila-
trilokāya namastubhyaṁ svāmine nityaparvaṇe ॥22॥

I bow to Thee who is my Master and in whose kingdom, festivals are being functioned every moment, continuously and uninterrupted. Every moment is filled with festivals and there is never sadness. Joy always appears there in Thy kingdom.

I bow to Thee who has filled the entire threefold universe by His uninterrupted and unlimited *ānanda-rasa*. You have filled Your bliss of consciousness in all the three worlds of mine. My wakefulness is overflowing with Your supreme bliss and so also is my dreaming state and dreamless state. So I am filled with that uninterrupted bliss.[2]

सुखप्रधानसंवेद्यसम्भोगैर्भजते च यत्।
त्वामेव तस्मैघोराय शक्तिवृन्दाय ते नमः ॥२३॥

sukhapradhānasaṁvedyasambhogairbhajate ca yat ।
tvāmeva tasmaighorāya śaktivṛndāya te namaḥ ॥23॥

O Lord, I don't bow to Thee, I bow to Thy class of energies, Thy innumerable energies which adore Thee only, by beautiful *śabda, sparśa, rasa, rūpa* and *gandha*. One strives to get beautiful

2. Threefold universe means *bhū-loka, bhuvaḥ-loka* and *svarga-loka* in the universal way of thinking and from individual point of view, *triloka* comprises the state of wakefulness, the dreaming state and the dreamless state.

things before one's eyes, one strives to hear beautiful sound through one's ears, one strives to smell beautiful fragrance of flowers through the nose and one also wants beautiful touch through the skin. All the five senses are the energies of Lord Śiva and these are bent upon carrying all the beautiful things inside and offering these to Lord Śiva who is residing in one's own heart. So I bow to these five senses.

The word *ghorāya* here is an *upalakṣaṇa* for *aghora-śakti* and it is frightful for those who are ignorant. It is not frightful for those who are not ignorant, who are attached to Lord Śiva, who are attached to His devotion.

One class of energies is *aghora* energies that carry one inside; the second class is *ghora* energies that make one stand still and the third class is *ghora-tarī* energies that push one down. These are the functions of the three energies of Lord Śiva.

Here the author implies *aghora* energies, which he says also act as *ghora* energies for those who are ignorant and who are not wholly devoted to Lord Śiva. They are kicked out. *Ghorāya* here refers to *aghora-śakti* because then all one's energies are carried towards the centre of the Universal consciousness. When one collects the pleasures of all the five senses and offers those pleasures to the Lord, then instead of being destroyed in the differentiated perception of the universe, one is carried to that oneness of the God-consciousness. So it is the function of *aghora* energies in the end.

मुनीनामप्यविज्ञेयं भक्तिसम्बन्धचेष्टिताः ।
आलिङ्गन्त्यपि यं तस्मै कस्मैचिद्भवते नमः ॥२४ ॥

munīnāmapyavijñeyaṁ bhaktisambandhaceṣṭitāḥ ।
āliṅgyantyapi yaṁ tasmai kasmaicidbhavate namaḥ ॥24 ॥

Those *ṛṣi*s and *muni*s who have discarded all pleasures of the universe, who have kept themselves away from worldly pleasures and directed their consciousness towards the recitation and meditation of Lord Śiva; those *ṛṣi*s and *muni*s also do not find Thee O Lord. You are absolutely away from their perception. You are not perceived by them. On the other hand, those who are Thy devotees, who are attached to Thee, who love Thee; although they are given to the activities of the universe, they do everything in their daily routine of life, they go through all the worldly activities, but still embrace You O Lord. They indulge in all the worldly activities but side by side embrace You. Those are Thy real devotees. I bow to Thee O Lord. Actually You are dear to me.

परमामृतकोशाय परमामृतराशये ।
सर्वपारम्यपारम्यप्राप्याय भवते नमः ॥२५॥

paramāmṛtakośāya paramāmṛtarāśaye ।
sarvapāramyapāramyaprāpyāya bhavate namaḥ ॥25॥

I bow to Thee O Lord who is the treasure of the supreme nectar of God-consciousness and who is the mass of the supreme nectar.

He is achieved only at the stage of the topmost centre of all tops, the transcendental top; the transcendental supreme limit. He is achieved at the supreme limit of transcendental state. He is realized only when the eyes, the perceptions, the five senses take journey to that end and reach that topmost transcendental point. I bow to Thee.

From Śaiva point of view, in other words, in each and every action, at the very source of each and every action He is realized. For instance when we perceive any object, for instance these spectacles, before that we perceive something like spectacles and before that we perceive some flow of perceiving.

There are no spectacles available there in our perceiving at that time; in the very beginning, there is only the force of coming out. That is the source, the source of each and every perception.

At the source of each and every perception You are observed, You are achieved my Lord. I bow to Thee. (That is *śāmbhavopāya*.)

महामन्त्रमयं नौमि रूपं ते स्वच्छशीतलम् ।
अपूर्वामोदसुभगं परामृतरसोल्वणम् ॥२६ ॥

mahāmantramayaṁ naumi rūpaṁ te svacchaśītalam ।
apūrvāmodasubhagaṁ parāmṛtarasolvaṇam ॥26 ॥

I bow to Thy form O Lord who is filled with supreme *mantra,* the supreme I-consciousness, the universal I-consciousness, who is only universal I-consciousness. I bow to Thee whose form is always transparent and cooling.

O Lord all the fires of the worldly desires are subsided in Your presence. These fires have no opportunity to rise when You are present. There is no question of these fires rising. So it is cooling. (It cools because there is no worry. All worldly worries create in us the fire that burns us with grief. For instance I like some girl but she doesn't like me, I burn with the fire of the desire, she has not accepted me, what should I do?) So one should divert totally towards Lord Śiva, everything will be solved.

Being transparent, the whole universe is reflected in His being because this universe is not separate from Him. Although it is separately perceived by us in fact if we go to the depth of this perception we will ultimately come to this conclusion that the whole universe is only a reflection in the mirror of God-consciousness. So we must feel that Lord Śiva is everywhere, in each and every being in this world that is fragrant with the unique aroma of God-consciousness. And that it is filled with and nourished with the supreme nectar.

स्वातन्त्र्यामृतपूर्णत्वदैक्यख्यातिमहापटे ।
चित्रं नास्त्येव यत्रेश तन्नौमि तव शासनम् ॥२७॥

svātantryāmṛtapūrṇatvadaikyakhyātimahāpaṭe ।
citraṁ nāstyeva yatreśa tannaumi tava śāsanam ॥27॥

O Lord I bow to Thy spiritual order in which order form nothing is written. It is only just a clear sheet order form from Lord Śiva. It is the perception of Your being, Your transcendental state which is filled with the nectar of independence. Your *svarūpa* is filled with the nectar of independence and that nectar of independence is the sheet on which You have written the order and on that sheet nothing is written. I bow to that sheet, that order sheet of Yours. So it means that this whole universe although it is perceived with differentiated perception (this is Mr X and that is Mrs Y, etcetera), but actually there is nothing like own or alien; there is nothing worthless and thus fit to be abandoned and nothing is beneficial and thus to be kept. It is only Universal consciousness and nothing else.

Although this is the picture, this is the writing, this is the order form from Lord Śiva, but actually it is not written at all. It is only blank white paper, whiteness shines everywhere. This is the position of the universe if one goes to the depth of understanding.

According to Śaiva point of view, although He writes this picture, to us it seems it is written, drawn, inscribed in consciousness, but if you go to the root of this picture, there is nothing written, only white sheet that will be perceived when you enter that transcendental state of God consciousness. You will perceive that there is nothing. This universe is only pervaded by God.

सर्वाशङ्काशनिं सर्वालक्ष्मीकालानलं तथा ।
सर्वामङ्गल्यकल्पान्तं मार्गं माहेश्वरं नुमः ॥२८ ॥

sarvāśaṅkāśaniṁ sarvālakṣmīkālānalaṁ tathā ।
sarvāmaṅgalyakalpāntaṁ mārgaṁ māheśvaraṁ numaḥ ॥28 ॥

I bow to the path of Lord Śiva, the avenue through which Lord Śiva would be achieved; I bow to that path of Lord Śiva, which acts like a thunderbolt and thus shatters and destroys all doubts. For all misfortunes, this path of Lord Śiva acts like the great fire of *kālāgni-rudra*. So all the misfortunes are burnt to ashes, all doubts are gone, all the absence of joy is destroyed paving the way for joy all around, when one just steps on to the path of Lord Śiva. All doubts and misfortunes are over.

I bow to that path of Lord Śiva.

जय देव नमो नमोऽस्तु ते सकलं विश्वमिदं तवाश्रितम् ।
जगतां परमेश्वरो भवान् परमेकः शरणागतोऽस्मि ते ॥२९ ॥

jaya deva namo namo 'stu te sakalaṁ viśvamidaṁ tavāśritam,
jagatāṁ parameśvaro bhavān paramekaḥ śaraṇāgato 'smi te. 29.

O Lord, victory be to Thee. I bow to Thee again and again; this entire universe is dependent on You. You are the Master of all the three worlds. I have taken refuge only in Thee.

॥ इति श्रीमदुत्पलदेवाचार्यविरचिते श्रीशिवस्तोत्रावल्यां सर्वात्मपरिभावनाख्यं द्वितीयं स्तोत्रम् ॥

॥ *iti śrīmadutpaladevācāryaviracite śrīśivastotrāvalyāṁ sarvātmaparibhāvanākhyaṁ dvitīyaṁ stotram* ॥

3

प्रणयप्रसादाख्यं तृतीयं स्तोत्रम्

Praṇayaprasāda Stotra

Supplication with Reverence

Praṇayaprasāda, the title of this chapter means supplication, to just attempt to please God through various humble ways, ask or beg for something earnestly, try to please the Lord through reverence, obeisance.

सदसत्त्वेन भावानां युक्ता या द्वितयी गतिः ।
तामुल्लङ्घ्य तृतीयस्मै नमश्चित्राय शम्भवे ॥१॥

sadasattvena bhāvānāṁ yuktā yā dvitayī gatiḥ ।
tāmullaṅghya tṛtīyasmai namaścitrāya śambhave ॥1॥

There are two aspects of the process of the universe; the universe moves in two ways, one universe is that of existence and the other universe is that of non-existence. The existing universe comprises the entire objective world around us and the non-existent universe comprises the imaginary things that we only imagine. As long as you perceive in your own mind, you can create things in dreaming state also which are non-existent. In the dreaming state, the world is non-existent; I ride a motor car in that non-existent world. The motor car is my own imagination and so is the road and so also is the point to which the motor car is being driven. So with my own imagination, I create this universe that is non-existent; that is found only in the dreaming state. Drunkards also create a world of their own and so do the lovers — they are always blind as it is! This universe is the creation of God whereas that is the creation of individual beings in their own minds. While the former comprises the existent world, the latter is the non-existent world.

When you cross these two, the existing and the non-existing world, then you get entry into the world which is the third world, third way of the world that is beyond both the existing and the non-existing world and cannot be described.

I bow to that Lord Śiva who is neither existing nor non-existing but beyond both these, the state which is beyond description, it is just wonderful. I bow to that wonderful and marvellous Lord Śiva.

आसुरर्षिजनादस्मिन्नस्वतन्त्रे जगत्त्रये ।
स्वतन्त्रास्ते स्वतन्त्रस्य ये तवैवानुजीविनः ॥२॥

āsurarṣijanādasminnasvatantre jagattraye ।
svatantrāste svatantrasya ye tavaivānujīvinaḥ ॥2॥

In this threefold universe, everyone is dependent, without independence. The whole body of the three worlds is dependent on one thing or the other. Right from *devarṣi*s to this earth all are seen to be dependent. In these three dependent worlds, those people alone are independent who serve Lord Śiva who is the embodiment of absolute independence. Only His devotees are independent in this otherwise wholly dependent universe. Lord Śiva is the sole embodiment of independence and those people who worship Lord Śiva, become independent. They get merged into Him.

अशेष-विश्वखचित-भवद्वपुरनुस्मृतिः ।
येषां भवरुजामेकं भेषजं ते सुखासिनः ॥३॥

aśeṣa-viśvakhacita-bhavadvapuranusmṛtiḥ ।
yeṣāṁ bhavarujāmekaṁ bheṣajaṁ te sukhāsinaḥ ॥3॥

Differentiated perception is the worst disease of the universe and cannot be cured by any medicine. There is only one remedy, the only dose to end the disease of perceiving differentially and that is to just memorize one's mind towards Thy *svarūpa,* Thy being of God-consciousness which is filled with universality. This whole universe in fact exists in God-consciousness and to put memory on that God-consciousness is the only remedy for getting rid of this disease. Memory here means the constant flow of awareness, uninterrupted flow of meditation. This is *śāktopāya.*

सितातपत्रं यस्येन्दुः स्वप्रभापरिपूरितः ।
चामरं स्वर्धुनीस्रोतः स एकः परमेश्वरः ॥४ ॥

sitātapatraṁ yasyenduḥ svaprabhāparipūritaḥ ।
cāmaraṁ svardhunīsrotaḥ sa ekaḥ parameśvaraḥ ॥4 ॥

He alone is Lord Śiva; He alone is the real Master of the universe who has used the moon as umbrella for Himself and the Milky Way as His fan. For whom the Milky Way is a fan and the moon serves as an umbrella, He is the only Master existing in this universe.

Second Meaning

When this universal objective state is infused by Your God-consciousness (Universal objective state is called moon from Śaiva point of view), Your God-consciousness is injected into that moon, that objective world, the moon will then possess another form, it will become the abode of nectar. He who has got the rise of *kuṇḍalinī* as the *cāmara,* as the fan; this universal objectivity injected with God-consciousness as the umbrella, He is the real Master and He is the real Lordship, there is no other Lordship.[1]

1. *Cāmara* is the bushy tail used as a fan or fly flap and is reckoned as an insignia of royality.

प्रकाशां शीतलामेकां शुद्धां शशिकलामिव।
दृशं वितर मे नाथ कामप्यमृतवाहिनीम्॥५॥

prakāśāṁ śītalāmekāṁ śūddāṁ śaśikalāmiva |
dr̥śaṁ vitara me nātha kāmapyamr̥tavāhinīm ||5 ||

O desired Lord, throw Your kind glance on me, that glance which is filled with light, which is filled with coolness and which is purified all-round just like the moonlight. Throw that unique glance on me O Lord, which throws floods of nectar.

त्वच्चिदानन्दजलधेश्च्युताः संवित्तिविप्रुषः।
इमाः कथं मे भगवन्नामृतास्वादसुन्दराः॥६॥

tvaccidānandajaladheścyutāḥ saṁvittiviprusạḥ |
imāḥ kathaṁ me bhagavānnāmr̥tāsvādasundarāḥ ||6 ||

This whole universe actually comprises the drops which have come out from the ocean of Thy being who is the embodiment of *cidānanda rasa*. This universe is actually created out of a few drops that have come out of the ocean of God-consciousness. Why don't I then taste from these that nectar of God-consciousness? Why is that nectar of God-consciousness absent here for me? Why don't I find God-consciousness in the entire objective world?

Kṣemarāja has commented upon this *śloka* in another way that I do not agree with.

He states that actually this whole universe has been formed out of the drops which have come out of that universal ocean of God-consciousness. The origin of this universal objective world lies in the drops that have come out of that ocean. How can this universe not become nectarized for me? He wants this universe to be nectarized with God-consciousness. He does not perceive the already nectarized state of this universe. His devotion is the desire for the universe to be nectarized.

This desire is neglected by the commentator, thus that is not the real commentary for this *śloka*.

त्वयि रागरसे नाथ न मग्नं हृदयं प्रभो ।
येषामहृदया एव तेऽवज्ञास्पदमीदृशाः ॥७॥

tvayi rāgarase nātha na magnaṁ hṛdayaṁ prabho I
yeṣāmahṛdayā eva te 'vajñāspadamīdṛśāḥ II7 II

O my Master, those who have not developed their minds, whose minds have not dived in the nectar of Thy devotion, from my point of view, those persons are absolutely mindless.[2] Such people deserve only contempt and need to be thrown away like ordinary stones.

प्रभुणा भवता यस्य जातं हृदयमेलनम् ।
प्राभवीणां विभूतीनां परमेकः स भाजनम् ॥८॥

prabhuṇā bhavatā yasya jātaṁ hṛdayamelanam I
prābhavīṇāṁ vibhūtīnāṁ paramekaḥ sa bhājanam II8 II

O my Master, one who has achieved the oneness of heart with Thee, he alone is the person worthy of Thy state of God-consciousness, Thy state of glory. He alone tastes the nectar of Thy glorious state.

Oneness of heart means achieving identical awareness; whatever the Master thinks of, the slave also must think of the same. The state of being a slave to the Master is not a joke. When you are slave to the Master, your Master need not ask you to do such and such a thing. You must know what is in His mind and you must do that. This is the actual position of being a slave. That is the oneness of heart. Whatever He thinks, that thought must come to your mind. You should not give Him the trouble of calling you and asking you to do a particular thing; beforehand you should act according to his choice which

2. Literally 'heartless.'

must be known to you. Then only can you claim to be His slave otherwise you are more like an engaged coolie who has to be every time told what is to be done or else he will keep sitting idle.

हर्षाणामथ शोकानां सर्वेषां प्लावकः समम् ।
भवद्ध्यानामृतापूरो निम्नानिम्नभुवामिव ॥९॥

harṣāṇāmatha śokānāṁ sarveṣāṁ plāvakaḥ samam ।
bhavaddhyānāmṛtāpūro nimnānimnabhuvāmiva ॥9॥

O Lord, the great flood of the nectar of Thy meditation levels all joys and sorrows just as the undulations of low and high ground are all levelled when these are inundated by floods. The flood waters even out the ups and downs of the ground and make it level; in the same way the flood of the nectar of Thy meditation keeps at the same level all joys, all sorrows and all tortures.

The term *dhyāna* here has been used in the higher sense of *samāveśa*.

केव न स्याद्दशा तेषां सुखसम्भारनिर्भरा ।
येषामात्माधिकेनेश न क्वापि विरहस्त्वया ॥१०॥

keva na syāddaśā teṣāṁ sukhasambhāranirbharā ।
yeṣāmātmādhikeneśa na kvāpi virahastvayā ॥10॥

O Lord, for those persons, those exceptional human beings, for whom You are more important than their own existence in this universe; for those persons, who love You more than their own lives, all states of their lives are constantly filled with excessive joy. Those devotees, for whom You are dearer than their own lives, who are not separated from You ever, who don't remain away from Your consciousness even for a moment; all states of their lives are always filled with excessive joy. They will never become sad.

गर्जामि बत नृत्यामि पूर्णा मम मनोरथाः ।
स्वामी ममैष घटितो यत्त्वमत्यन्तरोचनः ॥११ ॥

garjāmi bata nṛtyāmi pūrṇā mama manorathāḥ ।
svāmī mamaiṣa ghaṭito yattvamatyantarocanaḥ ॥11 ॥

You are always dearest to me, I love You; I always crave for You. Now that You have come and You are always present with me, my only problem of longing to attain You has been solved and I have achieved You. Hence I will emit a deep thundering sound with joy, I will dance. I will shatter all the limitations of my body away now that You are solved and achieved. You are the only one I was craving for.

नान्यद्वेद्यं क्रिया यत्र नान्यो योगो विदा च यत् ।
ज्ञानं स्यात् किन्तु विश्वैकपूर्णा चित्त्वं विजृम्भते ॥१२ ॥

nānyadvedyaṁ kriyā yatra nānyo yogo vidā ca yat ।
jñānaṁ syāt kintu viśvaikapūrṇā cittvaṁ vijṛmbhate ॥12 ॥

Where there is no other object for perception, where there is no other action to be performed, where there is no other practice of *yoga*, where there is no other way of thinking and where there is no knowledge other than the knowledge of Thy own nature; there alone the kingdom of consciousness is glorified, it shines from all sides. This whole differentiated world becomes one offering in that fire of consciousness. In one *svāhā* this whole differentiated perception of the world is finished.

दुर्जयानामनन्तानां दुःखानां सहसैव ते ।
हस्तात्पलायिता येषां वाचि शश्वच्छिवध्वनिः ॥१३ ॥

durjayānāmanantānāṁ duḥkhānāṁ sahasaiva te ।
hastātpalāyitā yeṣāṁ vāci śaśvacchivadhvaniḥ ॥13 ॥

Those persons in whose speech the sound "Śiva" resides eternally; those who recite this *mantra* of Śiva in continuity without any break, those persons have instantaneously escaped from the grip of unlimited and uncontrollable tortures of this universe. Those persons who have *Śiva-dhvani* continuously flowing from their mouth, have all of a sudden escaped the grip of the countless and uncontrollable tortures which cannot be conquered otherwise. They are at once relieved of the worldly tortures.

When you utter the sound of Śiva with its meaning even in *vaikharī*, it will in the end carry you to that God-consciousness. Utpaladeva here refers to *parāmarśa* primarily. *Śiva-dhvani* means entry in Śiva in the real sense.

उत्तमः पुरुषोऽन्योऽस्ति युष्मच्छेषविशेषितः ।
त्वं महापुरुषस्त्वेको निःशेषपुरुषाश्रयः ॥१४ ॥

uttamaḥ puruṣo 'nyo 'sti yuṣmaccheṣaviśeṣitaḥ ।
tvaṁ mahāpuruṣastveko niḥśeṣapuruṣāśrayaḥ ॥14 ॥

In this world of action, grammatically there are three persons, namely the first person, the second person and the third person, indicating respectively I, you and he. It is already an admitted norm in this world of action that whenever three persons do some work jointly, and a query is addressed individually to them, each one is bound to reply — "we are working jointly" and not — "I am working jointly." So the first person is predominant in all these three persons from grammatical point of view. So we attribute first person for all these three persons and we say "we are doing it." In the same way the *uttama-puruṣa* is supreme *vis-à-vis* the second and the third person.

But O Lord, You are neither the first person, nor the second person and nor the third person; You are the *mahāpuruṣa* the supreme spirit, because You are the life, the basis of all these three people. All these three persons flow out in this manifestation because of You.

जयन्ति ते जगद्वन्द्या दासास्ते जगतां विभो।
संसारार्णव एवैष येषां क्रीडामहासरः ॥१५॥

jayanti te jagadvandyā dāsāste jagatāṁ vibho ।
samsārārṇava evaiṣa yeṣāṁ kṝḍāmahāsaraḥ ॥15॥

O Lord of the three worlds, those persons who are Thy slaves, are victorious. Although they are Your slaves, they are respected and revered by all the three worlds. Everybody honours them because they are Thy slaves. The one who prostrates before Lord Śiva, before him the whole universe prostrates. Everybody takes refuge in him because he has taken refuge in that Supreme Being, the creator of this universe. For Thy slaves, this universe, which for others is the great ocean of torture, sorrow, sadness, ups and downs, is like a pleasure lake. The sojourn through this universe appears to them like the enjoyment one gets in a bathing pool.

आसतां तावदन्यानि दैन्यानीह भवज्जुषाम्।
त्वमेव प्रकटीभूया इत्यनेनैव लज्ज्यते ॥१६॥

āsatāṁ tāvadanyāni dainyānīha bhavajjuṣām ।
tvameva prakaṭībhūyā ityanenaiva lajjyate ॥16॥

Those who are Thy devotees, who have taken refuge in Your Being, have only one problem, only one request from You, and that is to reveal Your nature, even if other miserable states and sorrows remain unsolved for them.

There are so many miserable states and sorrows in this universe to be resolved like I want a wife, I don't get a wife; I want money but I don't get money; I want peace of mind but I don't get peace of mind, etcetera.

O Lord, let all those miserable states of the universe remain unresolved for the time being. I am not going to solve those miserable states. Only one thing needs to be solved and that is everything for me. Reveal Your nature to me. I want Thy presence before me. If You reveal Your nature to me, all those miserable states will automatically vanish.

मत्परं नास्ति तत्रापि जापकोऽस्मि तदैक्यतः।
तत्त्वेन जप इत्यक्षमालया दिशसि क्वचित् ॥१७॥

matparaṁ nāsti tatrāpi jāpako 'smi tadaikyataḥ ।
tattvena japa ityakṣamālayā diśasi kvacit ॥17॥

O Lord, there is a picture of Thy form wherein Lord Śiva is shown sitting cross-legged, eyes closed, moving beads and thinking of something else. The picture shows Lord Śiva in *samādhi,* made out to be worshipping some other deity, contemplating on some Being higher than His. Through this You reveal to us, make us understand that "there is no other being higher than Me, still I recite *mantra*s, not for any other Lord, but for My own Self. I am reciting *mantra*s for My own nature. I am not diverted towards any other higher being. There is no other being higher than Me, even then I recite *mantra*s." In fact, recitation of *mantra*s means reciting *mantra*s to reveal your own Self, you must recite *mantra*s for your own Self, and you must recognize your own nature.

सतोऽवश्यं परमसत्सच्च तस्मात्परं प्रभो।
त्वं चासतस्सतश्चान्यस्तेनासि सदसन्मयः ॥१८॥

sato 'vaśyaṁ paramasatsacca tasmātparaṁ prabho ।
tvaṁ cāsatassataścānyastenāsi sadasanmayaḥ ॥18॥

O Master, it is a fact that the existent object is absolutely other than a non-existent object and that a non-existent object is other than the existent object. But you are something else. You are neither existent nor non-existent. You are above the existent and non-existent in the logical sense.

If you say : He exists, it means you reject His non-existent nature. But Lord Śiva, according to Kashmir Śaivism is both existent and non-existent because of the complete embodiment of Lord Śiva, as He is complete as well as incomplete. The one, who is only complete and not incomplete, is not complete; he is incomplete because the state of incompleteness is not there. When incompleteness and completeness both exist, that is the complete state; that is the full state. That is *mahāsat.*

You are above this existent and non-existent. That is why You are both existing as well as non-existing.

सहस्रसूर्यकिरणाधिकशुद्धप्रकाशवान् ।
अपि त्वं सर्वभुवनव्यापकोऽपि न दृश्यसे ॥१९॥

sahasrasūryakiraṇādhikaśuddhaprakāśavān ।
api tvaṁ sarvabhuvanavyāpako 'pi na dṛśyase ॥19॥

O Lord, although You are more brilliant and shining than the rays of simultaneous rise of one thousand suns and more vividly revealed in each and every corner of this universe and although You have pervaded this whole universe, existent universe as well as non-existent imaginary universe, yet it is a wonder for me, how is it that You are not seen anywhere. Nobody can perceive You in this universe. You have kept Yourself an absolute secret.

That *prakāśa* is absolutely pure, universal. It cannot be objective. The one who is absolutely pure, purely subjective, will never become object of anybody. He will never be revealed because He is the Revealer. He sees everything but cannot be seen. The Knower cannot be known. The Knower knows everybody but nobody knows the Knower. The knower is the thing. This is the embodiment of knowership.

जडे जगति चिद्रूपः किल वेद्येऽपि वेदकः ।
विभुर्मितेच येनासि तेन सर्वोत्तमो भवान् ॥२०॥

jaḍe jagati cidrūpaḥ kila vedye 'pi vedakaḥ ।
vibhurmite ca yenāsi tena sarvottamo bhavān ॥20 ॥

O Lord, in the world of unconsciousness, You are filled with consciousness. In the unaware world, You alone are aware, You are filled with awareness. In the world of objectivity, You are the Knower. You are the Knower in the world of the known. In the objective world, You are the subject. As You are all-pervading in the world of limitation, You are the Unlimited. With these qualifications You are the greatest and the highest being existing in this universe.

अलमाक्रन्दितैरन्यैरियदेव पुरः प्रभोः ।
तीव्रं विरौमि यन्नाथ मुह्याम्येवं विदन्नपि ॥२१ ॥

alamākranditairanyairiyadeva puraḥ prabhoḥ ।
tīvraṁ viraumi yannātha muhyāmyevaṁ
vidannapi ॥21 ॥

I always weep and cry bitterly for Thee, for achieving Thy nature. I am always filled with lamentations to achieve Thee. I am always distressed because of Thy separation.

O Lord, I want to weep bitterly and cry loudly before You only for one purpose. Although I know how to attain You, although I know how to hold You, yet I leave You aside and go for worldly pleasures for the time being. Why am I going astray? I ought not have done this. I should have only sought Your presence all around, everywhere.

॥ इति श्रीमदुत्पलदेवाचार्यविरचिते श्रीशिवस्तोत्रावल्यां
प्रणयप्रसादाख्यं तृतीयं स्तोत्रम् ॥

॥ *iti śrīmadutpaladevācāryaviracite śrīśivastotrāvalyāṁ*
praṇayaprasādākhyaṁ tṛtīyaṁ stotram ॥

4

सुरसोद्बलाख्यं चतुर्थं स्तोत्रम्

Surasodbala Stotra

The Strength of Divine Nectar

SURASODBALA means to strengthen the real taste of that supreme nectar. *Su+rasa+udbala* means that *rasa,* that attachment to the Lord comes by itself, it doesn't come by adoption of any means. He infuses strength in that nectar of devotion. It just comes on its own, you can't make it come. It is the divine grace that makes it flow and the grace does not depend on your actions, good or bad. Even if you keep doing good actions, you cannot be sure of receiving that grace. Similarly even if you keep indulging in bad actions, it is not certain that you wouldn't receive grace. You can get grace anytime, anywhere; whenever He so wishes.

Destiny does't matter. Destiny is the result of your *karma*s, your past actions; whereas receiving grace has got nothing to do with your actions, it just comes. It is called *haṭha-śaktipāta,* that grace which makes you go, even if you don't agree, even if you are not prepared, even if you don't like, it will carry you forcibly. It is *tīvra-śaktipāta.*

The joy experienced at the time of receiving the grace is billions of times the joy relating to the gratification of normal physiological instincts. It would shatter your body to pieces and make you enter into that real divine bliss. When the grace comes, you can't help it, you can't do anything about it.

Afterwards you don't like anything. That is why those Śaivite *yogīs* have turned to that consciousness.

चपलमसि यदपि मानस तत्रापि श्लाघ्यसे यतो भजसे।
शरणानामपि शरणं त्रिभुवनगुरुमम्बिकाकान्तम् ॥१॥

capalam asi yadapi mānasa
tatrāpi ślāghyase yato bhajase ।
śaraṇānāmapi śaraṇaṁ
tribhuvanagurumambikākāntam ॥1॥

O my mind, although you are flickering, always restless, yet you are glorified because at times whenever you direct your nature towards the remembrance of Lord Śiva, you direct it wholeheartedly so you are glorified. You are victorious because you achieve the nearness of Lord Śiva, the Master of the three worlds; spiritually, the world of wakefulness, the world of dreaming state and the world of dreamless state.

In the beginning you must achieve *svapna-svātantrya,* mastery over the dreaming state; that is you dream only whatever you wish to dream according to your own choice and not according to the choice of *niyati śakti* of Lord Śiva. Next you must achieve mastery over *suṣupti,* the state of dreamless sound sleep. Mastering the state of sound sleep means to be aware that you are in *suṣupti* peacefully as long as you remain in *suṣupti;* that is *vijñānākala.* Having attained mastery over these two states, you can gain mastery over the state of wakefulness and when you have once gained mastery over wakefulness, you are none other than Lord Śiva, you are Lord Śiva Himself.

Although you are restless in the real sense, always going astray here and there, still you are victorious because at times, you remember the Lord of lords who is the master of all the three states, the refuge of all the refugees, the Master of the three worlds; who is dear to Pārvatī, embraced by the supreme *śakti* that is *parā-śakti*, Pārvatī, the Consciousness.

उल्लङ्घ्य विविधदैवतसोपानक्रममुपेयशिवचरणान् ।
आश्रित्याप्यधरतरां भूमिं नाद्यापि चित्रमुज्झामि ॥२॥

ullaṅghya vividhadaivata-
sopānakramamupeyaśivacaraṇān ।
āśrityāpyadharatarāṁ bhūmiṁ
nādyāpi citramujjhāmi ॥2॥

O Lord, this is the story of great torture for me. I have crossed all those steps of yogic exercises, yogic practices, all *sādhanās*, and have come to the supreme state, the uppermost limit of the stepless state and not only that, I have achieved, I have touched the lotus feet of Lord Śiva also, but I still go after these worldly sensual pleasures. After achieving this highest state also, I hanker after these worldly pleasures. This is the great story of my torture.

प्रकटय निजमध्वानं स्थगयतरामखिललोकचरितानि ।
यावद्भवामि भगवंस्तव सपदि सदोदितो दासः ॥३॥

prakaṭaya nijamadhvānaṁ
sthagayatarāmakhilalokacaritāni ।
yāvadbhavāmi bhagavaṁ-
stava sapadi sadodito dāsaḥ ॥3॥

O my Lord, O my Master, there is one request for You, keep Your avenues open for me for the time being as long as I would pass through them and reach Your lotus feet; and simultaneously, keep all the doors of the world of torture, the world of differentiated perception, the world of hankering after sensual pleasures closed for the time being as long as I would become Your slave. Till then You have to do these two things for me, namely, keep Your avenues wide open and simultaneously keep those hindrances and diversions at bay.

Although I have developed desire and devotion for Lord Śiva, at the same time, on the other side there appears some attractive figure, some attractive smell or some attractive taste and my attention is diverted to these.

O Lord, please keep the doors closed on those diversions until I would reach Your lotus feet. Please make it possible for me to reach Your lotus feet now. Always attentive, I want to serve You wholeheartedly. This is the only pleasure for me.

शिव शिव शम्भो शङ्कर शरणागतवत्सलाशु कुरु करुणाम्।
तव चरणकमलयुगलस्मरणपरस्य हि सम्पदोऽदूरे ॥४॥

śiva śiva śambho śaṅkara
śaraṇāgatavatsalāśu kuru karuṇām ।
tava caraṇakamalayugala-
smaraṇaparasya hi sampado 'dūre ॥4॥

O Lord Śiva, O Śambhu, O Śaṅkara; O beloved of those who have sought refuge in You, please bestow Your grace on me quickly. Don't hesitate to bless me right now because if You don't bless me soon, I will be blessed automatically as it is because I crave so much to get Your blessings that I can't remain without it, I can't live without Your grace.

So if You want to maintain Your honour and prestige, You must bless me at the earliest. Otherwise I would be blessed naturally as it is because I am craving so much for that. There is no other way out as I am bent upon remembering Your nature and reciting Your *mantra*. I have diverted my whole attention on Thy divine form, because those glories of being with You are very near to me so it is for You to decide if You do it Yourself or have it done automatically.

तावकाङ्घ्रिकमलासनलीना ये यथारुचि जगद्रचयन्ति।
ते विरिञ्चिमधिकारमलेनालिप्तमस्ववशमीश हसन्ति ॥५॥

tāvakāṅghrikamalāsanalīnā
ye yathāruci jagadracayanti ।
te viriñcimadhikāramalenā-
liptamasvavaśamīśa hasanti ॥5 ॥

You know the functioning of Brahmā? He creates, but cannot protect, destroy, conceal or reveal. His job is only to create the universe. Brahmā resides in the lotus that comes from the navel of Viṣṇu who is resting on the couch of those thousand heads of Śeṣanāga. That is why Brahmā is called *kamalāsana,* one whose seat is the lotus.

Addressing Lord Śiva, the author says that there are other Brahmās also who reside in Thy lotus-like feet.

O Lord Śiva, those Brahmās who reside in Thy lotus feet, not only create the universe like the creator Brahmā, but they create the universe, protect the universe, destroy the universe, conceal their nature and reveal their nature to people. They do all the five actions just like Śiva. They just scorn that Brahmā who is bent upon only creating but cannot protect, destroy, conceal or reveal. They hold him in very low esteem as he can only create as per *karmas,* but Brahmās residing in Thy lotus feet can create with their free will instead. This is the difference between those Brahmās and the creator Brahmā.

त्वत्प्रकाशवपुषो न विभिन्नं किंचन प्रभवति प्रतिभातुम् ।
तत्सदैव भगवन् परिलब्धोऽसीश्वर प्रकृतितोऽपि विदूरः ॥६ ॥

tvatprakāśavapuṣo na vibhinnaṁ
kiñcana prabhavati pratibhātum ।
tatsadaiva bhagavan parilabdho-
'sīśvara prakṛtito 'pi vidūraḥ ॥6 ॥

O Lord, nothing can exist if it is separated from Your glorious form of *cit,* all consciousness, all knowledge, all bliss. Thus everything that exists is one with that being of Your consciousness. So I should not worry that I have not attained You. I have already attained You wherever You are; You are everywhere so I have already attained You. Although internally You may be away from me, I don't see You but still I am with You.

As nothing can exist that is separated from You, it is obvious that I am with You. Everything is united with You so I am also united with You. Thus I have also achieved You. So I am not worried about that achievement but still You are away from me.

पादपङ्कजरसं तव केञ्चिद् भेदपर्युषितवृत्तिमुपेताः ।
केचनापि रसयन्ति तु सद्यो भातमक्षतवपुर्द्वयशून्यम् ॥७॥

pādapaṅkajarasaṁ tava keṁcid
bhedaparyuṣitavṛttimupetāḥ ।
kecanāpi rasayanti tu sadyo
bhātamakṣatavapurdvayaśūnyam ॥7॥

Thy devotees are classified in two ways: one class comprises those who drink the nectar of Your lotus feet by sips. Just drink one sip, then do something else, then another sip, and then do some other thing, then another sip, and so on. They drink the nectar of Thy lotus feet successively so it does not remain so fresh. The freshness of that nectar is ruined for those people who drink that nectar that way. But the other class of Thy devotees drink that nectar in such a way that when they just begin to drink it, they drink it for ever. They never are separated from drinking that nectar. So those are the real godly persons.

The first class of devotees drink that nectar intermittently, with the drinking sessions interspersed with various worldly activities. This kind of drinking is not so fresh. Freshness will come only to devotees who drink it altogether without doing any other job; they just go on drinking without any interruption. That nectar always remains fresh for them.

नाथ विद्युदिव भाति विभा ते या कदाचन ममामृतदिग्धा ।
सा यदि स्थिरतरैव भवेत्तत् पूजितोऽसि विधिवत्किमुतान्यत् ॥८ ॥

nātha vidyudiva bhāti vibhā te
yā kadācana mamāmṛtadigdhā ।
sā yadi sthirataraiva bhavettat
pūjito 'si vidhivatkimutānyat ॥8 ॥

O Master, Your shining form which is soaked with the supreme nectar of joy and ecstasy does appear to me sometimes. It appears to me momentarily just like the lightning of clouds, finished in a flash. Before I can get to worship You, it is gone.

Now, O Master, I would like to perceive that formation which is soaked in that supreme nectar, and I would like it to remain established for some more time, to remain stationary for some more time and not go away quickly just like lightning. O Lord, then I would be able to worship You.

When I perceive You, when I see the flash of lightning, I want to worship You, but before I can do that it is gone. How can I worship You O Lord? If it remained for some more time, then I would be able to worship Thee. So please do that for me. It is not so much of a job for You, You could very easily do it.

सर्वमस्त्यपरमस्ति न किंचिद् वस्त्ववस्तु यदि वेति महत्या ।
प्रज्ञया व्यवसितोऽत्र यथैव त्वं तथैव भव सुप्रकटो मे ॥९ ॥

sarvamasyaparamasti na kiñcid
vastvavastu yadi veti mahatyā ।
prajñayā vyavasito 'tra yathaiva
tvaṁ tathaiva bhava suprakaṭo me ॥9 ॥

From the Śaivite point of view, this is absolutely true that You reside in each and every object and that You are everywhere and there is nothing existing except You. This is a fact as discussed and proved in Śaivism. I have also concluded that this is the real fact that You are everywhere, You are everything and You are residing in each and every object; but then, why don't You appear like that to me? I would like You to appear like that. Theoretically I understand it, but it must appear to me practically also. That is what I am longing for.

स्वेच्छयैव भगवन्निजमार्गे कारितः पदमहं प्रभुणैव ।
तत्कथं जनवदेव चरामि त्वत्पदोचितमवैमि न किंचित् ॥१० ॥

svecchayaiva bhagavannijamārge
kāritaḥ padamahaṁ prabhuṇaiva ।
tatkathaṁ janavadeva carāmi
tvatpadocitamavaimi na kiṁcit ॥10 ॥

I have never told You to put me on the road to Your spiritual abode. I never asked You to carry me on Thy path. You have done it Yourself. You have put me on the path and now You are refusing to appear. If I have been kept and carried on Thy path, why do I act like ordinary worldly people, why don't I sing in that glamour of Thy glory filled with consciousness and bliss? How is it?

कोऽपि देव हृदि तेषु तावको जृम्भते सुभगभाव उत्तमः ।
त्वत्कथाम्बुदनिनादचातका येन तेऽपि सुभगीकृताश्चिरम् ॥११ ॥

ko 'pi deva hṛdi teṣu tāvako
jṛmbhate subhagabhāva uttamaḥ ।
tvatkathāmbudaninādacātakā
yena te 'pi subhagīkṛtāściram ॥11 ॥

This is Thy greatness O Lord, O Master, that in the hearts of those blessed devotees of Thine, such fineness of Thy devotion appears, that although they are away from Thy consciousness, yet when some other person puts and explains the fineness of Your joy and bliss before them; by hearing only they get entry into God-consciousness at once. Such is the fineness of their heart that if they are only explained the ways of God-consciousness, by hearing alone of the ways of God-consciousness, they get entry into that God-consciousness. This is the fineness of the heart they have acquired.

त्वज्जुषां त्वयि कयापि लीलया राग एष परिपोषमागतः ।
यद्वियोगभुवि सङ्कथा तथा संस्मृतिः फलति संगमोत्सवम् ॥१२॥

tvajjuṣāṁ tvayi kayāpi līlayā
rāga eṣa paripoṣamāgataḥ ।
yadviyogabhuvi saṁkathā tathā
saṁsmṛtiḥ phalati saṅgamotsavam ॥12॥

By Thy divine grace, the attachment for Thee in those devotees of Thine is so intense, not by their actions or efforts, not by their continuous practice of *yoga*, but by Your grace, by that supreme play of Thine; it is Your play, You have not to put any effort to bestow grace on somebody. It is just a matter of play for You. You could do it any time; You could do it even now.

So, when You induce that grace in some person, they are so much intensely attached to Thee later that although they may be away from You, they may not be in *samādhi*, even in their routine worldly activities, when someone reminds them about Lord Śiva, they at once get entry into God-consciousness. They don't remain in *samādhi* always; while they are talking, walking, smiling, laughing, or doing any other household work, there and then itself, at that very point, they get entry. This is the greatness of the attachment that is created in their heart through Your divine grace.

It is only grace that can carry you to God-consciousness. It is not your own effort, no action would do. Action is always limited. Action done by a limited soul will always remain limited. How can that limited action carry you to that unlimited abode of truth? For achieving that unlimited abode of truth, you need unlimited grace and that will be divine, and that will come only from your Master, Lord Śiva.

यो विचित्ररससेकवर्धितः शङ्करेति शतशोऽप्युदीरितः ।
शब्द आविशति तिर्यगाशयेष्वप्ययं नवनवप्रयोजनः ॥१३॥

yo vicitrarasasekavardhitaḥ
śaṅkareti śataśo 'pyudīritaḥ ।
śabda āviśati tiryagāśaye-
ṣvapyayaṁ navanavaprayojanaḥ ॥13॥

When this sound "Śiva" is recited a hundred times (Śaṅkara, Śaṅkara, Śaṅkara, . . . like that) and this sound enters the hearts of animal kingdom, that is all animal-like persons, all duffers who have beastly understanding, when this sound of Śiva (Śaṅkara) is recited hundred times and it gets entry in those animal-like hearts; in those hearts also it creates always fresh and new profits and glamour. They find some new and joyful application being applied in their hearts. Those animals, those duffers also feel the joy of something happening to them. This is the greatness of this sound "Śiva."

ते जयन्ति मुखमण्डले भ्रमन् अस्ति येषु नियतं शिवध्वनिः ।
यः शशीव प्रसृतोऽमृताशयात् स्वादु संस्रवति चामृतं परम् ॥१४॥

te jayanti mukhamaṇḍale bhraman
asti yeṣu niyataṁ śivadhvaniḥ ।
yaḥ śaśīva prasṛto 'mṛtāśayāt
svādu saṁsravati cāmṛtaṁ param ॥14॥

Those persons on whose lips this sound "Śiva" resides always;

while walking, talking, bathing, drinking, eating, meditating, not meditating, doing everything, they alone are glorified. The greatness of that sound is that when you utter that sound of Śiva only once, you feel it has flown out from the abode of nectar just like moonlight which has come from the abode of nectar. When you look at the moon, it soothes your heart; it soothes you, making you comfortable and peaceful. In the same way, when that sound is uttered only once, you feel it has flown out of the abode of nectar and it sprinkles you with that nectar and bathes you in nectar in fullness. Those persons who recite this sound for twenty-four hours, are actually glorified.

परिसमाप्तमिवोग्रमिदं जगद् विगलितोऽविरलो मनसो मलः ।
तदपि नास्ति भवत्पुरगोपुरार्गलकवाटविघट्टनमण्वपि ॥१५॥

parisamāptamivogramidaṁ jagad
vigalito 'viralo manaso malaḥ ।
tadapi nāsti bhavatpuragopurā-
rgalakavāṭavighaṭṭanamaṇvapi ॥15॥

O Lord, this whole universe of differentiated perception (this is Mr X, that is Mr Y, etcetera), has totally come to its end for me. It is a fact. I feel this differentiated perception is gone for good. That subtle internal impurity of *āṇava-mala* too is finished for me. So it is due that You must appear to me now.

The differentiated perception, the mode of differentiated perception is also finished so You must appear to me. It is now due because this differentiated perception exists no more and *āṇava-mala* also does not exist any more. I have no impurity now. *Kārma-mala* and *māyīya-mala* are already gone. Whatever impressions of *āṇava-mala* there were, those impressions too are now shattered to pieces. Now Your appearance to me is due. But even then the external gate of Your abode of kingdom does not open a bit yet. Not even a narrow crack is there. I am left confused about what has happened to me. I have done everything. I have overcome all these things; this differentiated perception is gone, this impurity is also over, still there is no hope of entering into that kingdom of Thine because there is not even the slightest chink in that gate.

सततफुल्लभवन्मुखपङ्कजोदरविलोकनलालसचेतसः ।
किमपि तत्कुरु नाथ मनागिव स्फुरसि येन ममाभि मुखस्थितिः ॥१६ ॥

satataphullabhavanmukhapaṅkajo-
daravilokanalālasacetasaḥ ।
kimapi tatkuru nātha manāgiva
sphurasi yena mamābhimukhasthitiḥ ॥16 ॥

O Lord, I have only one craving. My mind longs to just see and get entry into the depth of Thy face which is like a lotus always in bloom, unlike ordinary lotuses that open up only during the day time and close at night. Thy lotus-like face is in bloom always, day and night. Only this much craving and longing is there always in my mind, to just watch the centre of that lotus, to just go on observing the depth of that lotus of Your face.

O my Master, please do something so that You somehow appear to me always face to face. This is my ambition and it is not much of a job but just a matter of play for You.

त्वदविभेदमतेरपरं नु किं सुखमिहास्ति विभूतिरथापरा ।
तदिह तावकदासजनस्य किं कुपथमेति मनः परिहृत्य ताम् ॥१७ ॥

tvadavibhedamateraparaṁ nu kiṁ
sukhamihāsti vibhūtirathāparā ।
tadiha tāvakadāsajanasya kiṁ
kupathameti manaḥ parihṛtya tām ॥17 ॥

O Lord, this is an admitted fact that perceiving oneness of

Thy nature is the real pleasure, the real glory. When that conclusive perception of perceiving oneness everywhere (*abheda-rasa*) appears in one's mind, what other pleasure could one have other than that, what better glory could one seek? That is the best glory and that is the best pleasure one could ask for.

O my Master, if I already know that, why then do I some times go after other worldly pleasures? Why am I at times attached to some worldly things? It should not have happened. My mind leaves aside the glamour of Thy nature and goes in pursuit of other worldly pleasures and sensual gratifications. Why does it happen? It should not have happened but it does happen to me.

क्षणमपीह न तावकदासतां प्रति भवेयमहं किल भाजनम् ।
भवदभेदरसासवमादरादविरतं रसयेयमहं न चेत् ॥१८ ॥

kṣaṇamapīha na tāvakadāsatāṁ
prati bhaveyamahaṁ kila bhājanam ।
bhavadabhedarasāsavamādarā-
daviratam rasayeyamahaṁ na cet ॥18 ॥

If I would not have tasted the nectar of Thy glorious lotus-like feet, if I would not have tasted the oneness of that *abheda-rasa* with great honour, with great love and affection and in continuity as I have, what would have happened to me?

Previously I have tasted the nectar of that oneness of Thy glory in continuity and with honour, with respect, with love, with affection. If I would not have done that, I would not have been honoured with becoming Your slave even for a second. (As if I have become now!) I have become your slave for one or two seconds in twenty-four hours. That is enough for me; that is really great for me. I am happy that way. I am fortunate at least I have got something.

I don't see You at all but I have become Your slave, that in itself is a great consolation for me. That I have become Your slave is due to my previous behaviour of having tasted the nectar of Your oneness with respect, with honour, with love and in continuity.

He had that experience of oneness earlier but is not experiencing it now; he has experienced becoming His slave, he is a slave, that is enough, that is everything. If once you are honoured to become His slave that is great. If you once experience that state of Śiva, even in a flash of only one second, it will soak you for the rest of your life in that joy. You will be always intoxicated, it is so joyous.

If I would not have gone through this exertion to drink the nectar of Your oneness with devotion, with honour and in continuity then I would not have been able to become Your slave even for one second, but for one second I am Your slave. Sometimes I see You for one minute in one year; even that is enough. That is a great thing for me. That overjoys me and intoxicates me for the rest of my life.

न किल पश्यति सत्यमयं जनस्तव वपुर्द्वयदृष्टिमलीमसः ।
तदपि सर्वविदाश्रितवत्सलः किमिदमारटितं न शृणोषि मे ॥१९॥

na kila paśyati satyamayaṁ jana-
stava vapurdvayadṛṣṭimalīmasaḥ ।
tadapi sarvavidāśritavatsalaḥ
kimidamāraṭitaṁ na śṛṇoṣi me ॥19॥

O Lord, I confess these worldly people are given to worldly pleasures and they are made impure by always residing in the field of differentiated perception. It is true.

So it is not possible for them to see You. They can't see You because they are kept away from God-consciousness by being attached to worldly pleasures and differentiated perceptions. It is true, I believe in this thing. But even then You know everything, You know the position of each and every soul in this universe, You know me also and the position I am living in. You are all knowing and You are the protector of those who have surrendered to You unconditionally. You protect them, that is also true.

Why don't my cries of seeking to be with You reach You? You do not hear my cries. For those people who are given to worldly enjoyments, their being separated from You is understandable, but for me it is not due. I always crave for You. You are everything for me and still this cry does not reach You. What shall I do?

स्मरसि नाथ कदाचिदपीहितं विषयसौख्यमथापि मयार्थितम्।
सततमेव भवद्वपुरीक्षणामृतमभीष्टमलं मम देहि तत्॥२०॥

smarasi nātha kadācidapīhitaṁ
viṣayasaukhyamathāpi mayārthitam ।
satatameva bhavadvapurīkṣaṇā-
mṛtamabhīṣṭamalaṁ mama dehi tat ॥20॥

My Lord, just try to recollect, just go deep into my past and try to remember if there ever is a single occasion when I have longed and craved for worldly enjoyment, if there is a moment even when I have acted or longed for worldly pleasures. You won't find a single moment like that. I have always been asking for Your love, for Your nearness. I want to get entry into You. I want nothing else in this world, I have no other taste. I promise You, if there is even one moment ever when I have longed for worldly pleasures then discard me, don't see me at all. I have always been longing for Your nearness and there is nothing else I have ever longed for. So grant me Thy nearness. I don't want anything else.

किल यदैव शिवाध्वनि तावके कृतपदोऽस्मि महेश तवेच्छया।
शुभशतान्युदितानि तदैव मे किमपरं मृगये भवतः प्रभो॥२१॥

kila yadaiva śivādhvani tāvake
kṛtapado 'smi maheśa tavecchayā ।
śubhaśatānyuditāni tadaiva me
kimaparaṁ mṛgaye bhavataḥ prabho ॥21॥

O my Lord, right from the moment I have been made to step on the path of Your supreme nectar, when I have been put on the path of Your abode, the path of *Śiva-bhāva* through Your free will, hundreds of thousands of glories have risen in my nature. Why should I crave for any other thing? I crave only for You.

I have not stepped on that path myself, it was Your will that I should step on that path; from that very moment itself hundreds of thousands of glories have risen in my nature. Why should I ask for any other thing from Thee, O my Lord? I only want You and nothing else.

यत्र सोऽस्तमयमेति विवस्वाँश्चन्द्रमः-प्रभृतिभिः सह सर्वैः।
कापि सा विजयते शिवरात्रिः स्वप्रभाप्रसरभास्वररूपा॥२२॥

yatra so 'stamayameti vivasvām̐-
ścandramaḥ-prabhṛtibhiḥ saha sarvaiḥ ।
kāpi sā vijayate śivarātriḥ
svaprabhāprasarabhāsvararūpā ॥22॥

That abode of Your nectarized residence is glorified where the functioning of the sun stops altogether (There is no sunlight there. External meaning is sunlight; internal meaning is when the outgoing breath has stopped); where the moonlight has also ended (External meaning is moonlight; internal meaning is when the ingoing breath has stopped); and all notions of thought also have stopped totally. All thoughts other than spirituality, other than Lord Śiva have ended and ingoing and outcoming breaths have also stopped. That is *Śivarātri*. That supreme *Śivarātri*, that unique *Śivarātri* is glorified.

The external *Śivarātri* is the fourteenth night of the dark half of the month of Phālguna. It is the darkest night. The internal *Śivarātri* is when the rise of *cidānanda*, the rise of God-consciousness takes place. The rise of God-consciousness will never take place when there is breathing in and out or when there are so many notions and thoughts residing in the mind. That *Śivarātri* will take place only when all these three things namely incoming breath, outgoing breath and all thoughts cease altogether. And that *Śivarātri* is shining with its own glory. It is not perceived through any foreign light, it is glorified by its own light. He does not say this to Lord Śiva but to his own self, that this is the glorious *Śivarātri*.

अप्युपार्जितमहं त्रिषु लोकेष्वाधिपत्यममरेश्वर मन्ये ।
नीरसं तदखिलं भवदङ्घ्रिस्पर्शनामृतरसेन विहीनम् ॥२३॥

apyupārjitamahaṁ triṣu loke-
ṣvādhipatyamamareśvara manye ।
nīrasaṁ tadakhilaṁ bhavadaṅghri-
sparśanāmṛtarasena vihīnam ॥23॥

O God of all gods, even if I attain the state of kingdom of all the three worlds, that whole kingdom appears to me dry and tasteless if I am detached from You. If I become the ruler of all the three worlds of *bhū-loka*, *bhuvaḥ-loka* and *svarga-loka* but am deprived of being in touch with Your lotus feet, that whole kingdom appears to me absolutely tasteless and it worries me. I would not like to have that kingdom if I don't get to touch Your lotus feet. The nearness of Your lotus feet is everything for me, I want nothing else.

बत नाथ दृढोऽयमात्मबन्धो भवदख्यातिमयस्त्वयैव क्लृप्तः।
यदयं प्रथमानमेव मे त्वामवधीर्य श्लथते न लेशतोऽपि ॥२४॥

bata nātha dṛḍho 'yam-ātmabandho
bhavadakhyātimayastvayaiva klṛptaḥ ।
yadayaṁ prathamānameva me tvā-
mavadhīrya ślathate na leśato 'pi ॥24 ॥

O my Master, this is the greatest worry in me, this bondage of impurity created by You is so strong, the knot of bondage is so tight that it does not get loosened a bit even when You are shining in front of me. It does not care for You. This bondage is so strong that it disregards You also. You appear to me but still it is so tight. You could have shattered it to pieces but that does not happen. Before You also it is not shattered. This is another problem for me.

महतामसरेश पूज्यमानोऽप्यनिशं तिष्ठसि पूजकैकरूपः।
बहिरन्तरपीह दृश्यमानः स्फुरसि द्रष्टृशरीर एव शश्वत्॥२५॥

mahatāmamareśa pūjyamāno-
pyaniśaṁ tiṣṭhasi pūjakaikarūpaḥ ।
bahirantarapīha dṛśyamānaḥ
sphurasi draṣṭṛśarīra eva śaśvat ॥25 ॥

O God of gods, there is one thing which is unique about Your nature. When You are worshipped by those great souls, Your devotees, You take the seat of worshipper and not the worshipped. There You are worshipper and not the worshipped. You are worshipped but in fact You are worshipper Yourself.

If great *yogī*s perceive You internally and externally quite vividly, there also You remain as perceiver and not as perceived. There You are perceiver and not the perceived. Although they perceive You in their hearts at the time of *samādhi*, actually You are not perceived, You are the perceiver. When they worship

You, actually You are not the worshipped, You are the worshipper. This is Śaivism; he has touched Śaivism here.

॥ इति श्रीमदुत्पलदेवाचार्यविरचिते श्रीशिवस्तोत्रावल्यां
सुरसोद्बलाख्यं स्तोत्रम् ॥

॥ *iti śrīmadutpaladevācāryaviracite śrīśivastotrāvalyāṁ surasodbalākhyaṁ stotram* ॥

5

स्वबलनिदेशनाख्यं पञ्चमं स्तोत्रम्

Svabalanideśana Stotra

Longing for One's Own Strength

THE fifth chapter is nominated *Svabalanideśana* (*sva+bala+nideśana*) which means just longing for his own nature, longing for the strength of his own nature, pointing out his own power, longing for strength to find out his own nature. As he is powerless, he cannot attain the power that he longs for. How can he reach there? He has attachment for the Lord's lotus feet but he cannot reach there. So he requests the Lord to drag him there.

त्वत्पादपद्मसम्पर्कमात्रसम्भोगसङ्गिनम् ।
गलेपादिकया नाथ मां स्ववेश्म प्रवेशय ॥१॥

tvatpādapadmasamparkamātrasambhogasaṅginam ।
galepādikayā nātha māṁ svaveśma praveśaya ॥1॥

O Master, I have got attachment and weakness for just enjoying the pleasure of touching Your lotus feet. Not only touch, I want to always be near Your lotus feet. As You know, I am always attached to Your lotus feet and this is my only weakness. I have no other weakness in this world. I want to reach there, but the problem is that I can't reach there. How can I reach there? How can individuality get entry into universality? Individual consciousness can never reach universal consciousness so there is no hope of me reaching there and to be near Your lotus feet.

So there is one request to You to fulfil, my Lord: that is to drag me to Thy abode without my desire. Even if I don't want to, even if I have no strength to go there, still You carry me there; You drag me there at once because I cannot go there by myself even though I am craving to be there.

भवत्पादाम्बुजरजोराजिरञ्जितमूर्धजः ।
अपाररभसारब्धनर्तनः स्यामहं कदा ॥२॥

bhavatpādāmbujarajorājirañjitamūrdhajaḥ ।
apārarabhasārabdhanartanaḥ syāmahaṁ kadā ॥2॥

When will that glorious day come, my Lord, when I shall be with You, remain with You, hold Your lotus feet and take the dust of Your lotus feet. I would then wholeheartedly apply that dust on my head and hair and get fully intoxicated and then dance with joy always. When will that glorious day come for me?

त्वदेकनाथो भगवन्नियदेवार्थये सदा ।
त्वदन्तर्वसतिर्मूको भवेयं मान्यथा बुधः ॥३॥

tvadekanātho bhagavanniyadevārthaye sadā ।
tvadantarvasatirmūko bhaveyaṁ mānyathā budhaḥ ॥3॥

I have only one Master and that is Thyself. You are my Master. I know You, I know nobody else. You are everything to me. You are my wife, You are my husband, You are my father, You are my mother, You are my everything.

O Lord, I crave only for this much: let me remain dumb, let me remain an idiot, but let me reside in You. I would like to reside in Your inner Self and be an idiot to others. I would prefer to be ignorant but be with You rather than be wise and knowledgeable but away from Thy nearness. I don't want that wisdom.

अहो सुधानिधे स्वामिन् अहो मृष्ट त्रिलोचन।
अहो स्वादो विरूपाक्षेत्येव नृत्येयमारटन्॥४॥

aho sudhānidhe svāmin aho mṛṣṭa trilocana ।
aho svādo virūpākṣetyeva nṛtyeyamāraṭan ॥4॥

O Lord, I wish to dance, I crave to dance wholeheartedly singing all the while in clear voice:

> O my Lord, You are the ocean of nectar for me,
> You are my Master; You are tasteful and sweet,
> You have got three eyes, O my Master,
> You are sweet in words and sweet in actions,
> You are compassionate; You have got a third eye.
> In this way I would like to sing Your glory and dance always.

त्वत्पादपद्मसंस्पर्शपरिमीलितलोचनः।
विजृम्भेय भवद्भक्तिमदिरामदघूर्णितः॥५॥

tvatpādapadmasaṁsparśaparimīlitalocanaḥ ।
vijṛmbheya bhavadbhaktimadirāmadaghūrṇitaḥ ॥5॥

O Lord, I would like to taste the liquor of Your devotion and get intoxicated by that devotion. How I wish after getting intoxicated, I would be near Your lotus feet and by the touch of Your lotus feet, my eyes would be closed altogether and I would be intoxicated for twenty-four hours. In that intoxication I would be near Your lotus feet, so there would be no other thought in me except Your lotus feet, all my organs would get closed. That is what I want. (Like when one tastes a very tasty thing, one just closes one's eyes.)

चित्तभूभृद्भुवि विभो वसेयं क्वापि यत्र सा।
निरन्तरत्वत्प्रलापमयी वृत्तिर्महारसा॥६॥

cittabhūbhṛdbhuvi vibho vaseyaṁ kvāpi yatra sā ।
nirantaratvatpralāpamayī vṛttirmahārasā ॥6॥

O Lord, I would like to reside in that isolated peak of the mountain of mind where no other thoughts come. I would like to reside there and then just cry for You, just cry for Your nearness. If I have already achieved Your nearness, I would still cry for You. I would like to cry and cry for You always. That is my ambition and that would be very tasteful for me.

यत्र देवीसमेतस्त्वमासौधादा च गोपुरात् ।
बहुरूपः स्थितस्तस्मिन्वास्तव्यः स्यामहं पुरे ॥७॥

yatra devīsametastvamāsaudhādā ca gopurāt ।
bahurūpaḥ sthitastasminvāstavyaḥ syāmahaṁ pure ॥7॥

O Lord, I want You to appear to me everywhere along with Your better half Pārvatī, not only where You are residing, not only in the secluded place of *samādhi*, not only in the secluded place of Your residential abode of God-consciousness, but from that point right up to the point of *vaikharī*, up to the point of worldly activities You should appear to me.

I want You to appear to me along with Your Pārvatī right from *samādhi* to worldly activities and in whatever I come across. For instance when I see a person on the roadside I would like to see You in that person, I would like to see You in every thing along with Pārvatī. (This is going from internal state to external state, *jagad-ānanda*.)

समुल्लसन्तु भगवन् भवद्भानुमरीचयः ।
विकसत्वेष यावन्मे हृत्पद्मः पूजनाय ते ॥८॥

samullasantu bhagavan bhavadbhānumarīcayaḥ ।
vikasatveṣa yāvanme hṛtpadmaḥ pūjanāya te ॥8॥

O Lord, I want to give You only one trouble, not forever but only for some definite limited period.

O Lord, You are shining just like the sun. Please go on

showering those rays of Thy grace on the lotus of my heart that is just shrunk; that is not yet in the state of blooming. My lotus-like heart needs the penetration of those rays of Your sun till such time it blooms nicely, after that You can withdraw Your rays. But let it bloom first. I am not asking for something for my own self. I have no motive but to offer it at Your lotus feet once it has bloomed. That supernatural sun is Lord Śiva.

प्रसीद भगवन् येन त्वत्पदे पतितं सदा।
मनो मे तत्तदास्वाद्य क्षीवेदिव गलेदिव ॥९॥

prasīda bhagavan yena tvatpade patitaṁ sadā ।
mano me tattadāsvādya kṣīvediva galediva ॥9॥

O Lord, be pleased with me so that my mind is always at Your lotus feet. May You be pleased with my mind. With Your pleasure, Your joy penetrating my mind, it will experience many supernatural states of being and get intoxicated and dissolved in some supreme being. So be pleased with my mind that way.

प्रहर्षाद्वाथ शोकाद्वा यदि कुड्याद्धटादपि।
बाह्यादथान्तराद्भावात्प्रकटीभव मे प्रभो ॥१०॥

praharṣādvātha śokādvā yadi kuḍyādghaṭādapi ।
bāhyādathāntarādbhāvātprakaṭībhava me prabho ॥10॥

O my Master, just appear to me, I don't mind whether You appear to me in happiness or in crisis; if I am happy and You appear to me, well and good, or I am in crisis and You appear to me, still well and good. Let me remain in crisis, but just appear to me. I don't mind if I am discarded by all my company and I have lost all my kith and kin. Appear to me. Whether You appear to me from a wall or from a pot, I don't mind. It is fine if You appear to me from outside or if You appear to me from inside, it is still fine. Just appear to me. I don't want anything else. I don't lay down any conditions. You must appear to me whether I am in pain or in pleasure, whatever it is. Even if I am put in crisis and You appear to me, that crisis also is nectar for me.

बहिरप्यन्तरपि तत्स्यन्दमानं सदास्तु मे ।
भवत्पादाम्बुजस्पर्शामृतमत्यन्तशीतलम् ॥११॥

bahirapyantarapi tatsyandamānaṁ sadāstu me ।
bhavatpādāmbujasparśāmṛtamatyantaśītalam ॥11॥

The nectar which appears by the touch of Your divine lotus feet, the nectar that rises from the touch of Your lotus feet is very soothing and cooling.

O Lord let that divine nectar always remain flowing to me from outside and inside. I would like to be attached with the touch of Your divine lotus feet because that produces nectar which is soothing and cooling. Let that nectar flow to me for twenty-four hours from outside and inside; outside in the worldly activities and inside in *samādhi* also at the time of meditation.

त्वत्पादसंस्पर्शसुधासरसोऽन्तर्निमज्जनम् ।
कोऽप्येष सर्वसम्भोगलङ्घी भोगोऽस्तु मे सदा ॥१२॥

tvatpādasaṁsparśasudhāsaraso 'ntarnimajjanam ।
ko 'pyeṣa sarvasambhogalaṅghī bhogo 'stu me sadā ॥12॥

I would always like to have that unique enjoyment, that unique pleasure of just drowning in the lake filled with the nectar of the touch of Your lotus feet. The touch of Your lotus feet is nectar, and in that lake filled with that nectar I would like to be drowned. If I am drowned in that lake that way, the resulting enjoyment is unique and overcomes all other enjoyments of the world. That enjoyment I would like to have always, for twenty-four hours a day.

निवेदितमुपादत्स्व रागादि भगवन्मया ।
आदाय चामृतीकृत्य भुङ्क्ष्व भक्तजनैः समम् ॥१३ ॥

niveditamupādatsva rāgādi bhagavanmayā ।
ādāya cāmṛtīkṛtya bhuṅkṣva bhaktajanaiḥ samam ॥13 ॥

O Lord, I am before You at Your feet, I am carrying a great present for You. Could You please accept it? This present is what I have attained so far in my life and I have come to offer it at Your feet. This present is the collection of the worldly pleasures, the craving for worldly enjoyments. I have been craving for worldly enjoyments from my very birth right up to this point when I am before You. I have collected only these cravings in my whole life and I want to offer these at Your feet. I don't want You to keep it for Yourself because You don't need it. I would like You to possess it for some time, nectarize that craving for worldly enjoyments with Your God-consciousness, consume a part of it and then distribute it amongst Your devotees; we will also then take it.

I don't want to have those worldly enjoyments in dryness. I would like to have these worldly enjoyments only when they are nectarized with Your God-consciousness. I have no hesitation to have these when they are nectarized. I would enjoy these after You also take some and share them with your devotees.

अशेषभुवनाहारनित्यतृप्तः सुखासनम् ।
स्वामिन् गृहाण दासेषु प्रसादालोकनक्षणम् ॥१४ ॥

aśeṣabhuvanāhāranityatṛptaḥ sukhāsanam ।
svāmin gṛhāṇa dāseṣu prasādālokanakṣaṇam ॥14 ॥

O Lord, now You may say "I have so much to do, so many things to be done, so many things to be adjusted, I can't attend to You so soon," but in fact You have already done all those things, You are always full. Your stomach is always full, because this whole universe is Your own food, You have already possessed that, You are seated peacefully now, so what is the harm if You listen to my grievances now?

Great kings, seated on the throne, attend to the grievances of their subjects one by one successively. As they have no time to do so many things, they ask someone to come the next day; directing yet another to come after a few days for their jobs to be done.

But You have no such compulsions, You have already finished with Your household chores, You have already had Your food, that is *jagad-ānanda,* You are always filled with *jagad-ānanda,* and You have performed all Your activities. You are always full and seated in peace, please divert Your attention towards us also and listen to our grievances.

अन्तर्भक्तिचमत्कारचर्वणामीलितेक्षणः ।
नमो मह्यं शिवायेति पूजयन् स्यां तृणान्यपि ॥१५॥

antarbhakticamatkāracarvaṇāmīlitekṣaṇaḥ ।
namo mahyaṁ śivāyeti pūjayan syāṁ tr̥ṇānyapi ॥15॥

O Lord, I would like to have that supreme state, when I would be experiencing the internal joy of God-consciousness, the internal joy of Your nearness and by experiencing that internal joy, all my organs would get closed and then I would be doing prostration to my own self. In this way I would like to prostrate before my own nature and then worship everything in this world, even the blades of grass.

He is seeking to know his own nature first and worship that and then to come out and worship everything else. For instance when he looks at Mr X, he wouldn't look at Mr X, he would look at his own nature; when he tastes something nice, he would taste God-consciousness, he would like to taste divine nectar of God-consciousness in each and every act of daily life.

अपि लब्धभवद्भावः स्वात्मोल्लासमयं जगत्।
पश्यन् भक्तिरसाभोगैर्भवेयमवियोजितः ॥१६॥

api labdhabhavadbhāvaḥ svātmollāsamayaṁ jagat ।
paśyan bhaktirasābhogairbhaveyamaviyojitaḥ ॥16॥

O Lord, when shall that glorious day come, when I would perceive this whole universe as the outcome of the glory of my own nature and I would become one with the ecstasy of *bhakti-rasa*, the ecstasy of tasting the nectar of devotion; I would be one with tasting the ecstasy of Your devotion. For me, when shall that day come?

आकाङ्क्षणीयमपरं येन नाथ न विद्यते।
तव तेनाद्वितीयस्य युक्तं यत्परिपूर्णता ॥१७॥

ākāṅkṣaṇīyamaparaṁ yena nātha na vidyate ।
tava tenādvitīyasya yuktaṁ yatparipūrṇatā ॥17॥

O Lord, the *śāstra*s hold that You are always full and I think that is a fact. He alone is full who has nothing to do, who has nothing to seek, who has nothing to get, who has nothing to achieve, He alone is full. And because You have nothing to achieve, You don't have desire for anything, as You have everything. You have possessed everything, so there is nothing to long for.

If this is the theory in connection with Thee, then O Lord, You are the only unique person who is filled with fullness, real fullness.

हस्यते नृत्यते यत्र रागद्वेषादि भुज्यते।
पीयते भक्तिपीयूषरसस्तत्प्राप्नुयां पदम् ॥१८॥

hasyate nṛtyate yatra rāgadveṣādi bhujyate ।
pīyate bhaktipīyūṣarasastatprāpnuyāṁ padam ॥18॥

O Lord, I would like to achieve that state of being where one is filled with laughter, one always laughs, one always dances, one always eats and drinks. Here eating means subsiding the craving for worldly enjoyments. So in the outward world real enjoyment lies in eating, dancing, laughing and drinking; those four things make you complete. The extent of completion of your life is gauged by the level of these four things; when you are laughing, when you are dancing, when you are eating all varieties and drinking.

Another meaning is as follows:

(a) *hasyate* means when you laugh at the worldly people, on what they are doing, on their total waste of time in going here and there. This is all false activity. So you laugh at them.

(b) *nṛtyate* means you shatter away all your limbs, all your bodily attachments. Bodily attachments imply those with your kith and kin, with your job, with your Master, with all your surroundings, with house, motor car, etcetera. These are your limbs. When all these are shattered to pieces, that is real dancing.

(c) *rāga dveṣa ādi bhujyate* means absorbing love, hatred, attachment and all such things. When these are absorbed, consumed in God-consciousness, that is real eating.

(d) *pīyate* means drinking, not Scotch whisky, but just being attached to your divine nature. When you are attached to your divine nature that is the real drinking.

Where all this is being done, I would like to achieve that state of being. When shall I achieve that state?

तत्तदपूर्वामोदत्वच्चिन्ताकुसुमवासना दृढताम्।
एतु मम मनसि यावन्नश्यतु दुर्वासनागन्धः ॥१९॥

tat tadapūrvāmoda-
tvaccintākusumavāsanā dṛḍhatām ।
etu mama manasi yāvan-
naśyatu durvāsanāgandhaḥ ॥19 ॥

O Master, in the space of my mind there is always foul smell of various desires, various thoughts of life, like I would want to do this or I would like to go for swimming or watch movies or listen to music, etcetera. All these desires have created a hell of bad smell in my mind. I would like to get rid of it, but it is not within my power, O Lord.

There is only one way of getting rid of the foul smell in my mind and that is remembering Your lotus feet always. I do try that. I do remember Your lotus feet always because divine fragrance flows out of Thy lotus feet when one remembers them. But this divine fragrance in my mind comes and goes and is not established in my mind. As soon as it goes, the foul smell arises again. It has created a hell of bad smell in which I get drowned. How can I get rid of that?

O my Lord, I would ask one favour from Thee and that is to just establish this remembrance of Thy lotus feet, this fragrance of Thy lotus feet in my mind. If it remains for two or three hours, only then would this foul smell get washed away. This is my desire.

क्व नु रागादिषु रागः क्व च हरचरणाम्बुजेषु रागित्वम्।
इत्थं विरोधरसिकं बोधय हितममर मे हृदयम्॥२०॥

kva nu rāgādiṣu rāgaḥ
kva ca haracaraṇāmbujeṣu rāgitvam ।
ittham virodharasikam
bodhaya hitamamara me hṛdayam ॥20 ॥

O Divine Lord, my mind is attached to two opposite things.

Sometimes it likes to be in enjoyment of worldly pleasures, sometimes it wants to meditate. Sometimes it so happens in my mind that there is a strong desire to just meditate wholeheartedly on that one-pointedness, sometimes there is a strong desire in my mind to go after worldly pleasures. There is no meeting place between the North Pole of being attached to Your lotus feet and the South Pole of attachment with worldly pleasures. Sometimes attachment with Your lotus feet arises in my mind but the very next moment attachment to worldly pleasures gets the better of my mind. So my mind is attached to two opposite things.

O my Lord, just initiate my mind not to do such mischievous things. I can't teach my mind, it is out of my control. My mind is always like this. So please teach my mind to be attached to only one point and not to go in two directions. There is no fun in being attached to God-consciousness on one hand and on the other to be degraded to be attached to worldly pleasures; two opposite things. It should not happen. My mind should be attached to God, it must remember that God is the highest being in the universe and above the universe.

O immortal Being, please teach my mind this so that it comes to senses.

विचरन्योगदशास्वपि विषयव्यावृत्तिवर्तमानोऽपि ।
त्वच्चिन्तामदिरामदतरलीकृतहृदय एव स्याम् ॥२१ ॥

vicaranyogadaśāsvapi
viṣayavyāvṛttivartamāno 'pi ।
tvaccintāmadirāmada-
taralīkṛtahṛdaya eva syām ॥21 ॥

I am roaming in various states of Yoga, I am bent upon diverting my mind from the attachment towards worldly pleasures, I am extracting my mind from the worldly enjoyments. Although it is true, yet I don't like this kind of struggle. I would like to be intoxicated only with the desire of being attached to Your lotus feet; that desire alone must remain, I don't like the states of this Yoga like the rise of various *cakras*, nor do I like the withdrawal of worldly thoughts from my mind. Focus your mind towards one point of God-consciousness.

I would not like to go through the botheration of withdrawing the worldly thoughts from my mind. Nor would I like the botheration of going through the states of experiences of Yoga, like sometimes *mūlādhāra cakra* is rising, sometimes *cakra* in the navel is rising, or *cakra* in the heart is rising, sometimes *cakra* in the throat is rising, sometimes *cakra* in *bhrūmadhya* is rising. One thing is experiencing the various states of Yoga and another thing is to withdraw from worldly pleasures and focus the mind towards one point of God-consciousness. Although I do both these things, it is true but there is no happiness in that. I would rather like to remember being attached to Your lotus feet all the time, twenty-four hours a day. That alone should be my job. I don't want to achieve anything, except just always remembering Your lotus feet, nearness of Your lotus feet. Mad after achieving those lotus feet, I would like to just be one with those. I don't want to propagate in the world that I am a powerful *yogī*, I don't like that. I would instead want to die in the nearness of these lotus feet.

वाचि मनोमतिषु तथा शरीरचेष्टासु करणरचितासु ।
सर्वत्र सर्वदा मे पुरःसरो भवतु भक्तिरसः ॥२२॥

vāci manomatiṣu tathā
śarīraceṣṭāsu karaṇaracitāsu ।

sarvatra sarvadā me
puraḥsaro bhavatu bhaktirasaḥ ॥22 ॥

O Lord I would like to have and possess effortlessly the nectar of Thy devotion in all my activities, in speech, in mind, in intellect, in bodily activities and in organic activities.

When I talk to others, when my mind is thinking about various things of the world, when my intellect is confirming what to do and what not to do, in the activities of my body, in speech, in mind, in intellect, in the activities of my body and in the activities of my organs: *śabda, sparśa, rasa, rūpa, gandha,* in seeing, in touching, in hearing, etcetera, in all these activities, I would like to achieve, easily and not with struggle, the nectar of Thy devotion. Let me always have the nectar of Your devotion in all these activities effortlessly.

शिव-शिव-शिवेति नामनि तव निरवधि नाथ जप्यमानेऽस्मिन्।
आस्वादयन् भवेयं कमपि महारसमपुनरुक्तम् ॥२३ ॥

śiva-śiva-śiveti nāmani
tava niravadhi nātha japyamāne 'smin ।
āsvādayan bhaveyaṁ
kamapi mahārasamapunaruktam ॥23 ॥

O my Master, I would like to endlessly recite Your name 'Śiva, Śiva' . . . continuously without a break. I would like to recite only this *mantra* of Śiva always, and internally I would like to experience the supreme nectar of that unique thing which I can't describe. It is beyond my explanation. I simply can't describe what would happen to me when I would recite Your name 'Śiva, Śiva' always in continuity.

स्फुरदनन्तचिदात्मकविष्टपे परिनिपीतसमस्तजडाध्वनि।
अगणितापरचिन्मयगण्डिके प्रविचरेयमहं भवतोऽर्चिता ॥२४ ॥

sphuradanantacidātmakaviṣṭape
parinipītasamastajaḍādhvani ।

agaṇitāparacinmayagaṇḍike
pravicareyamahaṁ bhavato 'rcitā ||24 ||

O Lord, I would like to live in that country which comprises numberless hutments of God-consciousness, where all cottages are filled with God-consciousness; only God-consciousness everywhere and nothing else. In such a country I would like to live and roam about.

Wherever I go, I would find small huts with God-consciousness; I would like to have numberless such huts; God-consciousness everywhere. Everywhere I go and whatever I do in my worldly life — *śabda, sparśa, rasa, rūpa* and *gandha;* I would like to get entry into the hutments of God-consciousness. For instance, when I talk to someone, it would make me enter into that hut of God-consciousness. If I then talk to some other, that would make me enter into another such hut of God-consciousness.

Those hutments would be producers of strength of awareness too. Awareness would also come out of those huts and dullness would be totally absent. In that country, for me, dullness would vanish in every manner from all walks of life. I am longing to taste the nectar of God-consciousness with awareness.

And should I like to just visit another country, other than this country of God-consciousness, I would not find any. I would like to remain, live and shine in that country of God-consciousness. This is *śāktopāya*.

स्ववपुषि स्फुटभासिनि शाश्वते स्थितिकृते न किमप्युपयुज्यते ।
इति मतिः सुदृढा भवतात् परं मम भवच्चरणाब्जरजः शुचेः ॥२५॥

svavapuṣi sphuṭabhāsini śāśvate
sthitikṛte na kimapyupayujyate |

iti matiḥ sudṛḍhā bhavatāt paraṁ
mama bhavaccaraṇābjarajaḥ śuceḥ ॥25॥

It is a fact that once one's nature appears clearly to oneself and when this appearance is firmly established and confirmed; when once one is established in that God-consciousness then nothing remains to be done. There is no doubt in this understanding and this understanding I have; still at times I go after worldly pleasures and that is not indicative of real establishment.

This understanding already exists in me but it is not confirmed, it is not established. Let it be established firmly, not because of my qualities, not because it is due to me. I have no qualities, but because I think of Your feet. Thinking of Your feet makes me eligible to remain confirmed in that state.

किमपि नाथ कदाचन चेतसि स्फुरति तद्भवदंघ्रितलस्पृशाम् ।
गलति यत्र समस्तमिदं सुधासरसि विश्वमिदं दिश मे सदा ॥२६॥

kimapi nātha kadācana cetasi
sphurati tadbhavadaṁghritalaspṛśām ।
galati yatra samastamidaṁ sudhā-
sarasi viśvamidaṁ diśa me sadā ॥26॥

O my Master, in the minds of those fortunate people who always reside near Your lotus feet, something unique happens which I cannot explain, something flows out and with that flow all other worries of the world are shattered to pieces and dissolved in that supreme ocean of nectar. Those fortunate devotees of Thee who always reside in Your lotus feet, sometimes during meditation, experience a unique indescribable state in their minds wherein the dualistic world gets dissolved in that ocean of nectar. I would like to achieve that state always. Please grant me that.

॥ इति श्रीमदुत्पलदेवाचार्यविरचिते श्रीशिवस्तोत्रावल्यां
स्वबलनिदेशनाख्यं पञ्चमं स्तोत्रम् ॥

॥ *iti śrīmadutpaladevācāryaviracite śrīśivastotrāvalyāṁ*
svabalanideśanākhyaṁ pañcamaṁ stotram ॥

6

अध्वविस्फुरणाख्यं षष्ठं स्तोत्रम्

Adhvavisphuraṇa Stotra

Clearing of the Path

THE sixth chapter is named *Adhvavisphuraṇa* wherein the author beseechingly pleads, "O Lord I am treading on Thy path just to achieve You, just to get entry into Your kingdom; please remove all the distractions." He wants his path to be clear of disturbances and distractions so that he could tread smoothly.

क्षणमात्रमपीशान वियुक्तस्य त्वया मम।
निबिडं तप्यमानस्य सदा भूया दृशः पदम्॥१॥

kṣaṇamātramapīśāna viyuktasya tvayā mama ।
nibiḍaṁ tapyamānasya sadā bhūyā dṛśaḥ padam ॥1॥

O Lord, when I am separated from Yourself even for a moment, You must understand, I at once catch fire of sadness. So it is worthwhile for You my Lord to remain in front of me always because when I am kept away from Yourself even for a moment, I get burnt in the fire of sadness. So please be in front of me always.

वियोगसारे संसारे प्रियेण प्रभुणा त्वया।
अवियुक्तः सदैव स्यां जगतापि वियोजितः॥२॥

viyogasāre saṁsāre priyeṇa prabhuṇā tvayā ।
aviyuktaḥ sadaiva syāṁ jagatāpi viyojitaḥ ॥2॥

It is a fact that the essence of this universe is to get separated.

Everybody will get separated in the end. But I have no attachment for my kith and kin, if I am separated from them, I don't mind, but I have attachment for Thee my Lord. You are the only personality I long for. I crave for You alone. I wish I was inseparable from Thee. I wish I was always one with Thee. This is the earnest desire in my mind.

कायवाङ्मनसैर्यत्र यामि सर्वं त्वमेव तत्।
इत्येष परमार्थोऽपि परिपूर्णोऽस्तु मे सदा ॥३॥

kāyavāṅmanasairyatra yāmi sarvaṁ tvameva tat ।
ityeṣa paramārtho 'pi paripūrṇo 'stu me sadā ॥3॥

This is the real science underlying our philosophy that wherever I go through body, speech or mind, that place is always one with Thee, thus I am never away from Thy presence. Wherever my body goes, whatever my speech says, whatever my mind thinks that is Your nature, that is Your divine self. This is the reality of our philosophy. It is a fact but I don't get satisfied. I would like to get satisfaction in this understanding. I understand this is true but to me this does not appear to be practical. I want it to appear to me in practical shape.

निर्विकल्पो महानन्दपूर्णो यद्वद्भवांस्तथा।
भवत्स्तुतिकरी भूयादनुरूपैव वाङ्मम ॥४॥

nirvikalpo mahānandapūrṇo yadvadbhavāṁstathā ।
bhavatstutikarī bhūyādanurūpaiva vāṅmama ॥4॥

O Lord, You are *nirvikalpa,* You have no *vikalpa* and You are filled with supreme ecstasy. This is the reality of Your nature. I am the singer of Your glory. I would like that whatever glory I sing of Thee, must also be like Thy nature. I must sing Your glory just as You are. You are *nirvikalpa,* my singing also must be *nirvikalpa;* You are filled with supreme ecstasy, my singing must also be filled with ecstasy. That is what I am longing for.

भवदावेशतः पश्यन् भावं भावं भवन्मयम्।
विचरेयं निराकाङ्क्षः प्रहर्षपरिपूरितः ॥५॥

bhavadāveśataḥ paśyan bhāvaṁ bhāvaṁ bhavanmayam ।
vicareyaṁ nirākāṅkṣaḥ praharṣaparipūritaḥ ॥5॥

My Lord, I would like one thing: just as a ghost possesses somebody and that person then becomes one with the ghost and afterwards he speaks also like a ghost, in the same way I want You to get entry into my body. When You enter my body, my perception would be absolutely different than it was before. I wish I would see, perceive each and every object as one with Thee and I would roam about this world without any desire and I would be filled with supreme joy. I would become one with You. This is my desire.

भगवन्भवतः पूर्णं पश्येयमखिलं जगत्।
तावतैवास्मि सन्तुष्टस्ततो न परिखिद्यसे ॥६॥

bhagavanbhavataḥ pūrṇaṁ paśyeyamakhilaṁ jagat ।
tāvataivāsmi santuṣṭastato na parikhidyase ॥6॥

O Lord, there is one desire in me which always knocks in the background of my consciousness and that is I would like to perceive this whole universe as filled with Your supreme consciousness. That is my ambition. Let my ambition be fulfilled that way. My Lord, I promise I won't afterwards trouble You by asking for more. This is the only thing that I am asking for, once and for all. Let me see this whole universe as one with Thee and I will be satisfied. I won't afterwards trouble You any more.

विलीयमानास्त्वय्येव व्योम्नि मेघलवा इव।
भावा विभान्तु मे शश्वत्क्रमनैर्मल्यगामिनः ॥७॥

vilīyamānāstvayyeva vyomni meghalavā iva I
bhāvā vibhāntu me śaśvatkramanairmalyagāminaḥ II7 II

Let me feel this objective world, this universe of objectivity, just like clouds lying in the ether of Your consciousness. As there are heaps of clouds in the sky, in the same way let me feel this universe as a mass of clouds in the sky of God-consciousness. Just as the clouds fade by and by and only the blue sky is left afterwards, only blue sky remains and clouds are seen no more; in the same way this universe should appear to me, purified and having become one with Thee in the end. Let me feel that way.

स्वप्रभाप्रसरध्वस्तापर्यन्तध्वान्तसन्ततिः ।
सन्ततं भातु मे कोऽपि भवमध्याद्भवन्मणिः ॥८ ॥

svaprabhāprasaradhvastāparyantadhvāntasantatiḥ I
santataṁ bhātu me ko 'pi bhavamadhyādbhavanmaṇiḥ II8 II

O Lord, I have this desire that all my ignorance, the whole mass of ignorance, many layers of the darkness of my ignorance should vanish with the effulgent light of the flow of Your consciousness always. And in the very action of this universe, I must find that great universal jewel of Thy formation. That great jewel must appear to me here in this universe itself.

कां भूमिकां नाधिशेषे किं तत्स्याद्यन्न ते वपुः ।
श्रान्तस्तेनाप्रयासेन सर्वतस्त्वामवाप्नुयाम् ॥९ ॥

kāṁ bhūmikāṁ nādhiśeṣe kiṁ tatsyādyanna te vapuḥ I
śrāntastenāprayāsena sarvatastvāmavāpnuyām II9 II

O Lord, which is the stage You don't possess? All stages are possessed by Thee. What is that formation which is not Your formation? All formations are possessed by You, all forms are Yours. But I can't find You, I am really exhausted. Let me perceive the presence of Your consciousness; let me perceive the presence of Your Being effortlessly, anywhere I wish to.

Your appearance is possible anywhere because You are present everywhere. So why not appear to me too here only, in my own room itself? I am actually exhausted now; I don't want to search any further.

भवदङ्गपरिष्वङ्गसम्भोगः स्वेच्छयैव मे ।
घटतामियति प्राप्ते किं नाथ न जितं मया ॥१० ॥

bhavadaṅgapariṣvaṅgasambhogaḥ svecchayaiva me ।
ghaṭatāmiyati prāpte kiṁ nātha na jitaṁ mayā ॥10 ॥

O Master, just by my will, not by action or effort, whenever I just desire, the joy of being embraced with You must appear to me automatically. I don't want to embrace You, You must embrace me. I must get embraced by You, that is my desire. And when that is achieved, when that appears to me, I have conquered everything that was there to conquer. (This is *śāmbhavopāya*. In *śāktopāya*, you have to embrace.)

प्रकटीभव नान्याभिः प्रार्थनाभिः कदर्थनाः ।
कुर्मस्ते नाथ ताम्यन्तस्त्वामेव मृगयामहे ॥११ ॥

prakaṭībhava nānyābhiḥ prārthanābhiḥ kadarthanāḥ ।
kurmaste nātha tāmyantastvāmeva mṛgayāmahe ॥11 ॥

O Master, please appear to me now, I am craving and longing for You. I only ask You to appear to me and in turn I promise that I will never ask for any other thing as long as I am in this world. I desire only You and nothing else. So You just appear before me.

॥ इति श्रीमदुत्पलदेवाचार्यविरचिते श्रीशिवस्तोत्रावल्यां
अध्वविस्फुरणाख्यं षष्ठं स्तोत्रम् ॥

॥ *iti śrīmadutpaladevācāryaviracite śrīśivastotrāvalyāṁ*
adhvavisphuraṇākhyaṁ ṣaṣṭhaṁ stotram ॥

7

विधुरविजयनामधेयं सप्तमं स्तोत्रम्

Vidhuravijaya Stotra

Overcoming Separation

THIS chapter is named *Vidhuravijaya*, a combination of two words: *vidhura* meaning helplessness, distress, lovelorn, separation, and *vijaya* meaning conquest, triumph, overcoming. He wants to conquer his helplessness due to separation from the Lord.

त्वय्यानन्दसरस्वति समरसतामेत्य नाथ मम चेतः ।
परिहरतु सकृदियन्तं भेदाधीनं महानर्थम् ॥१ ॥

tvayyānandasarasvati
samarasatāmetya nātha mama cetaḥ ।
pariharatu sakṛdiyantaṁ
bhedādhīnaṁ mahānartham ॥1 ॥

O my Master, I would like my mind to act this way, it should first get entry, it should first dive in the lake of Your consciousness, and then it should leave aside all ups and downs of duality for good, the differentiated perceptions in the world. I would like it to dive in that lake of God-consciousness and then discard altogether its habit of perceiving in duality, the differentiated perception.

एतन्मम न त्विदमिति रागद्वेषादिनिगडदृढमूले ।
नाथ भवन्मयतैक्यप्रत्ययपरशुः पतत्वन्तः ॥२ ॥

etanmama na tvidamiti
rāgadveṣādinigaḍadṛḍhamūle |
nātha bhavanmayataikya-
pratyayaparaśuḥ patatvantaḥ ||2 ||

O my Master, there is another problem in me; my mind is tied down with the chains of the bondage of attachment and detachment, attachment like "this is mine," "this is my property," "this is my son so he is mine," "this thing is going to give me pleasure so I should get it," etcetera; detachment like "this is not mine," "this is his son so he is not mine," "this thing is going to give me pain so I should not get it," etcetera. This *rāga* and *dveṣa*, to be attached in one way and to be detached in another way, is a great bondage that has tied down my mind.

O my Master, I would like to have the perception of perceiving one God-consciousness on both the sides. Let the axe of the oneness of God-consciousness fall on that chain of the bondage that has bound my mind and let it be cut into pieces so that all the *rāga* and *dveṣa* is removed.

You should perceive in only one manner, for instance either perceive that everybody is mine or perceive nobody is mine and not be selective like "this thing is mine" but "that thing is not mine." This way you should not perceive. As long as you perceive "this is my razor and that is his," that is attachment, being away from God-consciousness. So either profess "everything is mine" or recognize "nothing is mine, I just use it, it is not mine." If you use his razor, the Śaivite feels it is also his face only that is being shaved in a universal way. The Śaivite can own just as I do!

गलतु विकल्पकलङ्कावली समुल्लसतु हृदि निरर्गलता ।
भगवन्नानन्दरसप्लुतास्तु मे चिन्मयी मूर्तिः ॥३॥

galatu vikalpakalaṅkāvalī
samullasatu hṛdi nirargalatā ।
bhagavannānandarasa-
plutāstu me cinmayī mūrtiḥ ॥3 ॥

O Lord, let the chain of this darkness of differentiated perceptions get destroyed altogether. Let unbounded universal freedom rise in my heart always. O my Lord, let this individuality of mine be soaked in the nectar of the bliss of God-consciousness.

Three things he wants here: first the black darkness of differentiated perception should be washed off; next, freedom from all sides should bloom in his heart; thirdly his individuality of self should be soaked in universal God-consciousness. And all these three things must happen simultaneously and not in a successive manner.

The freedom in the heart implies aligning one's will with the will of God, everything I am doing is the will of God, whatever happens is divine.

रागादिमयभवाण्डकलुठितं त्वद्भक्तिभावनाम्बिका तैस्तैः ।
आप्याययतु रसैर्मां प्रवृद्धपक्षो यथा भवामि खगः ॥४ ॥

rāgādimayabhavāṇḍaka-
luṭhitaṁ tvadbhaktibhāvanāmbikā taistaiḥ ।
āpyāyayatu rasairmāṁ
pravṛddhapakṣo yathā bhavāmi khagaḥ ॥4 ॥

I am just like a bird's egg, an egg in this universe, an egg whose outer shell is made up of the substances of attachment and detachment, *kāma, krodha, lobha* and *moha, rāga* and *dveṣa,* all these differentiated things of the universe. And inside that egg I am moving here and there. When it rolls, the substance inside also moves implying that sometimes I am born, then I am a child, then comes the youth, then I am old and then comes death after which I am born again, then again childhood, again youth, then old age and then death once again. And like this I keep moving within this egg. I am entangled inside this egg. That is my problem.

I want a mother bird to help me out of this egg, and that mother bird is Your devotion. O Lord, Your devotion is the mother bird that will make me shine in this and solve my problem. That mother bird of Thy devotion must come and warm this egg with its warm sparks of devotion. It must continue putting those sparks on that shell, hatching it, so that I am able to come out of this shell, become a bird and then fly away in the sky of God-consciousness. Let this devotion keep increasing.

त्वच्चरणभावनामृत रससारास्वादनैपुणं लभताम् ।
चित्तमिदं निःशेषितविषयविषासङ्गवासनावधि मे ॥५॥

tvaccaraṇabhāvanāmṛta-
rasasārāsvādanaipuṇaṁ labhatām ।
cittamidaṁ niḥśeṣita-
viṣayaviṣāsaṅgavāsanāvadhi me ॥5॥

There is another problem in me. My mind does not know how to taste the nectar of remembering Your lotus feet. It does not know what is to be done in this world to taste the nectar of remembering Your lotus feet always. It doesn't know the technique of tasting the nectar of Your lotus feet.

Please teach my mind the technique of tasting the nectar of remembering Your lotus feet and the trick of understanding that technique. Let that technique be taught to my mind not only for now, but up to that point till in my mind all the differentiated attachment to worldly pleasures gets destroyed for good; up to that point You have to keep teaching my mind the technique.

त्वद्भक्तितपनदीधितिसंस्पर्शवशान्ममैष दूरतरम्।
चेतोमणिर्विमुञ्चतु रागादिकतप्तवह्निकणान् ॥६॥

tvadbhaktitapanadīdhiti-
saṁsparśavaśānmamaiṣa dūrataram ।
cetomaṇirvimuñcatu
rāgādika-taptavahnikaṇān ॥6॥

My mind is just like a magnifying glass but the sun is not always visible. What shall it burn? It will burn nothing. Let this magnifying glass of my mind be penetrated by the rays of the sun of Your devotion. Let the sun of Thy devotion keep on producing rays in continuity without the disturbance of clouds in between so that the magnifying glass of my mind burns all the attachments, detachments, pleasures and pains; sorrow and sadness, everything will get burnt altogether and thrown away as sparks of fire. It will only produce sparks and all those things will get removed. As long as the magnifying glass of my mind does this function, that sun of Thy devotion must go on producing the rays on that glass so that it burns everything.

तस्मिन्पदे भवन्तं सततमुपश्लोकयेयमत्युच्चैः।
हरिहर्यश्वविरिञ्चा अपि यत्र बहिः प्रतीक्षन्ते ॥७॥

tasminpade bhavantaṁ
satatamupaślokayeyamatyuccaiḥ ।
hariharyaśvaviriñcā
api yatra bahiḥ pratīkṣante ॥7॥

Although I am crazy in putting this problem before You, yet it is a problem for me and must be solved. I would like to reside at that point of divinity and sing Your glory inside that abode of God-consciousness where even Indra, Nārāyaṇa, Brahmā and all those gods also are not allowed entry, but made to wait outside. There I would like to sing Your glory.

भक्तिमदजनितविभ्रमवशेन पश्येयमविकलं करणैः ।
शिवमयमखिलं लोकं क्रियाश्च पूजामयी सकलाः ॥८ ॥

bhaktimadajanitavibhrama-
vaśena paśyeyamavikalaṁ karaṇaiḥ ।
śivamayamakhilaṁ lokaṁ
kriyāśca pūjāmayī sakalāḥ ॥8 ॥

There is another problem. I want to turn absolutely mad for Thy devotion, I want madness for Your love and by that madness, I must see everything in an absolutely different way, I must feel absolutely differently from others because mad people don't see things the way normal people do. A mad person may see a big mountain when he is intoxicated where there is actually none and a real big mountain he may perceive as a small clod. Such is the perception of those mad people. I want to become mad like that by tasting the nectar of Thy devotion and then my point of view of perceiving would change altogether. Then if I see two persons actually quarrelling with each other over worldly matters, I would feel that they are quarrelling for attaining God-consciousness. If I see people indulging in sensual gratifications, I would feel they are going into divinity.

As I would get maddened by Your devotion, I would feel everything happening in the outside world to be all divine. I would feel that all actions whatsoever, good or bad, are just Thy worship and nothing else.

मामकमनोगृहीतत्वद्भक्तिकुलाङ्गनाणिमादिसुतान् ।
सूत्वा सुबद्धमूला ममेति बुद्धिं दृढीकुरुताम् ॥९ ॥

māmakamanogṛhīta-
tvadbhaktikulāṅganāṇimādisutān ।
sūtvā subaddhamūlā
mameti buddhiṁ dṛḍhīkurutām ॥9 ॥

My mind is just like a young man in his perfect youth and my mind, that man has possessed as his wife a beautiful girl, that is Your devotion. Although he is married to that wife the problem is that this girl always goes astray, she does not always remain with me. She always goes out without informing where she was going while I keep waiting, wasting my time for my wife. This is my problem. She does not get focussed.

I understand the reason for her behaviour is that she has no issues. If she had an issue, she would always stay home. So let her have those issues namely *aṇimā, mahimā, laghimā,* etcetera, those eight great yogic powers. All those sons, the eight great yogic powers, must be produced by that wife that is Your devotion. Where would she go afterwards? She would get entangled in my own household and would always stay with me then. She will be encouraged and will encourage me also.

॥ इति श्रीमदुत्पलदेवाचार्यविरचिते श्रीशिवस्तोत्रावल्यां
विधुरविजयनामधेयं सप्तमं स्तोत्रम् ॥

॥ *iti śrīmadutpaladevācāryaviracite śrīśivastotrāvalyāṁ vidhuravijayanāmadheyaṁ saptamaṁ stotram* ॥

8

अलौकिकोद्बलनाख्यमष्टमं स्तोत्रम्

Alaukikodbalana Stotra

The Transcendent Power

यः प्रसादलव ईश्वरस्थितो या च भक्तिरिव मामुपेयुषी।
तौ परस्परसमन्वितौ कदा तादृशे वपुषि रूढिमेष्यतः ॥१॥

yaḥ prasādalava īśvarasthito
yā ca bhaktiriva māmupeyuṣī ।
tau parasparasamanvitau kadā
tādṛśe vapuṣi rūḍhimeṣyataḥ ॥1॥

O Lord, one thing is the droplets of nectar of being blessed by Lord Śiva, very tiny particles of the blessings of Lord Śiva; and the other thing that is residing in me is in some manner my devotion, my attachment for You. I devote all my time to remembering You and that devotion is residing in me. It is not real devotion, it is not actual devotion in me, it is justg so-called devotion, because if it were exactly devotion, then it would have borne fruit, the fruit of Your nearness. As long as Your nearness does not happen to me, even if the devotion is there, that is only nominal devotion. This nominal devotion is residing in me and the grace is residing in You.

O Lord, when shall that time come, when shall that golden opportunity come, when these two things would be united with each other? I will continue with my devotion and You will keep showering grace on me, both these will work simultaneously and will be established in me. As long as I continue with my devotion for Thee, the grace will continue to be showered on me. This is what I would like to have. I would not like that kind of devotion wherein I devote all my time to You but nothing happens.

त्वत्प्रभुत्वपरिचर्वणजन्मा कोऽप्युदेतु परितोषरसोऽन्तः ।
सर्वकालमिह मे परमस्तु ज्ञानयोगमहिमादि विदूरे ॥२॥

tvatprabhutvaparicarvaṇajanmā
ko 'pyudetu paritoṣaraso 'ntaḥ ।
sarvakālamiha me paramastu
jñānayogamahimādi vidūre ॥2॥

Let the taste of that real satisfaction rise always in me, when I would be really satisfied, when I would get myself filled with the satisfaction that I have a Master and that is Lord Śiva; that I have Lord Śiva as my Master. Let this satisfaction always reside in me. I would like to taste that perception. I would like this kind of taste to always reside in me that my Master is Lord Śiva.

Being informed in Śaivism, being informed in Vedānta, Trika, all these philosophies, or meditating, practising *prāṇāyāma*, breath control, let these remain away from me. I only wish this kind of *rasa* that I have got the Master and that is Lord Śiva.

लोकवद्भवतु मे विषयेषु स्फीत एव भगवन्परितर्षः ।
केवलं तव शरीरतयैतान् लोकयेयमहमस्तविकल्पः ॥३॥

lokavadbhavatu me viṣayeṣu
sphīta eva bhagavanparitarṣaḥ ।
kevalaṁ tava śarīratayaitān
lokayeyamahamastavikalpaḥ ॥3॥

O Lord, I don't want this hankering after the worldly pleasures to be discarded by me. Let this passion for worldly objects in me remain like in other people. I don't want my yearning for worldly objects to vanish altogether. I don't want to discard those desires. Let those desires remain in me but only with one difference: I should perceive these desires for worldly objects just as one with You, as Your body of universal consciousness.

देहभूमिषु तथा मनसि त्वं प्राणवर्त्मनि च भेदमुपेते।
संविदः पथिषु तेषु च तेन स्वात्मना मम भव स्फुटरूपः ॥४॥

dehabhūmiṣu tathā manasi tvaṁ
prāṇavartmani ca bhedamupete ।
saṁvidaḥ pathiṣu teṣu ca tena
svātmanā mama bhava sphuṭarūpaḥ ॥4॥

There are four sections of states. The first section is of *dehapramātṛbhāva* or *dehabhūmi,* when one is residing in wakefulness; the second section is of *svapna* or *mānasī,* when one is residing in the world of thought, the dreaming state; the third section is *prāṇavartmani,* the world of *prāṇa,* when one is residing in *suṣupti,* the dreamless state, and the fourth state is the *saṁvid-pathiṣu* or *turīya,* the path of knowledge, the path of perception, real perception.

O Lord, in all these four sections, let me remain one with You. I don't want the state of oneness shining only in *turīya,* the path of consciousness. Let me have oneness with You in my wakefulness, let oneness with You remain in dreaming state, let oneness with You remain in dreamless state and let oneness with You remain in *turīya.*

निजनिजेषु पदेषु पतन्त्विमाः करणवृत्तय उल्लसिता मम।
क्षणमपीश मनागपि मैव भूत् त्वदविभेदरसक्षतिसाहसम् ॥५॥

nijanijeṣu padeṣu patantvimāḥ
karaṇavṛttaya ullasitā mama ।

kṣaṇamapīśa manāgapi maiva bhūt
tvadavibhedarasakṣatisāhasam ॥5॥

O Lord, let my organs work in their own senses. I don't want to withdraw them from the sensual pleasures. Let them flow out on their respective sense objects because it is their nature to flow out; the mood of organs is to flow out to their respective sense objects. Let them do that, I have no objection to that, but only on one condition: namely Your oneness must shine along with this function, Your oneness of God-consciousness must shine when this organic function takes place, and if it does not shine even for one moment, if it breaks even for a moment let me lose my courage. I want to lose my courage altogether if I am away from it even for one second.

Let the sensual pleasures happen to me, but sensual pleasures must take place in Your oneness. The oneness with You must shine altogether in these sensual pleasures and if there is break of oneness with You in this act, let me lose courage that very moment; let me not pacify myself that time: "don't worry, next time you will sure get oneness with God after a while." No, I shall not have that much courage. One hundredth part of a moment also must not be without that oneness and if it is, I must lose my courage. I must get a great shock and die at that very moment, I must lose my body and I must lose everything. I must not tolerate separation from You even for a moment.

So the oneness with You must continue during the enjoyment of worldly pleasures too.

लघुमसृणसिताच्छशीतलं भवदावेशवशेन भावयन् ।
वपुरखिलपदार्थपद्धतेर्व्यवहारानतिवर्तयेय तान् ॥६॥

laghumasṛṇasitācchaśītalaṁ
bhavadāveśavaśena bhāvayan ।

vapurakhilapadārthapaddhate-
rvyavahārānativartayeya tān ||6 ||

I must perceive the path of these worldly objects, the formation of the entire objective world in this way: very light, very soft, spotlessly white, very pure and cooling. During the enjoyment of worldly sensations, I must get entry into Your nature. The entry in Your nature is soft, it is light, it is absolutely white, it is pure and it is cooling. It cools down the body, the mind and the formation of all worldly objects as these enter in Your God-consciousness. I will get rid of all those differentiated perceptions of the world.

विकसतु स्ववपुर्भवदात्मकं समुपयान्तु जगन्ति ममाङ्गताम्।
व्रजतु सर्वमिदं द्वयवल्गितं स्मृतिपथोपगमेऽप्यनुपाख्यताम्॥७॥

vikasatu svavapurbhavadātmakaṁ
samupayāntu jaganti mamāṅgatām |
vrajatu sarvamidaṁ dvayavalgitaṁ
smṛtipathopagame 'pyanupākhyatām ||7 ||

Let my individuality shine in the *svarūpa* of Your universality. Let my individual consciousness shine in the *svarūpa* of Your universal consciousness. Let all the three worlds become part and parcel of my universal body and let even the memory of the differentiated perception which existed prior to this experience, this perception, vanish. Let even the impressions of that dualistic perception not remain in the memory of the past. I am so much terrified by this dualistic perception that now I wouldn't even want to remember at all that there once was dualistic perception. I must not even think of that. This memory also must totally vanish.

समुदियादपि तादृशतावकाननविलोकपरामृतसम्प्लवः।
मम घटेत यथा भवदद्वयाप्रथनघोरदरीपरिपूरणम्॥८॥

samudiyādapi tādṛśatāvakā-
nanavilokaparāmṛtasamplavaḥ |

mama ghaṭeta yathā bhavadadvayā-
prathanaghoradarīparipūraṇam ॥8 ॥

Let me be flooded with the great flood of that supreme nectar by just observing Your face. Whenever I perceive Your divine face,[1] I should be flooded with the *rasa* of that nectar. Will that flood ever come to me in this lifetime? I am not insisting for it to happen just now. If ever this kind of flood takes place in me it would fill up that great abyss created by Your separation, Your being away from me.

Your separation has created in my mind such kind of deep wounds which I want to get filled with that nectar.

If there is a terrible wound that does not receive timely treatment, it prolongs and goes deeper and deeper and then it becomes an abyss and subsequently it cannot be cured.

अपि कदाचन तावकसङ्गमामृतकणाच्छुरणेन तनीयसा।
सकललोकसुखेषु पराङ्मुखो न भवितास्म्युभयच्युत एव किम्॥९॥

api kadācana tāvakasaṅgamā-
mṛtakaṇācchuraṇena tanīyasā ।
sakalalokasukheṣu parāṅmukho
na bhavitāsmyubhayacyuta eva kim ॥9 ॥

O Lord, the nearness of Thy consciousness, the experience of that divine nectar takes place in my mind very seldom, that too very scantily. It does not take place always, not each day. The mere sprinkling of the divine nectar of the nearness of Your consciousness is not only insufficient but it is showered very rarely.

Ever since I experienced the first sprinkling of that nectar, I lost the charm for all the worldly excitements. I have moved

1. Face here refers to five energies namely, *cit, ānanda, icchā, jñāna,* and *kriyā śakti.*

totally away from hankering after worldly pleasures. Those worldly pleasures have really ended at that very point. Actually nearness of God-consciousness is such a dense nectar that you lose taste for all worldly pleasures that very moment. So this is a fact that I have no interest left in worldly pleasures, well and good, but there must be something in its place; that sprinkling must come again but that does not come.

Now there is apprehension in my mind that I may become deprived of both the things, deprived of the divine nectar of God-consciousness and I have already become deprived of the worldly pleasures as it is. There is a possibility of my being deprived of both things. But that must not happen. Won't I get ruined from both the sides for good?

सततमेव भवच्चरणाम्बुजाकरचरस्य हि हंसवरस्य मे।
उपरि मूलतलादपि चान्तरादुपनमत्वज भक्तिमृणालिका ॥१०॥

satatameva bhavaccaraṇāmbujā-
karacarasya hi haṁsavarasya me ।
upari mūlatalād api cāntarā-
dupanamatvaja bhaktimr̥ṇālikā ॥10॥

I am just like that swan found always swimming in the lakes full of lotuses and whose ambition is to find the fibrous stalk at the root of the lotus stem (*nadrū* in Kashmiri). *Nadrū* is the desired object, it is his food and he is very fond of it.

I am just like that swan; I swim, I roam about, I reside not in that lake where these gross *nadrū*s are found. I reside in the lake of Your lotus feet. I am that kind of swan and I must get that *nadrū* there. I don't want Your lotus feet as those are lotuses; I want to find the *nadrū*, the root from where these lotuses grow. And the root of Thy lotus feet is Thy devotion; intense love for You is the root of those lotus feet. Those lotuses will grow when there is intense love for Thee and that intense love is the *nadrū*.

So I don't want to dive there and go to the bottom, find *nadrū* there and eat it. *Nadrū*, Your intense devotion must appear to me not only at the place of the root but at the place of the lotus, the upper surface of that plant, and in the centre also. I must get *nadrū*, the intense devotion everywhere. Thy devotion must appear to me at Your lotus feet, in the centre of Your lotus feet, in the root of Your lotus feet. I must observe only devotion; I want that devotion. I don't want to see lotus without devotion. O eternal Lord, Your lotus feet must appear to me with devotion everywhere.

उपयान्तु विभो समस्तवस्तून्यपिचिन्ताविषयं दृशः पदं च ।
मम दर्शनचिन्तनप्रकाशामृतसाराणि परं परिस्फुरन्तु ॥११ ॥

upayāntu vibho samastavastūnyapi-
cintāviṣayaṁ dṛśaḥ padaṁ ca ।
mama darśanacintanaprakāśā-
mṛtasārāṇi paraṁ parisphurantu ॥11 ॥

O my Master, I don't want to discard this objective world. Let the impressions, thoughts or the desires about the objective world be there. Let me perceive it, let thoughts regarding the same come to me, let this objective world remain present before me for ever, I don't want to discard or not to perceive this objective world. But appearing of this objective world and the state of utilizing this objective world must come to me, must appear to me as the shining of Your *svarūpa*. That divinity, that taste and the shining of Your form must appear to me in each and every act of this universe. This is what I want.

परमेश्वर तेषु तेषु कृच्छ्रेष्वपि नामोपनमत्स्वहं भवेयम् ।
न परं गतभीस्त्वदङ्गसङ्गादुपजाताधिकसम्मदोऽपि यावत् ॥१२ ॥

parameśvara teṣu teṣu kṛcchre-
ṣvapi nāmopanamatsvahaṁ bhaveyam ।

na paraṁ gatabhīstvadaṅgasaṅgā-
dupajātādhikasammado 'pi yāvat ॥12॥

O Lord Śiva, let all those crises, depressions and the disasters of the world befall me, let all those unbearable disastrous things crush me, I welcome those. Let me be soaked in these, I don't mind, but I must be embraced by You. By being in Your arms, I will not only be fearless, but I will also become intoxicated by those disastrous and catastrophic states that befall me. I will love them, I will welcome them.

भवदात्मनि विश्वमुम्भितं यद् भवतैवापि बहिः प्रकाश्यते तत्।
इति यद्दृढनिश्चयोपजुष्टं तदिदानीं स्फुटमेव भासताम्॥१३॥

bhavadātmani viśvamumbhitaṁ yad
bhavataivāpi bahiḥ prakāśyate tat ।
iti yaddṛḍhaniścayopajuṣṭaṁ
tadidānīṁ sphuṭameva bhāsatām ॥13॥

From the philosophical point of view I have understood that this whole universe is one with You. Like the beads woven into a thread, this whole universe is interwoven in Your consciousness. That is a fact I have read in all the spiritual books. But only a person who is fully aware feels that way.

This is my conclusion in understanding the way the universe exists. This is only my understanding, I have understood this way of existence of the universe. But I want to experience it, let me get the capacity to experience this practically. Let me experience this actual position of the universe. I enjoyed this in the form of a conviction; let me now experience it in manifestation.

॥ इति श्रीमदुत्पलदेवाचार्यविरचिते श्रीशिवस्तोत्रावल्यां
अलौकिकोद्बलनाख्यमष्टमं स्तोत्रम्॥

॥ *iti śrīmadutpaladevācāryaviracite śrīśivastotrāvalyāṁ*
alaukikodbalanākhyamaṣṭamaṁ stotram ॥

9

स्वातन्त्र्यविजयाख्यं नवमं स्तोत्रम्

Svātantryavijaya Stotra

The Glory of Freedom

NOTHING is in the hands of the devotee; he wants to possess everything, all powers. But he has no power to do anything that he likes. Throughout this chapter the devotee asks the Lord, when shall that time come, when shall that day come?

कदा नवरसार्द्रार्द्रसम्भोगास्वादनोत्सुकम् ।
प्रवर्तेत विहायान्यत् मम त्वत्स्पर्शने मनः ॥१ ॥

kadā navarasārdrārdra –
sambhogāsvādanotsukam ।
pravarteta vihāyānyat
mama tvatsparśane manaḥ ॥1 ॥

O Lord, my mind is craving to just enjoy the taste of ever fresh nectar of Thy devotion. My mind is yearning to taste the nectar of God-consciousness. My mind's only qualification is that it is fond of taking that nectar which is always new and always fresh; which is always wet and wherein there is no dryness. That is the *rasa* of love of God-consciousness, love and attachment for God; affection for God creates that ever fresh *rasa*. This is the position of my mind, but it does not get that joy ever. My mind wants to own that *svātantrya*. But that *rasa* will come only when I touch Your spiritual body.

O Lord, my mind is yearning to attain and taste the *rasa* of Your devotion but that devotion would come only with Your touch, when my mind would touch Your spiritual body. I want to embrace You and that embrace would give me the joy of tasting that *rasa*. When shall that time come, when I would leave all other worldly activities and be totally focussed onto that point, only to just embrace You and taste the nectar of the nearness of that devotion and love? When shall that day come?

त्वदेकरक्तस्त्वत्पादपूजामात्रमहाधनः ।
कदा साक्षात्करिष्यामि भवन्तमयमुत्सुकः ॥२॥

tvadekaraktastvatpāda-
pūjāmātramahādhanaḥ ।
kadā sākṣātkariṣyāmi
bhavantamayamutsukaḥ ॥2॥

I am yearning, I am always attached to You. Adoring You is the only wealth I possess and that is my lone qualification. I have no attachment for anything except for Thee. I have no wealth other than being attached to Thee. I have only this wealth of Your devotion and of adoring You. And that is all I want to possess. So when shall that day come, when I would see You, when I would perceive You, when I would own You?

गाढानुरागवशतो निरपेक्षीभूतमानसोऽस्मि कदा ।
पटपटिति विघटिताखिलमहार्गलस्त्वामुपैष्यामि ॥३॥

gāḍhānurāgavaśato
nirapekṣībhūtamānaso 'smi kadā ।
paṭapaṭiti vighaṭitākhila-
mahārgalastvāmupaiṣyāmi ॥3॥

O Lord, just hear one word from me. I love You but You don't love me. I am Yours but You are not mine; like the tide belongs to the ocean but the ocean doesn't belong to the tide.

When shall that day come, when with the intensity of Your love, by the density of my love and attachment for You, my mind will vacate all other thoughts and that big door between You and me which is already bolted, locked and barred, which separates me from You, keeps me out of Your residence, shall be thrown wide open? By my mere presence there, with the qualifications of the intensity of Thy devotion and exclusion of all other anxieties, attachments and thoughts from my mind, this bolted and barred door will break into pieces and I will embrace You. By my presence it will break itself into pieces and You will be seated in my lap. When shall that day come?

स्वसंवित्सारहृदयाधिष्ठानाः सर्वदेवताः ।
कदा नाथ वशीकुर्यां भवद्भक्तिप्रभावतः ॥४॥

svasaṁvitsārahṛdayā-
dhiṣṭhānāḥ sarvadevatāḥ ।
kadā nātha vaśīkuryāṁ
bhavadbhaktiprabhāvataḥ ॥4॥

O Lord, all these organic deities — my eyes, my ears, my nose, my throat, my tongue, my body, my skin, actually they are residing in one's own consciousness.

When shall that day come, when, by the glory of Your devotion, I will get all these organs under my control. The cause of controlling my organs will of course be Thy intense devotion. Please tell me when shall that time come?

कदा मे स्याद्विभो भूरि भक्त्यानन्दरसोत्सवः ।
यदालोकसुखानन्दी पृथङ्नामापि लप्स्यते ॥५॥

kadā me syādvibho bhūri
bhaktyānandarasotsavaḥ ।
yadālokasukhānandī
pṛthaṅnāmāpi lapsyate ॥5॥

O Lord, when shall that day come, when I will experience the intense festival of the bliss of Your devotion? That is the only festival for me; to get Your devotion, to achieve Your devotion. I have no other festival; I have no charm in any other festival.

When shall that festival appear to me? I want to ask You. When shall I get entry in *prathamābhāsa;* when shall I experience the appearance of God-consciousness in universal objectivity? When shall I get entry into universal God-consciousness; and when shall the differentiated names, forms and speeches also vanish for good?

ईश्वरमभयमुदारं पूर्णमकारणमपह्नुतात्मानम् ।
सहसाभिज्ञाय कदा स्वामिजनं लज्जयिष्यामि ॥६ ॥

īśvaramabhayamudāraṁ
pūrṇamakāraṇamapahnutātmānaṁ ।
sahasābhijñāya kadā
svāmijanaṁ lajjayiṣyāmi ॥6 ॥

O Lord Śiva, You are fearless, You are extravagant; You spend in Your own way, You don't seek anybody's decision on how much should You spend; and still You are always full, there is nothing lacking.

You have no father and no mother, that is why You have possessed so many disqualifications. You are disqualified because You don't fear anybody, You are extravagant and the misfortune for me is that You are always full, I can't even offer You anything, You don't accept anything. You have kept Yourself hidden because You are not worth being known to anybody because of these disqualifications.

O my Master, there is one longing in me: when shall that day come for me, when I would perceive You instantaneously, and I would take You around in a cart everywhere so that everybody sees You? You would be ashamed, I will shame

You everywhere, my Master. I will tell everyone everywhere about Your disqualifications of being debauch, extravagant, and without father and mother; so You will be ashamed everywhere. I will make a scandal of You. I will show You to everybody.

It means that Ācarya Utpaladeva had this thought at the background of his mind that everybody should perceive God.

[On being asked if it was not outrageous to say such things about God, *Swāmījī* clarified], *"Bhakti viṣaye na kaścin doṣaḥ."* Everything is fine because it is through love; with love and devotion you could say anything. So many people have smashed shoes on the heads of their *iṣṭadeva*s out of love and it is absolutely fine.

A Master had instructed one of his disciples to hit the *Śivaliṅga* with his shoes eleven times each day which he faithfully complied with every day. He would go there everyday, hit the *Śivaliṅga* and come back. It was his *pūjā*, *sādhanā*. One day the entire place got flooded, that *Śivaliṅga* had gone under water. How could he reach there? But that day also he swam and somehow reached there and hit the *Śivaliṅga* with shoes as he had been instructed. That very moment Lord Śiva appeared to him and showed him His real divine form.

कदा कामपि तां नाथ तव वल्लभतामियाम् ।
यया मां प्रति न क्वापि युक्तं ते स्यात्पलायितुम् ॥७॥

kadā kāmapi tāṁ nātha
tava vallabhatāmiyām ।
yayā māṁ prati na kvāpi
yuktaṁ te syātpalāyitum ॥7॥

Alright leave everything aside, don't come to me but I have a request to make. I want to ask You something.

I want to know when I would possess that intense love for You. When shall that state of extreme love for Thee rise in me? When shall that day come, when there would be in me such extreme love for Thee that there would be no excuse, no chance for You to hide from me? The intensity of my love would make You remain in front of me always. When shall that day come?

तत्त्वतोऽशेषजन्तूनां भवत्पूजामयात्मनाम् ।
दृष्ट्यानुमोदितरसाप्लावितः स्यां कदा विभो ॥८॥

tattvato 'śeṣajantūnāṁ
bhavatpūjāmayātmanām ।
dṛṣṭyānumoditarasā-
plāvitaḥ syāṁ kadā vibho ॥8॥

O Lord, it is a fact that everybody, knowingly or unknowingly worships You. Even if a person is abusing another person, he is just worshipping You. If a person is gratifying his sensual urge, he too is just worshipping You. If two persons are quarrelling with each other, they are worshipping You. In fact, in the real sense, whatever is done, is nothing but Your worship. Everybody is in fact on the course of Your worship.

O Lord, when shall that time come when I will actually feel that only You are being worshipped everywhere and that whatever is being done by anybody is just Your worship? I would feel it myself; I would confirm it in my mind that really only the Lord is being worshipped everywhere. When shall that day come when I shall be flooded by this joy that the Lord alone is being worshipped everywhere; whatever is being done anywhere by anybody, is just Your worship? When shall that day come when I will be flooded with the joy of the nectar of the confirmation that Your adoration alone is being adopted everywhere in whatever is being done and nothing else?

ज्ञानस्य परमा भूमिर्योगस्य परमा दशा।
त्वद्भक्तिर्या विभो कर्हि पूर्णा मे स्यात्तदर्थिता ॥९॥

jñānasya paramā bhūmir-
yogasya paramā daśā ।
tvadbhaktiryā vibho karhi
pūrṇā me syāttadarthitā ॥9 ॥

O all-pervading Lord, really Your devotion is the supreme state of knowledge and the supreme state of *yoga*. Your love is all. When shall that devotion rise in me, when shall that love shine in me and when shall that longing for that love be fulfilled?

When shall that day come when my longing for that love, which is the supreme state of knowledge, supreme state of *yoga* would be fulfilled in me?

सहसैवासाद्य कदा गाढमवष्टभ्य हर्षविवशोऽहम्।
त्वच्चरणवरनिधानं सर्वस्य प्रकटयिष्यामि ॥१०॥

sahasaivāsādya kadā
gāḍhamavaṣṭabhya harṣavivaśo 'ham ।
tvaccaraṇavaranidhānaṁ
sarvasya prakaṭayiṣyāmi ॥10 ॥

O Lord, the supreme treasure of Your divine feet is really never known in succession, it is never known in successive steps; when it is known, it is known just at once. In the spiritual field of Your science, knowing Your feet, the treasure of Your feet is not successive in nature; when it is revealed, it is revealed in one go, the revelation is sudden, at once.

When shall that day come when I will all of a sudden come to understand the treasure of Your divine feet and embrace those? I will hold that treasure with my own nature; when that supreme joy will flow in me, I wouldn't know how to handle that. I will distribute amongst the whole world that treasure when that day comes. It is my ambition that everybody knows that treasure.

(The revelation is sudden, unlike a bank account wherein the accumulation takes place in successive steps.)

परितः प्रसरच्छुद्धत्वदालोकमयः कदा ।
स्यां यथेश न किञ्चिन्मे मायाच्छायाबिलं भवेत् ॥११ ॥

paritaḥ prasaracchuddha-
tvadālokamayaḥ kadā ।
syāṁ yatheśa na kiñcinme
māyācchāyābilaṁ bhavet ॥11 ॥

O Lord, when shall that day come when I would be so flooded by Thy light of consciousness that I would become one with that light and by that light there would be no traces of any darkness of illusion left? When shall that day come?

आत्मसात्कृतनिःशेषमण्डलो निर्व्यपेक्षकः ।
कदा भवेयं भगवंस्त्वद्भक्तगणनायकः ॥१२ ॥

ātmasātkr̥taniḥśeṣa-
maṇḍalo nirvyapekṣakaḥ ।
kadā bhaveyaṁ bhagavaṁ-
stvadbhaktagaṇanāyakaḥ ॥12 ॥

O Lord, I would like to achieve that state when I would be united with this universe; universal consciousness would be united with me. O Lord when shall that day come, when I would be united with the universal consciousness and I would be the leader of all Thy devotees, leading them towards Your abode? I would command them "Come on, come on this way I will lead you." I want to become the leader of all Your devotees. When shall that day come?

नाथ लोकाभिमानानामपूर्वं त्वं निबन्धनम् ।
महाभिमानः कर्हि स्यां त्वद्भक्तिरसपूरितः ॥१३॥

nātha lokābhimānānāma-
pūrvaṁ tvaṁ nibandhanam ।
mahābhimānaḥ karhi syāṁ
tvadbhaktirasapūritaḥ ॥13॥

O Lord, this sensation of ego which is found in each and every individual in this universe has in fact descended from You. You have produced this ego in each and every being. But I don't want that kind of ego; I would like that universal I-consciousness, the ego of universal I-consciousness. When shall that day come when I would achieve that ego of universal I-consciousness and I would be soaked in the nectar of Your devotion?

अशेषविषयाशून्यश्रीसमाश्लेषसुस्थितः ।
शयीयमिव शीताङ्घ्रिकुशेशययुगे कदा ॥१४॥

aśeṣaviṣayāśūnya-
śrīsamāśleṣasusthitaḥ ।
śayīyamiva śītāṅghri-
kuśeśayayuge kadā ॥14॥

O Lord, Your two feet, which are very cooling, are just like two lotuses; I would like to sleep on these. When shall that day come when I would get to sleep on these two lotuses already having embraced the woman of liberation, woman which is the embodiment of liberation? As I lie down on those lotus feet of Yours, I would be liberated. I would embrace that beautiful girl Lakṣmī, the Goddess of spiritual wealth on that bed of Your lotus feet, that bed which is not deprived of the worldly enjoyments, where all worldly enjoyments are existing.

That liberation he has nominated as the beautiful girl Lakṣmī, the goddess of spiritual wealth.

भक्त्यासवसमृद्धायास्त्वत्पूजाभोगसम्पदः ।
कदा पारं गमिष्यामि भविष्यामि कदा कृती ॥१५॥

bhaktyāsavasamṛddhāyā-
stvatpūjābhogasampadaḥ ।
kadā pāraṁ gamiṣyāmi
bhaviṣyāmi kadā kṛtī ॥15॥

Thy devotion, Thy worship is great wealth; it is the real great treasure. That worship rises by taking the liquor of being attached to You. Thy attachment is liquor and I take that liquor, I remain attached to You and by that attachment this enjoyment of worshipping You rises.

When shall that day come when I would reach the last resting point of that worship and when shall that day come when all my desires would get fulfilled like that?

आनन्दबाष्पपूरस्खलितपरिभ्रान्तगद्गदाक्रन्दः ।
हासोल्लासितवदनस्त्वत्स्पर्शरसं कदाप्स्यामि ॥१६॥

ānandabāṣpapūra-
skhalitaparibhrāntagadgadākrandaḥ ।
hāsollāsitavadana-
stvatsparśarasaṁ kadāpsyāmi ॥16॥

O Lord, when shall the nectar of Thy embrace shine in me; when shall I enjoy the fragrance, the sweetness of Your embrace? When shall I achieve that? By that great joy, tears would roll down my cheeks, those will block my vision and I would not be able to perceive anyone in front of me. I would be intoxicated, I would be sobbing and I would be laughing loudly at the same time. All this would take place simultaneously. When shall that day come?

पशुजनसमानवृत्तामवधूय दशामिमां कदा शम्भो ।
आस्वादयेय तावकभक्तोचितमात्मनो रूपम् ॥१७॥

paśujanasamānavr̥ttām-
avadhūya daśāmimāṁ kadā śambho ।
āsvādayeya tāvaka-
bhaktocitamātmano rūpam ॥17॥

O Lord Śiva, it is really disgraceful not only for me, but for You too it is disgraceful. You know I am Your devotee still I am roaming from door to door just like any other ordinary ignorant worldly person. This degraded state which I ought not to have fallen into by virtue of being Your devotee, but have possessed through Your negligence does not behove You. It is not appropriate that I am in this degraded state.

So when shall that day come when I would discard this degraded state and enjoy the reality of the nectar of Your nearness that is due to Your devotees? Your devotees must have that.

लब्धाणिमादिसिद्धिर्विगलितसकलोपतापसन्त्रासः ।
त्वद्भक्तिरसायनपानक्रीडानिष्ठः कदासीय ॥१८॥

labdhāṇimādisiddhir-
vigalitasakalopatāpasantrāsaḥ ।
tvadbhaktirasāyanapāna-
krīḍāniṣṭhaḥ kadāsīya ॥18॥

O my Lord, when shall that day come when I would have possessed, achieved all those eight great yogic powers and all the sorrow, torture and fear would have vanished and I would be playful and joyful in drinking the nectar of Your devotion? When shall I reach that state?

नाथ कदा स तथाविध आक्रन्दो मे समुच्चरेद् वाचि ।
यत्समनन्तरमेव स्फुरति पुरस्तावकी मूर्तिः ॥१९॥

nātha kadā sa tathāvidha
ākrando me samuccared vāci ।
yatsamanantarameva
sphurati purastāvakī mūrtiḥ ॥19 ॥

O my Master, when shall that day come when I would cry in only one word, "O my Lord" in such a way that You would have no excuse to ignore me? When shall I be able to produce such a cry? One such cry and You would just appear in front of me.

When shall I cry that way so that the very next moment, Your beautiful form, Your beautiful body would appear in front of me, by that single cry only? When shall I utter such a cry? When will that day come when I would utter such a cry; only one cry and You would have no excuse to hide?

गाढगाढभवदङ्घ्रिसरोजालिङ्गनव्यसनतत्परचेताः ।
वस्त्ववस्त्विदमयत्नत एव त्वां कदा समवलोकयितास्मि ॥२० ॥

gāḍhagāḍhabhavadaṅghrisarojā-
liṅganavyasanatatparacetāḥ ।
vastvavastvidamayatnata eva
tvāṁ kadā samavalokayitāsmi ॥20 ॥

O Lord, there is one desire in me, I would like to repeatedly embrace tightly Thy lotus feet, just embrace again and again, and by that action I would achieve Thee. Then I would effortlessly see this existent and non-existent universe as one with You. When shall that day come?

॥ इति श्रीमदुत्पलदेवाचार्यविरचिते श्रीशिवस्तोत्रावल्यां
स्वातन्त्र्यविजयाख्यं नवमं स्तोत्रम् ॥

॥ *iti śrīmadutpaladevācāryaviracite śrīśivastotrāvalyāṁ*
svātantryavijayākhyaṁ navamaṁ stotram ॥

10

अविच्छेदभङ्गाख्यं दशमं स्तोत्रम्

Avicchedabhaṅga Stotra

Breaking the Continuity

THE tenth chapter is nominated as *Avicchedabhaṅga,* meaning the devotee feels the continuity of God-consciousness does not remain established, does not continue firmly. He wants it to persist but it breaks every now and then. In this chapter he is crying for it to remain firmly established.

न सोढव्यमवश्यं ते जगदेकप्रभोरिदम् ।
माहेश्वराश्च लोकानामितरेषां समाश्च यत् ॥१॥

na soḍhavyamavaśyaṁ te jagadekaprabhoridam ।
māheśvarāśca lokānāmitareṣāṁ samāśca yat ॥1॥

O the only Lord of this universe, how do You tolerate that Your slaves, Your devotees and other worldly people reside at the same level. It should not happen that Your devotees tread on the same path and remain at the same level as the ordinary worldly people do. How do You tolerate this? You should not tolerate this.

ये सदैवानुरागेण भवत्पादानुगामिनः ।
यत्र तत्र गता भोगांस्ते कांश्चिदुपभुञ्जते ॥२॥

ye sadaivānurāgeṇa bhavatpādānugāminaḥ ।
yatra tatra gatā bhogāṁste kāṁścidupabhuñjate ॥2॥

O Lord, those people who with Your devotion always follow

and tread the pathway on which Your lotus feet travel, they keep following that pathway with great love and affection, never mind the worldly state they are situated in. Irrespective of the physical state they are in, they enjoy some supreme spiritual taste. They don't worry about that.

भर्ता कालान्तको यत्र भवांस्तत्र कुतो रुजः ।
तत्र चेतरभोगाशा का लक्ष्मीर्यत्र तावकी ॥३॥

bhartā kālāntako yatra bhavāṁstatra kuto rujaḥ ।
tatra cetarabhogāśā kā lakṣmīryatra tāvakī ॥3॥

Where Lord Śiva, Kālāntaka, who is the destroyer of Kāla the Lord of death, remains with a helping hand, where can there be a possibility of any disease or sorrow. No disease or sorrow can appear when Lord Śiva, the destroyer of death is there to protect. Where there is Your Lakṣmī, the Goddess of Your devotion, the Goddess of spiritual wealth, there is no possibility of any desire for worldly pleasures. All the enjoyments end there. All worldly enjoyments seem nothing before the spiritual wealth showered by Lakṣmī of Lord Śiva.

क्षणमात्रसुखेनापि विभुर्येनासि लभ्यसे ।
तदैव सर्वः कालोऽस्य त्वदानन्देन पूर्यते ॥४॥

kṣaṇamātrasukhenāpi vibhuryenāsi labhyase ।
tadaiva sarvaḥ kālo 'sya tvadānandena pūryate ॥4॥

When Thy Lordship is achieved by some person even though for half a second only; even if that flash of super-sexual joy rises in a person only for a moment, the rest of his lifespan is filled with the intoxication of that joy.

If that super-sexual joy of Your *svarūpa*, Your existence is experienced by anybody even if only for a moment, and no matter if he does not achieve that joy again afterwards till the time of his death, yet the whole span of his lifetime is filled with the intoxication of that joy. Such is the greatness of that joy that having experienced it even only once, it persists for the entire lifetime, right up to the time of death.

आनन्दरसबिन्दुस्ते चन्द्रमा गलितो भुवि ।
सूर्यस्तथा ते प्रसृतः संहारी तेजसः कणः ॥५॥

ānandarasabinduste candramā galito bhuvi ।
sūryastathā te prasṛtaḥ saṁhārī tejasaḥ kaṇaḥ ॥5॥

बलिं यामस्तृतीयाय नेत्रायास्मै तव प्रभो ।
अलौकिकस्य कस्यापि माहात्म्यस्यैकलक्ष्मणे ॥६॥

baliṁ yāmastṛtīyāya netrāyāsmai tava prabho ।
alaukikasya-kasyāpi māhātmyasyaikalakṣmaṇe ॥6॥

O Lord, this moon that shines in the sky, is only a tiny drop of the nectar of Your spiritual bliss; it is just one drop that shines and that shining moonlight is so pleasing and so soothing to everybody. This is only one drop of that super-sexual joy that has entered in the substance of the moon.

The sun that shines in the sky is only one spark of Your *prakāśa*, your destructive light; just a spark of Your majestic brilliance exists in the sun. That glory is so destructive that it can blind whosoever dares to even look at it.

But I leave these two sources of this *prakāśa* aside; I have got nothing to do with these two *prakāśa*s. One is filled with joy and the other is filled with destructive light. This moon represents Your left eye; and the sun represents Your right eye. I have nothing to do with these two eyes of Yours shining in this world.

There is a third eye situated in between Your two eyebrows and that is the eye of fire, *pramātṛ bhāva;* I want to offer everything of mine to that fire; to Your third eye which is beyond this universe, above this universe and is the sign of Thy glory, and has great glory in it.

(The appropriate Kashmiri word for *balim yāmaḥ* is *balāyi-lagun,* just to sacrifice everything in its name without any reservations.)

तेनैव दृष्टोऽसि भवद्दर्शनाद्योऽतिहृष्यति ।
कथञ्चिद्यस्य वा हर्षः कोऽपि तेन त्वमीक्षितः ॥७ ॥

tenaiva dṛṣṭo 'si bhavaddarśanādyo 'tihṛṣyati ।
kathañcidyasya vā harṣaḥ ko 'pi tena tvamīkṣitaḥ ॥7 ॥

He who has actually perceived and seen You, by seeing You his joy will know no bounds. That person becomes so enraptured; his joy is so great that he can't explain anything. In fact, he has perceived You. That joy does not come just by meditating; it comes only by the grace of God, by *śaktipāta.* So he alone has actually seen You, perceived You and not anyone else.

It is not that when you perceive God-consciousness and you will explain your perception before your Master, "O Master, I have seen God-consciousness today by your grace and it was so nice, it was very beautiful." This is not the way of experiencing that. When you experience it and narrate it to your Master, you can't relate anything. You just weep, you can't say even one word, you will be so filled with joy, you can't speak, you can't utter a word. You just weep before him and that is the sign that you have perceived that God-consciousness. If you say I perceived it and it was very beautiful, it is all fraud!

येषां प्रसन्नोऽसि विभो यैर्लब्धं हृदयं तव ।
आकृष्य त्वत्पुरात्तैस्तु बाह्यमाभ्यन्तरीकृतम् ॥८ ॥

yeṣāṁ prasanno 'si vibho yairlabdhaṁ hṛdayaṁ tava ।
ākṛṣya tvatpurāttaistu bāhyamābhyantarīkṛtam ॥8 ॥

O Lord, those with whom You are actually pleased and those

who have achieved and perceived Your internal heart, those persons alone have extracted this whole universe from Your nature of God-consciousness and then soaked it again in that God-consciousness. They have extracted this universe from the state of God-consciousness and then have again united it with God-consciousness.

This duality does not come from duality. This duality comes from unity. From unity they have extracted this duality and then again they have united this duality with unity. Those people have done this with whom You are pleased and who have actually perceived Your essence.

त्वदृते निखिलं विश्वं समदृग्यातमीक्ष्यताम्।
ईश्वरः पुनरेतस्य त्वमेको विषमेक्षणः ॥९॥

tvadṛte nikhilaṁ viśvaṁ samadṛgyātamīkṣyatām ।
īśvaraḥ punaretasya tvameko viṣamekṣaṇaḥ ॥9॥

Without Thee everybody sees, observes this whole universe with two eyes in a dualistic way. But You are the only one who perceives it in the monistic way with only one eye, the third eye. This is the difference.

आस्तां भवत्प्रभावेण विना सत्तैव नास्ति यत्।
त्वद्दूषणकथा येषां त्वदृते नोपपद्यते ॥१०॥

āstāṁ bhavatprabhāveṇa vinā sattaiva nāsti yat ।
tvaddūṣaṇakathā yeṣāṁ tvadṛte nopapadyate ॥10॥

This is a fact that without Thy glory, without the appearance of Your glory, nothing can exist in this universe.

For instance if this pen exists, it exists only because of His glory.

But then there are people, the atheists, who deny Your existence. Denial of Your existence by those persons cannot be explained without Your existence. Their denial of Your existence, refusal to acknowledge Your existence; their explanation of the denial of Your existence cannot exist without Your existence. There also they need Your existence to deny You. To say that there is no God, this saying also will exist only when God is there.

बाह्यान्तरान्तरायालीकेवले चेतसि स्थितिः ।
त्वयि चेत्स्यान्मम विभो किमन्यदुपयुज्यते ॥११॥

bāhyāntarāntarāyālīkevale cetasi sthitiḥ ।
tvayi cetsyānmama vibho kimanyadupayujyate ॥11॥

O Lord, if my mind becomes established in Thyself, and my mind takes the position of being detached from the outward universe (of differentiated perception), the inverted universe (of internal confusion, ambiguity, whether to do or not to do a thing) and the void universe (of obstacles, impediments, *pralaya-kāla*, the time of universal destruction); what else do I need then?

My mind will be absolutely away from these three sections of the universe; outward universe, inward universe and void universe; these will not exist in that mind. And if You prevail, in that mind Your existence shines and is established, what else do I need then? I don't need anything, any means then. My needs are fulfilled altogether.

अन्ये भ्रमन्ति भगवन्नात्मन्येवातिदुःस्थिताः ।
अन्ये भ्रमन्ति भगवन्नात्मन्येवातिसुस्थिताः ॥१२॥

anye bhramanti bhagavannātmanyevātiduḥsthitāḥ ।
anye bhramanti bhagavannātmanyevātisusthitāḥ ॥12॥

There are two meanings of *bhramanti*. First is that they just waste their time going here and there. The second *bhramanti* means *vikasanti*, they enjoy.

O Lord, in this world, there are some ignorant people who are situated in that being which is not actually God. They remain there with scattered mind, always miserable and keep going around ceaselessly in the vicious cycle of repeated births and deaths. They just keep wasting their time in going here and there.

And, O Lord, there are some wise people who shine, who are glorified because they are established in their own nature.

अपीत्वापि भवद्भक्तिसुधामनवलोक्य च ।
त्वामीश त्वत्समाचारमात्रात्सिद्ध्यन्ति जन्तवः ॥१३॥

apītvāpi bhavadbhaktisudhāmanavalokya ca ।
tvāmīśa tvatsamācāramātrātsiddhyanti jantavaḥ ॥13॥

O Lord, there are some people who have not tasted the nectar of Your oneness, who have not tasted the nectar of Your devotion, who have not experienced the state of Your God-consciousness, but even by just hearing Your name also from outside world they get entry into God-consciousness.

They are such people that without getting entry into God-consciousness and without adopting any means for Thee; they have not tasted the nectar of Your devotion, they have not entered into the state of God-consciousness but still they are so close to You that by hearing Your name from the outside, they get entry. They are so great.

भृत्या वयं तव विभो तेन त्रिजगतां यथा ।
बिभर्ष्यात्मानमेवं ते भर्त्तव्या वयमप्यलम् ॥१४॥

bhṛtyā vayaṁ tava vibho tena trijagatāṁ yathā ।
bibharṣyātmānamevaṁ te bharttavyā vayamapyalam ॥14॥

O Lord, we are Your slaves, there is no doubt in that. And as it is obvious that You take care of all the three worlds considering these as Your slaves, in the same way it is Your duty to take care of us and see that all our needs are met. You have to fulfil and complete all our needs. You have to do that because You are our Master.

Bhṛtya does not mean paid servant. *Bhṛtya* means slave, unpaid servant completely supported by his Master; who is looked after in each and every respect by his Master. He has no support other than his Master. So he is a slave and depends completely on his Master. He doesn't need any remuneration; he just needs the support of the Master.

परानन्दामृतमये दृष्टेऽपि जगदात्मनि ।
त्वयि स्पर्शरसेऽत्यन्ततरमुत्कण्ठितोऽस्मि ते ॥१५॥

parānandāmṛtamaye dṛṣṭe 'pi jagadātmani ।
tvayi sparśarase 'tyantataramutkaṇṭhito 'smi te ॥15॥

O Lord, although I have seen You and I have experienced the state of Your being which is filled with the supreme nectar of bliss, still there is a desire in my mind: I want to just embrace You. This desire is always tickling in the background of my mind that I want to embrace You.

देव दुःखान्यशेषाणि यानि संसारिणामपि ।
धृत्याख्यभवदीयात्मयुतान्यायान्ति सह्यताम् ॥१६॥

deva duḥkhānyaśeṣāṇi yāni saṁsāriṇāmapi ।
dhṛtyākhyabhavadīyātmayutānyāyānti sahyatām ॥16॥

O Lord, the tortures, pains, sorrows, sadness encountered by a person in this universe are tolerated only because of Your nearness, because You are near them. Otherwise, nobody would tolerate any sadness, any torture in this universe. It is tolerated only because of Thy presence. Since You are always sweet, Your presence makes these tolerable. Even the person with no love for God would have some attachment for I-consciousness. They tolerate these because of the existence of I-consciousness.

सर्वज्ञे सर्वशक्तौ च त्वय्येव सति चिन्मये ।
सर्वथाप्यसतो नाथ युक्तास्य जगतः प्रथा ॥१७ ॥

sarvajñe sarvaśaktau ca tvayyeva sati cinmaye ।
sarvathāpyasato nātha yuktāsya jagataḥ prathā ॥17 ॥

The existence of this universe in fact is non-existent. The existence of the universe by all means is false. It is in every way unreal. It should not exist. Why does it exist then? This pair of spectacles should not exist, why does it exist? It exists only when You are there, when Your existence is shining. This existence of the non-existent universe is possible only when You are shining. So everything is fine when You are shining. It doesn't make sense to imagine a world independent simply in time, space and form. It has no authority to exist on those grounds. This universe should not exist because duality is non-existent; duality exists only when non-duality is shining in duality. This is Śaivism.

त्वत्प्राणिताः स्फुरन्तीमे गुणा लोष्टोपमा अपि ।
नृत्यन्ति पवनोद्धूताः कार्पासपिचवो यथा ॥१८ ॥

tvatprāṇitāḥ sphurantīme guṇā loṣṭopamā api ।
nṛtyanti pavanoddhūtāḥ kārpāsapicavo yathā ॥18 ॥

यदि नाथ गुणेष्वात्माभिमानो न भवेत्ततः ।
केन हीयेत जगतस्त्वदेकात्मतया प्रथा ॥१९ ॥

yadi nātha guṇeṣvātmābhimāno na bhavettataḥ ।
kena hīyeta jagatastvadekātmatayā prathā ॥19 ॥

O Lord, these senses, the five senses of action and the five senses of cognition, they are just like a lump of earth. All these ten senses have no life of their own; they are just like lumps of earth, just dead. But when You inject Your consciousness in them, they perform their respective actions, they shine, they vibrate, they do everything.

The eyes are just like clods of earth, lifeless and dead; but when You inject Your God-consciousness in the eyes, they perceive each and every form. In the same way all the organs perform when they are injected with Your God-consciousness; then they dance just like small particles of cotton fibre blown here and there in ether by the force of wind. So You are that wind.

In the same way, if there would not have been adjustment of God-consciousness in these ten organs, nobody would come down from the state of God-consciousness. Everybody would always have clung to God-consciousness and nobody would come in this universal existence. It means we are enjoying the worldly life with the five organs of action and the five organs of cognition we possess. Nobody would accept enjoying worldly life if God-consciousness would not have been adjusted in this state also. Nobody would care for this universe. The joy comes from that I-consciousness. God establishes that self-identity in these organs. So God-consciousness is there. If they would not have found God-consciousness in this state of life, nobody would have come down in this state of life; everybody would have remained in God-consciousness always. Who would abandon that state of spirituality of God-consciousness? No one would have abandoned that place but everybody has, because they have found that God-consciousness here also, so they enjoy.

वन्द्यास्तेऽपि महीयांसः प्रलयोपगता अपि ।
त्वत्कोपपावकस्पर्शपूता ये परमेश्वर ॥२० ॥

vandyāste 'pi mahīyāṁsaḥ pralayopagatā api ।
tvatkopapāvakasparśapūtā ye parameśvara ॥20 ॥

O Lord, although Rāvaṇa, Tripurāsura, Mahākāla the lord of death, Kāmadeva the lord of love, etcetera, were killed by

You, still Your nearness was there so they are worth salutations from us. They were sanctified and liberated by the touch of the fire of Your wrath. We salute them because they had Your nearness. You had fought with them with Your hands. Your divine hands touched them.

महाप्रकाशवपुषि विस्पष्टे भवति स्थिते ।
सर्वतोऽपीश तत्कस्मात्तमसि प्रसराम्यहम् ॥२१ ॥

mahāprakāśavapuṣi vispaṣṭe bhavati sthite ।
sarvato 'pīśa tatkasmāttamasi prasarāmyaham ॥21 ॥

O Lord, it is a fact that Your existence is found everywhere because it is all light, all consciousness everywhere. Although it is found by me also everywhere, yet why do I roam in darkness every now and then? What is the cause of my existence in darkness, dense darkness?

अविभागो भवानेव स्वरूपममृतं मम ।
तथापि मर्त्यधर्माणामहमेवैकमास्पदम् ॥२२ ॥

avibhāgo bhavāneva svarūpamamṛtaṁ mama ।
tathāpi martyadharmāṇāmahamevaikamāspadam ॥22 ॥

Actually You are universal, You are everywhere and my body is one with Your nectarized body, but still it is a wonder to me as to why I am given to all mortal problems, like I got headache, I have got nasal trouble, I have got boils, I have got all the sadness, all sorrows. This is a wonder for me. You are my essential real nature.

महेश्वरेति यस्यास्ति नामकं वाग्विभूषणम् ।
प्रणामाङ्कश्च शिरसि स एवैकः प्रभावितः ॥२३ ॥

maheśvareti yasyāsti nāmakaṁ vāgvibhūṣaṇam ।
praṇāmāṅkaśca śirasi sa evaikaḥ prabhāvitaḥ ॥23 ॥

Blessed are those persons whose tongue is glorified with Thy name, whose tongue always recites Your name: "O Maheśvara,

O Bhagavān, O Śiva, O my Dearest, O Lord," and on whose forehead is the sign of bowing down on the ground before You. Those people whose tongue is glorified by constant recitation of Your name and whose forehead is glorified by the sign of bowing before You, they are actually fortunate and no one else.

सदसच्च भवानेव येन तेनाप्रयासतः ।
स्वरसेनैव भगवंस्तथा सिद्धिः कथं न मे ॥२४ ॥

sadasacca bhavāneva yena tenāprayāsataḥ ।
svarasenaiva bhagavaṁstathā siddhiḥ kathaṁ na me ॥24 ॥

O Lord, this is a fact that You are existing in existent objects, and You exist in non-existent objects. In those objects which are fully lighted, You exist. In those objects which are dark, You exist. You are there in the darkness and You are there in the light. Why don't I perceive You without any effort then?

If it is a fact that You are existing everywhere, in existing things as well as in non-existent things, then why don't I perceive Your state without any effort, why should I have to make an effort to perceive You? This is my problem.

शिवदासः शिवैकात्मा किं यन्नासादयेत्सुखम् ।
तर्प्योऽस्मि देवमुख्यानामपि येनामृतासवैः ॥२५ ॥

śivadāsaḥ śivaikātmā kiṁ yannāsādayetsukham ।
tarpyo 'smi devamukhyānāmapi yenāmṛtāsavaiḥ ॥25 ॥

I am a slave of Lord Śiva, it is a fact. I am not only just a slave, I am myself Śiva. And that person, who has become like that, will enjoy all sorts of enjoyment, all sorts of bliss. So it is a fact that all those five great lords have to come and bow to me, five lords of five great actions namely, creation, protection, destruction, concealing and revealing.

Lord of creation is Brahmā, Lord of protection is Nārāyaṇa, Lord of destruction is Rudra, Lord of concealing is Īśvara and Lord of revealing is Sadāśiva, and these five great *kāraṇas*, these five great Lords have to come and prostrate before me. They have to adore me. They are bound to worship me with that liquor which is filled with divine nectar.

हृन्नाभ्योरन्तरालस्थः प्राणिनां पित्तविग्रहः ।
ग्रससे त्वं महावह्निः सर्वं स्थावरजङ्गमम् ॥२६ ॥

hṛnnābhyorantarālasthaḥ prāṇināṁ pittavigrahaḥ ।
grasase tvaṁ mahāvahniḥ sarvaṁ
sthāvarajaṅgamam ॥26 ॥

O Lord, You have become that fire which exists in the centre of the belly of each and every being, and there You eat everything, whatever is moving and whatever is not moving. You eat everything. Everything is digested by You.

For instance You want to drink nectar, You drink milk You take it in the form of a baby. You want to eat meat; You take it in the form of tigers, lions, beasts. Actually all those who take meat are beasts as it is!

॥ इति श्रीमदुत्पलदेवाचार्यविरचिते श्रीशिवस्तोत्रावल्यां
अविच्छेदभङ्गाख्यं दशमं स्तोत्रम् ॥

॥ *iti śrīmadutpaladevācāryaviracite śrīśivastotrāvalyāṁ*
avicchedabhaṅgākhyaṁ daśamaṁ stotram ॥

11

औत्सुक्यविश्वसितनामैकादशं स्तोत्रम्

Autsukyaviśvasita Stotra

Longing for Assurance

THIS chapter is nominated as *Autsukyaviśvasita* comprising two words, namely *autsukya* which means desire, longing for the nearness of God, and *viśvasita* which stands for consolation, assurance and confidence. First the longing and then the assurance, don't worry it will come.

जगदिदमथ वा सुहृदो बन्धुजनो वा न भवति मम किमपि।
त्वं पुनरेतत्सर्वं यदा तदा कोऽपरो मेऽस्तु ॥१॥

jagadidamatha vā suhṛdo
bandhujano vā na bhavati mama kimapi ।
tvaṁ punaretatsarvaṁ
yadā tadā ko 'paro me 'stu ॥1॥

In this whole universe, no one is mine; rather I have no one in this world. My kith and kin, my friends, my relatives aren't mine. I have no concern with anybody here in this universe. You are my Master, to me You are everything. You are my friend, You are my kith and kin, not only at this moment of intense desire for Your nearness but for ever. Always You are my everything; I have no one other than You.

स्वामिन्महेश्वरस्त्वं साक्षात्सर्वं जगत्त्वमेवेति।
वस्त्वेव सिद्धिमेत्विति याच्ञा तत्रापि याच्ञैव ॥२॥

svāminmaheśvarastvaṁ sākṣātsarvaṁ
jagattvameveti ।
vastveva siddhimetviti yācñā tatrāpi yācñaiva ॥2 ॥

O my Master, it is a fact that You are the Lord of lords. This whole universe is just one with You. Why should I ask for anything from You? I don't want a particular thing, give me everything. You are Maheśa; You are the Lord of lords, bestower of everything, why should I then ask for one particular thing.

Asking for "everything" here means being one with the universal consciousness. He won't ask for petty things like a better job for his son.

त्रिभुवनाधिपतित्वमपीह यत्तृणमिव प्रतिभाति भवज्जुषः ।
किमिव तस्य फलं शुभकर्मणो भवति नाथ भवत्स्मरणादृते ॥३ ॥

tribhuvanādhipatitvamapīha yat-
tṛṇamiva pratibhāti bhavajjuṣaḥ ।
kimiva tasya phalaṁ śubhakarmaṇo
bhavati nātha bhavatsmaraṇādṛte ॥3 ॥

O Master, those who are devoted to Thee, if they are provided with the kingdom of all the three worlds, that kingdom even appears to them just like a neglected blade of grass. They have nothing to long for except just remembering You always. They don't want the kingdom of the three worlds. O Master, in this world the kingdom of all the three worlds appears to Thy devotees, Thy adorers, those who taste You, not better than a neglected blade of dried grass.

That devotee who performs this divine action of adoring You, worshipping You, what better fruit will he own other than just remembering You. He enjoys only that. What better enjoyment will that person who is conducting that divine action of Thy worship possess, other than Thy remembrance?

येन नैव भवतोऽस्ति विभिन्नं किञ्चनापि जगतां प्रभवश्च ।
त्वद्विजृम्भितमतोऽद्भुतकर्मस्वप्युदेति न तव स्तुतिबन्धः ॥४॥

yena naiva bhavato 'sti vibhinnaṁ
kiñcanāpi jagatāṁ prabhavaśca ।
tvadvijṛmbhitamato 'dbhutakarma-
svapyudeti na tava stutibandhaḥ ॥4॥

It is a fact that there is nothing outside Your *svarūpa*. Nothing exists without Thee. Only You are existing in this world and nothing else. Those five handlers of this universe, creator, protector, destroyer, concealer and revealer, namely Brahmā, Viṣṇu, Rudra, Īśvara and Sadāśiva respectively; these great gods also are just the offshoots of Your divinity, just the sparks of Your divinity only.

In this universe, whatever great things You are doing, whatever wonderful things You are doing, even for those great things too there is no scope for singing Your glory because nothing is a wonder for You. Everything is so very easy for You because expansion of those sparks of Your divinity is found in those five great gods who are handling this universe. So in Your surprising acts also, we are not supposed to sing Your glory that You have done or You are doing such miracles. It is Your very nature to do so, it is nothing new for You.

त्वन्मयोऽस्मि भवदर्चननिष्ठः सर्वदाहमिति चाप्यविरामम् ।
भावयन्नपि विभो स्वरसेन स्वप्नगोऽपि न तथा किमिव स्याम् ॥५॥

tvanmayo 'smi bhavadarcananiṣṭhaḥ ।
sarvadāhamiti cāpyavirāmam ।
bhāvayannapi vibho svarasena
svapnago 'pi na tathā kimiva syām ॥5॥

O Lord, there is still one problem in me.

There is no such moment when I don't adore You wholeheartedly. I am always with You, thinking of You, possessing You. Every now and then I am with You and I perceive that I am worshipping You always as my dearest Lord. I do all these things and perceive You all the time, but when I go to sleep, I get merged in the dreaming world and dream of some peculiar things not related to You at all. That should not happen.

From early in the morning till very late in the night, I am always with You and after that, in whatever little rest I take, I dream of things not concerned with You. This should not happen to me. I must worship You in the dreaming state also. This is my problem.

ये मनागपि भवच्चरणाब्जोद्भूतसौरभलवेन विमृष्टाः ।
तेषु विस्रमिव भाति समस्तं भोगजातममरैरपि मृग्यम् ॥६ ॥

ye manāgapi bhavaccaraṇābjod-
bhūtasaurabhalavena vimṛṣṭāḥ ।
teṣu visramiva bhāti samastaṁ
bhogajātamamarairapi mṛgyam ॥6 ॥

To those people who have been just touched by even the smallest quantity, smallest droplet, even a microscopic grain of the pollen of the fragrance that has come out from Thy lotus feet, all the pleasures enjoyed by the gods in the heaven appear like foul smell. All that world of enjoyment appears to them with foul smell once they have been even slightly touched by that pollen of fragrance which has come out from Thy lotus feet. Just thinking of the world of enjoyment arouses distaste and disgust in them; they can't even look at it, they find all other enjoyments absolutely tasteless, the desire for worldly pleasures automatically vanishes from their mind.

हृदि ते न तु विद्यतेऽन्यदन्यद्वचने कर्मणि चान्यदेव शंभो ।
परमार्थसतोऽप्यनुग्रहो वा यदि वा निग्रह एक एव कार्यः ॥७ ॥

hṛdi te na tu vidyate 'nyadanyad-
vacane karmaṇi cānyadeva śaṁbho ।
paramārthasato 'pyanugraho vā
yadi vā nigraha eka eva kāryaḥ ॥7 ॥

You see I am a simple man; I have no fraud in me and You know that. You too must be straightforward, but at times You seem to be a fraud. Whatever one has in mind, the same thing must be there in the speech and the same thing must be reflected in one's actions also. But I feel You have thought of something else with regard to Your devotees. Outwardly You say You would do it but internally You have thought of not doing it and in action You do still something else. It should not happen that You resolve something in your mind, have something else in speech and do still something else through actions.

O Lord, I am a simple man, You must also be like that. If You have not to uplift me, If You have not to elevate me, put me down once for all. If You have to elevate me, think that way in Your mind, say so through Your speech and do that through Your actions. Don't tease me by doing contradictory things. Just tell me frankly that You would not like to do it and I would sit in some corner and repent for the rest of my life. Your false assurances that You would do it, do it tomorrow or do it day after tomorrow and having resolved internally not to do it at all, will lead me nowhere.

Either elevate me (*anugraha*) or destroy me (*nigraha*).

मूढोऽस्मि दुःखकलितोऽस्मि जरादिदोष-
भीतोऽस्मि शक्तिरहितोऽस्मि तवाश्रितोऽस्मि ।
शम्भो तथा कलय शीघ्रमुपैमि येन
सर्वोत्तमां धुरमपोज्झितदुःखमार्गः ॥८ ॥

mūḍho 'smi duḥkhakalito 'smi jarādidoṣa-
bhīto 'smi śaktirahito 'smi tavāśrito 'smi ।
śambho tathā kalaya śīghramupaimi yena
sarvottamāṁ dhuramapojjhitaduḥkhamārgaḥ ॥8 ॥

O Lord, I am dull-headed, actually I don't know how to talk with You and am always overwhelmed with sadness. I am scared of the pains of this universe, namely ill health, old age and death. Nothing is within my power; there is no way I can exercise any control over these. I am dull and this dullness won't go even with my effort. I am overwhelmed with sadness, sorrows and torture but I can't get out of that torture. I am afraid of these three things, namely old age, disease and death and I am powerless.

O Lord, I have taken shelter in You, so please act in such a way, that I instantaneously achieve the highest and the greatest state of being which will free me from all tortures, where there is no torture at all.

त्वत्कर्णदेशमधिशय्य महार्घभाव-
माक्रन्दितानि मम तुच्छतराणि यान्ति ।
वंशान्तरालपतितानि जलैकदेश-
खण्डानि मौक्तिकमणित्वमिवोद्वहन्ति ॥९ ॥

tvatkarṇadeśamadhiśayya mahārghabhāva-
mākranditāni mama tucchatarāṇi yānti ।
vaṁśāntarālapatitāni jalaikadeśa-
khaṇḍāni mauktikamaṇitvamivodvahanti ॥9 ॥

When the drops of soft rain fall in the hollow spaces in bamboos, after some time these are converted into pearls. Consider the bamboos have been burnt by the forest fire and there are some bamboo stumps left and in those hollows the rain drops fall. After some particular period, these are converted into pearls. This water in those droplets has no fun in itself; it does not have any value of its own. But these become valuable only when these fall in the hollow spaces of those bamboo stumps and take the form of pearls.

O Lord, in the same way my crying and weeping for You and Your nearness is useless, it has no value; but when this cry reaches the hollow part of Your ears, it becomes valuable, it becomes precious just like those drops of water become pearls and jewels in the hollows of the bamboo stumps. In the same way my otherwise useless crying becomes valuable and bears the fruit of liberation, and I get liberated.

किमिव च लभ्यते बत न तैरपि नाथ जनैः
क्षणमपि कैतवादपि च ये तव नाम्नि रताः ।
शिशिरमयूखशेखर तथा कुरु येन मम
क्षतमरणोऽणिमादिकमुपैमि यथा विभवम् ॥१० ॥

kimiva ca labhyate bata na tairapi nātha janaiḥ
kṣaṇamapi kaitavādapi ca ye tava nāmni ratāḥ ।
śiśiramayūkhaśekhara tathā kuru yena mama
kṣatamaraṇo 'ṇimādikamupaimi yathā vibhavam ॥10 ॥

O Lord, those people who have diverted their minds to Your remembrance can achieve anything whatever is possible and whatever is impossible. Even those people who are not devoted to You but who recite Your name not from the core of their hearts but just for curiosity, just to please You, just to flatter You, just for the sake of making money; who even fraudulently recite Your name, also achieve great things. So great is Your name that those pretentious persons also achieve everything. Those hypocrites given to Your name for even one moment, also achieve great heights. So great is Thy name.

O Lord, Your forehead is beautified with that crescent moon; please do something for me so that I am delivered from the fear of old age, disease and death and I achieve those eight great internal yogic powers.

शम्भो शर्व शशाङ्कशेखर शिव त्र्यक्षाक्षमालाधर
श्रीमन्नुग्रकपाललाञ्छन लसद्भीमत्रिशूलायुध ।
कारुण्याम्बुनिधे त्रिलोकरचनाशीलोग्रशक्त्यात्मक
श्रीकण्ठाशु विनाशयाशुभभरानाधत्स्व सिद्धिं पराम् ॥११ ॥

śambho śarva śaśāṅkaśekhara śiva
tryakṣākṣamālādhara
śrīmannugrakapālalāñchana
lasadbhīmatriśūlāyudha ।
kāruṇyāmbunidhe trilokaracanāśīlograśaktyātmaka
śrīkaṇṭhāśu vināśayāśubhabharānādhatsva
siddhiṁ parām ॥11 ॥

O Lord Śiva, O destroyer of the whole universe, O holder of the crescent moon on Your forehead, O Śiva, O holder of three eyes, O holder of beads (*jayamālā),* O holder of the wealth of liberation, O holder of the terrifying skull (of Brahmā that is filled with Viṣṇu's blood), O holder of terrifying trident as the weapon in Your hand, You are the ocean of compassion, You arrange the three worlds (*prameya, pramāṇa* and *pramātā*), O holder of terrifying energies, O Śrīkaṇṭanātha (these are all appelations), please destroy all my tortures, the burden of crises existing in me, and please bestow Your divinity of God-consciousness on me, the ultimate *siddhi.*

तत्किं नाथ भवेन्न यत्र भगवान्निर्मातृतामश्नुते
भावः स्यात्किमु तस्य चेतनवतो नाशास्ति यं शङ्करः ।
इत्थं ते परमेश्वराक्षतमहाशक्तेः सदा संश्रितः
संसारेऽत्र निरन्तराधिविधुरः क्लिश्याम्यहं केवलम् ॥१२ ॥

tatkiṁ nātha bhavenna yatra
bhagavānnirmātṛtāmaśnute

bhāvaḥ syātkimu tasya cetanavato nāśāsti yaṁ
śaṅkaraḥ ।
itthaṁ te parameśvarākṣatamahāśakteḥ sadā
saṁśritaḥ
saṁsāre 'tra nirantarādhividhuraḥ
kliśyāmyahaṁ kevalam ॥12 ॥

O Lord, which is that object, where You are not the creator; You are the creator of everything that exists in this universe. And which is that object which is not governed by You, O Śaṅkara. In this way I have taken refuge in Thee who possesses all unending eternal power, and still it is shameful for You, not for me, that in this world I am overwhelmed and shattered by mental tortures in continuity; this is my state. This is the fruit of my taking refuge in Thee. I have become the object of only pain and sorrow. I don't experience any joy in this world. This is the fruit of my surrendering everything to You and taking refuge in You. Why should it be so?

You are the greatest, You have got the highest and never-ending power; whatever object exists in this world, You are its creator and You are ruling it, You are governing it. So You are the governor of this whole universe and You have got that supreme unending power. I have taken refuge in Thee but in turn I am tortured with unending pain and sorrow. Why should it be so? Is this Your greatness?

यद्यप्यत्र वरप्रदोद्धततमाः पीडाजरामृत्यवः
एते वा क्षणमासतां बहुमतः शब्दादिरेवास्थिरः ।
तत्रापि स्पृहयामि सन्ततसुखाकाङ्क्षी चिरं स्थास्नवे
भोगास्वादयुतत्वदङ्घ्रिकमलध्यानाग्र्यजीवातवे ॥१३ ॥

yadyapyatra varapradoddhatatamāḥ
pīḍājarāmṛtyavaḥ
ete vā kṣaṇamāsatāṁ bahumataḥ śabdādirevāsthiraḥ ।

tatrāpi spṛhayāmi santatasukhākāṅkṣī ciraṁ
sthāsnave
bhogāsvādayutatvadaṅghrikamaladhyānāgryajīvātave ||13 ||

O bestower of boons, O Lord Śiva, in this universe crises, pain, unending pain, old age, and death are supposed to be extremely frightening, fearful, and unbearable. Let us not touch upon this. Let these three things namely sadness, old age and death remain aside. There was some sense of pleasure also in this universe through *śabda* (hearing), *sparśa* (touch), *rasa* (taste), *rūpa* (form) and *gandha* (smell). But the pleasure that we get through these is also not stable. That too is waning.

So in this position, in fact I am such a person, who needs pleasure that will remain established always, till eternity. I want long lasting joy; such joy which will remain established forever. That joy will come only by maintaining and possessing a delightful life consisting of enjoying the nectar of Your worship. I would like that kind of life in which I would always worship only You and enjoy that action of worshipping You for my entire life. That is what I need in this universe as the pain, old age and death are so fearful and the worldly enjoyments also don't last, these are very temporary in nature.

हे नाथ प्रणतार्तिनाशनपटो श्रेयोनिधे धूर्जटे
दुःखैकायतनस्य जन्ममरणत्रस्तस्य मे साम्प्रतम्।
तच्चेष्टस्व यथा मनोज्ञविषयास्वादप्रदा उत्तमाः
जीवन्नेव समश्नुवेऽहमचलाः सिद्धीस्त्वदर्चापरः ॥१४॥

he nātha praṇatārtināśanapaṭo śreyonidhe dhūrjaṭe
duḥkhaikāyatanasya janmamaraṇatrastasya me
sāmpratam |
tacceṣṭasva yathā manojñaviṣayāsvādapradā uttamāḥ
jīvanneva samaśnuve 'hamacalāḥ
siddhīstvadarcāparaḥ ||14 ||

O my Master, O my Lord You are bent upon removing and destroying the torture of those who have taken refuge in You.

O ocean of peace and beatitude, the final liberation, You have got matted locks. O such Lord, I have become victim of only pain, sorrow, sadness and torture; I am afraid of repeated births and deaths. So at present You should act in such a way for me that in this very life I would get those great tasteful powers I have been longing for; those permanent tasteful powers to just worship You. I should achieve those powers in this very life, in my lifetime only and not after my death.

नमो मोहमहाध्वान्तध्वंसनानन्यकर्मणे ।
सर्वप्रकाशातिशयप्रकाशायेन्दुलक्ष्मणे ॥१५ ॥

namo mohamahādhvānta-
dhvaṁsanānanyakarmaṇe ।
sarvaprakāśātiśaya-
prakāśāyendulakṣmaṇe ॥15 ॥

O Lord, I bow to Thee who has only this much to do; You have only one work and that is to remove the illusion, the forgetfulness of one's being, one's existence. You are bent upon removing that great dense darkness. You have only this much to do; it is Your sole work.

I bow to Thee who is very delightful, who possesses more radiant light than all other lights, namely the light of fire, the light of the moon and the light of the sun, that light which is more effulgent than all these three lights and who sports the mark of the crescent moon on His forehead. I bow to Thee.

॥ इति श्रीमदुत्पलदेवाचार्यविरचिते श्रीशिवस्तोत्रावल्यां
औत्सुक्यविश्वसितनामैकादशं स्तोत्रम् ॥

॥ *iti śrīmadutpaladevācāryaviracite śrīśivastotrāvalyāṁ*
autsukyaviśvasitanāmaikādaśaṁ stotram ॥

12

रहस्यनिर्देशनाम द्वादशं स्तोत्रम्

Rahasyanirdeśa Stotra

Revealing the Secret

THIS chapter is nominated as *Rahasyanirdeśa* which is composed of two words: *rahasya* and *nirdeśa*. The author is bent upon revealing the secret of the sovereign, independent, free will of God. He beseeches the Lord to unfold to him the supreme secret.

सहकारि न किञ्चिदिष्यते भवतो न प्रतिबन्धकं दृशि ।
भवतैव हि सर्वमाप्लुतं कथमद्यापि तथापि नेक्षसे ॥१॥

sahakāri na kiñcidiṣyate
bhavato na pratibandhakaṁ dṛśi ।
bhavataiva hi sarvamāplutaṁ
kathamadyāpi tathāpi nekṣase ॥1॥

My Lord, for finding You out, for experiencing Your nature, for perceiving You, there is no need to adopt any means. You are perceived, just without any adoption, without any meditation, without prayers, without concentration, without maintaining any discipline. For realizing Thee, nothing is needed, neither meditation nor discipline, nor *brahmacarya*, nor *satya*, nor *asteya*; all these things are useless there.

For realizing You there is nothing to be adopted and there is no obstacle also in realizing You. You are free to be realized. The path of Your realization is clear, so there is nothing to stop one from realizing Your nature because You have pervaded the whole world. You have pervaded the world of means and You have pervaded the world of obstacles. Obstacles are shining because You are shining in obstacles, and means are also shining because You are shining there too.

But the problem is that I am still kept away from Your realization. There ought to have been no problem in the real sense as the path was quite clear; but I still do not realize You. You are still not seen, You are still not perceived. This is the problem.

[Question: Why to do anything then?]

[Answer:] It is just to keep oneself busy, there is nothing to be done actually. It is not that if one kept oneself busy with these things, one was sure to realize God, it might not come at all. It comes by itself. In Śaivism, there is actually nothing needed to perceive God. This is a fact that when God is perceived, He is just perceived without the adoption of any means.

What are means, *upāyas*? *Upāyas* are just living a disciplined life following *brahmacarya, satya, asteya,* etcetera. It is a normal belief that all these measures are to be adopted and only then God is revealed. But as per Śaivism, God is revealed without adoption of these things. When God is revealed, He is just revealed, by Himself. This is the secret. There is no cause and effect relationship. He is not realized with effort. When you make effort for realizing Him, you may still remain far away from His nature. When you abandon all your efforts, you may still remain far away from His nature. God is revealed just when He so wills. *Śaktipāta* is not in your hands.

अपि भावगणादपीन्द्रियप्रचयादप्यवबोधमध्यतः ।
प्रभवन्तमपि स्वतः सदा परिपश्येयमपोढविश्वकम् ॥२॥

api bhāvagaṇādapīndriya-
pracayādapyavabodhamadhyataḥ ।
prabhavantamapi svataḥ sadā
paripaśyeyamapoḍhaviśvakam ॥2 ॥

O Lord, from the objective world, from the collection of the organic world and from the centre of the cognitive world, I would always like to feel You automatically; I would like to see You, perceive You where all dualities vanish, where all dualistic realization ends. I would like to see You that way not only in *samādhi*, but also from the objective world and from the organic world. I would also like to automatically see You from the centre of the cognition, without having to make any effort. Having overcome the dualistic perception, I would like to see You everywhere.

कथं ते जायेरन्कथमपि च ते दर्शनपथं
व्रजेयुः केनापि प्रकृतिमहताङ्केन खचिताः ।
तथोत्थायोत्थाय स्थलजलतृणादेरखिलतः
पदार्थाद्यान्सृष्टिस्रवदमृतपूरैर्विकिरसि ॥३ ॥

katham̐ te jāyerankathamapi ca te darśanapatham̐
vrajeyuḥ kenāpi prakr̥timahatāṅkena khacitāḥ ।
tathotthāyotthāya sthalajalatr̥ṇāderakhilataḥ
padārthādyānsr̥ṣṭisravadamr̥tapūrairvikirasi ॥3 ॥

O Lord, how can those fortunate persons be born again in this universe and how can those fortunate persons be understood by ordinary worldly people? Worldly people can never understand them; they are beyond the understanding of the worldly people. Worldly people cannot understand that they are so highly elevated and how can they again come into this universe? They are marked with that unique and extraordinary sign of greatness; how can they be born in this universe again and how can they be understood by ordinary people?

You elevate those people from the objective world. You take them out from the sticky mud of these worldly pleasures and sprinkle them with the flows of super-sexual joy of God-consciousness. You shower on them that nectar of God-consciousness after getting them out of this lower universal field; always raising them from all this sticky situation of the worldly state.

You elevate them as You elevate Your own nature; You elevate them and at the same time You elevate Your own nature. You consider this whole universe as one body of Yours, so You elevate them as You elevate Yourself. How You elevate them is not by their activity, not by their meditating effort but by adopting *śaktipāta*, by just Your independent will. You take them out of this objective world and then soak them in Your nectar of God-consciousness. How can those people be born again in this world? How can those people be understood by the ordinary worldly people? They become divine. They are for ever liberated from the cycle of the repeated births and deaths. They become *jīvanamukta.*

साक्षात्कृतभवद्रूपप्रसृतामृततर्पिताः ।
उन्मूलिततृषो मत्ता विचरन्ति यथारुचि ॥४ ॥

sākṣātkṛtabhavadrūpaprasṛtāmṛtatarpitāḥ ।
unmūlitatṛṣo mattā vicaranti yathāruci ॥4 ॥

In this world I have found some mad people who enjoy roaming about here and there according to their own choice, with their own independent will; they have no longing for anything, they have no thirst for any object (*śabda, sparśa, rasa, rūpa* and *gandha*). Without any thirst they enjoy in this world just like mad people, because they have drunk the nectar which has flown out of experiencing Your nature. By drinking that nectar they have become so contented and full that they roam about in this world without any objective. They have nothing to do in this world. They just roam about.

न तदा न सदा न चैकदेत्यपि सा यत्र न कालधीर्भवेत् ।
तदिदं भवदीयदर्शनं न च नित्यं न च कथ्यतेऽन्यथा ॥५॥

na tadā na sadā na caikade-
tyapi sā yatra na kāladhīrbhavet ।
tadidaṁ bhavadīyadarśanaṁ
na ca nityaṁ na ca kathyate 'nyathā ॥5॥

O Lord, realizing You is beyond the normal sense of time, beyond the comprehension of time. It is neither eternal nor can it be called the absence of eternity.

In the real sense, this is the only sign of experiencing Your nature: In experiencing Your nature there is no that time, there is no this time, there is no simultaneous time, there no past time, there is no present time, there is no future time, there is no eternity and there is no absence of eternity. That really is Your state of realization. It is not eternal and it is not absence of eternity also. It is always shining. You can't say always also.

त्वद्विलोकनसमुत्कचेतसो योगसिद्धिरियती सदास्तु मे ।
यद्विशेयमभिसन्धिमात्रतस्त्वत्सुधासदनमर्चनाय ते ॥६॥

tvadvilokanasamutkacetaso
yogasiddhiriyatī sadāstu me ।
yadviśeyamabhisandhimātratas-
tvatsudhāsadanamarcanāya te ॥6॥

O Lord, I want to own only one yogic power and I must own it for ever; just one small thing which I want to own, only one *yogasiddhi* and I am fit for that *yogasiddhi*. You must grant me that only desire in my mind and that is just to see You always. This desire to just see You always knocks in the background of my mind, in the background of my consciousness. My mind is always restless to see You.

I don't want those eight great yogic powers, I want only one *yogasiddhi* and that is I must get entry into the palace, the abode of Your nature; not by any effort nor by adopting any means, but whenever I wish to, I must get entry by mere desire, just by my will. I have not to ask You for anything else. I want to worship You and that is the only desire tickling in the background of my consciousness. I want to see You. I just want to worship You and then I am satisfied; You have nothing to worry about. I won't ask for anything else, no boons, no *anugraha*, no peace of mind, no *yoga*, nothing, I just want to worship You. That is my joy.

निर्विकल्पभवदीयदर्शनप्राप्तिफुल्लमनसां महात्मनाम् ।
उल्लसन्ति विमलानि हेलया चेष्टितानि च वचांसि च स्फुटम् ॥७॥

nirvikalpabhavadīyadarśana-
prāptiphullamanasāṁ mahātmanām ।
ullasanti vimalāni helayā
ceṣṭitāni ca vacāṁsi ca sphuṭam ॥7॥

Those are great souls whose mind has bloomed by the achievement of Your *nirvikalpa darśana*, their speech and their activities seem to be filled with divinity. Whatever they talk is divine, they may talk kind and compassionate words, that is divine; they may talk harsh and abusive words, they may talk nonsense, that is also divine. Everything becomes divine for those who have achieved that *nirvikalpa darśana* of Thee and whose mind has bloomed. Their activity and their words shine in such a way that they become pure and divine, filled with divinity. Their speech is pure, spontaneous and divine.

भगवन्भवदीयपादयोर्निवसन्नन्तर एव निर्भयः ।
भवभूमिषु तासु तास्वहं प्रभुमर्चेयमनर्गलक्रियः ॥८॥

bhagavanbhavadīyapādayor-
nivasannantara eva nirbhayaḥ ।
bhavabhūmiṣu tāsu tāsvahaṁ
prabhumarceyamanargalakriyaḥ ॥8 ॥

O Lord, there is one problem with me. I want to reside, I want to live under Your divine feet where there is no fear of anything in this world because You are fearlessly there. Nothing negative, nothing bad can happen to me there when I am situated under Your divine feet; there won't be any fire, there won't be any earthquake, there would be no theft, no disease, and no trouble whatsoever.

I don't want to remain there always like that, the problem is that I want to live there but I would also like to experience worldly states, worldly enjoyments and in those worldly enjoyments, I would like to adore Thy feet at the same time. I would come out from under Thy feet, just open my eyes and experience worldly pleasures and then if I get filled with some torture, I would again go under Your feet so that I would always be happy. I want to adore You always like that.

भवदङ्घ्रिसरोरुहोदरे परिलीनो गलितापरैषणः ।
अतिमात्रमधूपयोगतः परितृप्तो विचरेयमिच्छया ॥९ ॥

bhavadaṅghrisaroruhodare-
parilīno galitāparaiṣaṇaḥ ।
atimātramadhūpayogataḥ
paritṛpto vicareyamicchayā ॥9 ॥

O Lord, I would like to rest under Your lotus feet where I would find no other desire left in me. No other desire would remain in me; all other desires would vanish altogether. That pollen of Your lotus feet, that nectar of God-consciousness, will drip on me and create intense joy in me. By adopting that intense joy, I would get fully satisfied and then I would roam about this world according to my own choice.

यस्य दम्भादिव भवत्पूजासङ्कल्प उत्थितः ।
तस्याप्यवश्यमुदितं सन्निधानं तवोचितम् ॥१० ॥

yasya dambhādiva bhavatpūjāsaṅkalpa utthitaḥ ।
tasyāpyavaśyamuditaṁ sannidhānaṁ tavocitam ॥10 ॥

Your worship is so great that a person who desires to adore Your nature even if only for curiosity sake, just to show people that he is an adorer of Lord Śiva, he worships You just fraudulently to show people that he is worshipping You; to him also You become divine. You will appear to him in the state of God-consciousness; he will also achieve God-consciousness. This is the greatness of Your nature that whosoever just touches it even with a crooked thought also attains that supreme joy.

भगवन्नितरानपेक्षिणा नितरामेकरसेन चेतसा ।
सुलभं सकलोपशायिनं प्रभुमातृप्ति पिबेयमस्मि किम् ॥११ ॥

bhagavannitarānapekṣiṇā
nitarāmekarasena cetasā ।
sulabhaṁ sakalopaśāyinaṁ
prabhumātṛpti pibeyamasmi kim ॥11 ॥

O Lord, there is one desire in me and that must be fulfilled. I want to swallow You up in my nature to my entire satisfaction. You who are found everywhere I want to swallow You at once, not with my mouth but with my mind. And my mind must not be diverted to any point other than the objective of just to swallow You. When will that day come when there would be no other desire in my mind but to swallow You?

I would like to swallow You, who is effortlessly found everywhere, to my entire satisfaction. When shall that day come?

त्वया निराकृतं सर्वं हेयमेतत्तदेव तु ।
त्वन्मयं समुपादेयमित्ययं सारसंग्रहः ॥१२॥

tvayā nirākṛtaṁ sarvaṁ heyametattadeva tu ।
tvanmayaṁ samupādeyamityayaṁ sārasaṁgrahaḥ ॥12॥

The essence of this philosophy in brief is that everything where You are not found is to be abandoned; whatsoever it may be, jewellery, gold, kingdom, sovereignty, etcetera, it is to be abandoned if You are not there. And when You are present, it may be anything absurd, it is worth having. This in brief is the essence of our philosophy.

भवतोऽन्तरचारि-भावजातं प्रभुवन्मुख्यतयैव पूजितं तत्।
भवतो बहिरप्यभावमात्रा कथमीशान भवेत्समर्च्यते वा ॥१३॥

bhavato 'ntaracāri-bhāvajātaṁ
prabhuvanmukhyatayaiva pūjitaṁ tat ।
bhavato bahirapyabhāvamātrā
kathamīśāna bhavetsamarcyate vā ॥13॥

O Lord, this whole universe entirely exists in Your own nature and this universe, the whole class of objectivity, is worth adoring because it is one with Your nature. Because anything non-existent, any object which does not exist is also felt in You, in Your nature. How can that non-existent object exist otherwise, how can that be worshipped?

This entire universe is one with You. So all action is worship, Your direct worship and not anybody else's worship.

Worship means just to know; when you know a thing, it is worshipped, to use these spectacles is the worship of these spectacles; just to see is to worship because there is unity there. When you eat food, chew it, you are worshipping food, when you kiss your beloved, it is worship.

निःशब्दं निर्विकल्पं च निर्व्याक्षेपमथानिशम्।
क्षोभेऽप्यध्यक्षमीक्षेयं त्र्यक्ष त्वामेव सर्वतः ॥१४॥

niḥśabdaṁ nirvikalpaṁ ca nirvyākṣepamathāniśam ।
kṣobhe 'pyadhyakṣamīkṣeyaṁ tryakṣa tvāmeva sarvataḥ ॥14॥

O holder of three eyes, O Lord Śiva, You are soundless, You are thoughtless, You are unwavering, without any distraction. I want to see You in the agitated state also of this objective world. When my mind is agitated and is taken away from God-consciousness, in that state also I would like to see You and observe Your presence there, everywhere.

प्रकटय निजधाम देव यस्मिंस्त्वमसि सदा परमेश्वरीसमेतः।
प्रभुचरणरजःसमानकक्ष्याः किमविश्वासपदं भवन्ति भृत्याः ॥१५॥

prakaṭaya nijadhāma deva yasmiṁs-
tvamasi sadā parameśvarīsametaḥ ।
prabhucaraṇarajaḥsamānakakṣyāḥ
kimaviśvāsapadaṁ bhavanti bhṛtyāḥ ॥15॥

O Lord, please reveal that abode of Yours where You reside along with Goddess Pārvatī; that private compartment in which You are residing along with Your better-half Pārvatī. I just want to enjoy the presence of both of You. I am Your slave and as such am I not worth even that particle of dust on Your feet, that has got entry into that compartment. As Your feet are already there, some dust particles also may be there. If these are allowed, I too should be allowed entry. You should trust me as You trust that particle of dust under Your feet. You must trust me, I am not a thief, I won't even touch any precious things there.

दर्शनपथमुपयातोऽप्यपसरसि कुतो ममेश भृत्यस्य।
क्षणमात्रकमिह न भवसि कस्य न जन्तोर्दृशोर्विषयः ॥१६॥

darśanapathamupayāto 'pyapasarasi
kuto mameśa bhṛtyasya ।
kṣaṇamātrakamiha na bhavasi
kasya na jantordṛśorviṣayaḥ ॥16॥

O Lord, it is my great fortune that You have come to see me today. You just opened the door of my hut to come in but You again returned from there itself. What is the fun in coming that way? You had come to see me, that is fine, that is my good fortune; but You are returning at once, what is the fun in seeing me this way?

Imagine I am here, I am God's devotee. God is coming; He has opened the door just to see me. Just after opening the door, he closes it and leaves. He intended to come in but doesn't; instead He just returns. That is the position he relates.

Now You will say "I had to just show you my face and having done that I return." But this way everyone perceives You.

For instance when you sneeze, at the start of the sneezing there is God-consciousness, you perceive God-consciousness that way. There is some joy. Similarly at the start of yawning, there is God-consciousness; this is the momentary meeting of God-consciousness.

In the same way You have come to see me and You return at once after just a momentary *darśana.*

There are many *yogīs* who experience God-consciousness like that for a flash of a second and then it is no more. But I am not satisfied with that momentary way of meeting God. You have come to see me, just come in and be with me for some time, we will discuss something. I am Your slave, why should You be afraid of me? What can I do? Please come in and give me some joy.

Now You will say "whatever joy I had to bestow upon you, I have already showered on you by just opening your door and returning," but this way the joy of Your meeting is experienced by everybody in this world. Those who are not Your slaves, they also perceive You like that, for instance at the time of yawning; or at the time of going from the state of wakefulness to sleep there is a point where God-consciousness is shining. Meeting this way does not satisfy me; I do not recognize this meeting at all. I consider You have not come at all. So You cannot say that You have done me a great favour; You have done nothing for me; this is a common place.

ऐक्यसंविदमृताच्छधारया सन्ततप्रसृतया सदा विभो ।
प्लावनात् परमभेदमानयंस्त्वां निजं च वपुराप्नुयां मुदम् ॥१७॥

aikyasaṁvidamṛtācchadhārayā
santataprasṛtayā sadā vibho ।
plāvanāt paramabhedamānayaṁ-
stvāṁ nijaṁ ca vapurāpnuyāṁ mudam ॥17॥

O Lord, this desire is knocking in the background of my mind that I should be overflooded by the stream of the nectar of oneness; I want to get flooded by that stream of non-dualism. That stream must flood me in continuity without any break; then there will be one great union of me with You and with bliss; we will become one. There will be highest beatitude of God-consciousness and with that highest beatitude of God-consciousness You will be united and with You, I will be united. We will become one. This is my desire.

अहमित्यमुतोऽवरुद्धलोकाद्भवदीयात्प्रतिपत्तिसारतो मे ।
अणुमात्रकमेव विश्वनिष्ठं घटतां येन भवेयमर्चिता ते ॥१८॥

ahamityamuto 'varuddhalokād-
bhavadīyātpratipattisārato me ।
aṇumātrakameva viśvaniṣṭhaṁ
ghaṭatāṁ yena bhaveyamarcitā te ॥18॥

O Lord, there is one desire in me, I would like to have just one tiny particle, the smallest particle from the essence of Your God-consciousness, from the essence of Your knowledge, from that unity of knowledge. I would like to have just a minute particle from that knowledge which is perfect universal I-consciousness, where all differentiated perceptions have vanished. I would only like to have just one smallest particle from that God-consciousness and that particle must not delete universal consciousness; universal consciousness must also he united with that God-consciousness.

I want union of God-consciousness to take place with universal consciousness; the universe and God-consciousness must appear to me as one. There is no selfishness of mine in that; I am not selfish to have it; I just want to adore You that way.

For instance I would perceive an object and the perception of that object would be Your worship; I would perceive You and that would be the worship of that object. Perceiving God is worshipping the objective world, and perceiving the objective world is in other words worshipping God. Worshipping God is perception of the objective world and perception of the objective world is the worship of God. That way I would like to worship You in and out.

अपरिमितरूपमहं तं तं भावं प्रतिक्षणं पश्यन्।
त्वामेव विश्वरूपं निजनाथं साधु पश्येयम्॥१९॥

aparimitarūpamahaṁ
taṁ taṁ bhāvaṁ pratikṣaṇaṁ paśyan ।
tvāmeva viśvarūpaṁ
nijanāthaṁ sādhu paśyeyam ॥19॥

This is the desire in me: I would like to perceive the entire objective world, all these worldly objects just in an infinite way. While perceiving an object, I must perceive everything in it. And when I perceive You, I must feel that I perceive all the hundred and eighteen worlds. Perception this way becomes tasty; I would like to have that taste.

(For instance, when I perceive these spectacles, I must feel that these spectacles are infinite, that there is everything lying in it; that there are all the one hundred and eighteen worlds in perceiving these spectacles.)

भवदङ्गगतं तमेव कस्मान्न मनः पर्यटतीष्टमर्थमर्थम् ।
प्रकृतिक्षतिरस्ति नो तथास्य मम चेच्छा परिपूर्यते परैव ॥२० ॥

bhavadaṅgagataṁ tameva kasmānna
manaḥ paryaṭatīṣṭamarthamartham ।
prakṛtikṣatirasti no tathāsya
mama cecchā paripūryate paraiva ॥20 ॥

Why should I abandon objective perception? I would never like to abandon the objective perception because the objective world, these worldly objects are Your own limbs, extension of Your own body. This whole objective perception is Your limbs. Perceiving that this is a pen and that is a box, this is Ernie, that is a tree, is only perceiving Your limbs, why should I then abandon this perception, I will never abandon this kind of perception.

Why should my mind not roam around in the whole objective world? Let it roam around everywhere, let it be scattered, let it go astray, but everywhere it goes, there would be Your presence. This way there won't be any need to control my mind. I will leave my mind free, let it go anywhere, but everywhere it reaches, it must feel it is just wandering in You; wherever it reaches it must perceive that all the objects are the limbs of God and that these are not away from You.

By nature the mind is restive, it won't be controlled, but

this way the mind will be at ease, wherever my mind wants to go, it will be free to go. My supreme desire to realize God-consciousness will also be fulfilled.

शतशः किल ते तवानुभावाद्भगवन्केऽप्यमुनैव चक्षुषा ये।
अपि हालिकचेष्टया चरन्तः परिपश्यन्ति भवद्वपुः सदाग्रे ॥२१॥

śataśaḥ kila te tavānubhāvād-
bhagavanke 'pyamunaiva cakṣuṣā ye ।
api hālikaceṣṭayā carantaḥ
paripaśyanti bhavadvapuḥ sadāgre ॥21॥

Now You would say that it was very difficult to have that state; and I know You would argue that it was very difficult to possess that kind of state, the state of *jagad-ānanda.*

But with Your grace, O Lord, I have seen hundreds of Thy devotees in that state, they are very unique, with these very eyes they see You while performing the routine degraded activities of the world like ploughing, etcetera. With my own eyes, I have seen hundreds of such people in this universe who while indulging in *hālika-ceṣṭā,* the mundane worldly activities also, always feel Your presence just near them. You could bestow this kind of state to me also. I have always been longing for You. This is the only desire at the back of my mind. Why should I not have this? What wrong have I done?

Hālika-ceṣṭā here does not mean ploughing alone, it implies and includes the mundane activities indulged in by those who have no inclination towards knowing God, for instance everything they do from morning through evening, that is to eat, drink, gratify their senses, plough, dig, sleep, etcetera.

न सा मतिरुदेति या न भवति त्वदिच्छामयी
सदा शुभमथेतरद्भगवतैवमाचर्यते।
अतोऽस्मि भवदात्मको भुवि यथा तथा सञ्चरन्
स्थितोऽनिशमबाधितत्वदमलाङ्घ्रिपूजोत्सवः ॥२२॥

na sā matirudeti yā na bhavati tvadicchāmayī
sadā śubhamathetaradbhagavataivamācaryate ।
ato 'smi bhavadātmako bhuvi yathā tathā sañcaran
sthito 'niśamabādhitatvadamalāṅghripūjotsavaḥ ॥22 ॥

Alright, don't grant me that kind of state; even if You don't grant me, I have already achieved that kind of state. (He is very rude to God!)

I will logically prove it to You, how I have achieved that state. That intellectual perception will not rise which is not one with You. In the real way of thinking, good desires and bad desires that arise in individuals are all handled by You. So I am always with You. Wherever I am going, wherever I am seated, I am with You. So my worshipping You is continuing. Don't give me anything, I am already there.

भवदीयगभीरभाषितेषु प्रतिभा सम्यगुदेतु मे पुरोऽतः ।
तदनुष्ठितशक्तिरप्यतस्तद्भवदर्चाव्यसनं च निर्विरामम् ॥२३ ॥

bhavadīyagambhīrabhāṣiteṣu
pratibhā samyagudetu me puro 'taḥ ।
tadanuṣṭhitaśaktirapyatastad-
bhavadarcāvyasanaṁ ca nirvirāmam ॥23 ॥

There is another problem with me. There is one desire in me. (He is again down!)

First let my intellect grasp and digest those Śāstras enunciating Your secret non-dualistic philosophy. Let my intellect first work and digest that understanding. I must first understand it fully. After understanding, I must have the capacity to follow that philosophy, I must practise that philosophy. And then I want to just worship You day and night without any break. I must exert myself in worshipping You to the extent of exhaustion.

Three things I would like to have: first the knowledge of the Śāstras and the philosophy contained therein; secondly the power of practising that theory, treading on that path, and thirdly I must worship You in continuity without any rest till I get exhausted. In a nutshell, I must possess first the knowledge, secondly the capacity and thirdly the devotion.

व्यवहारपदेऽपि सर्वदा प्रतिभात्वर्थकलाप एष माम्।
भवतोऽवयवो यथा न तु स्वत एवादरणीयतां गतः ॥२४॥

vyavahārapade 'pi sarvadā
pratibhātvarthakalāpa eṣa mām ।
bhavato 'vayavo yathā na tu
svata evādaraṇīyatāṁ gataḥ ॥24॥

O Lord, let all the worldly objects appear to me as these appear to other people who are not realized. Like that, let these worldly objects appear to me, but with only one restriction, that these must appear to me as the limbs of Your own body, these must not appear to me as separate from God-consciousness. These must appear to me as Your own limbs. In my routine worldly activities also these must appear to me as one with You and I must regard these as such. I must not regard these only from the pleasure point of view.

मनसि स्वरसेन यत्र तत्र प्रचरत्यप्यहमस्य गोचरेषु।
प्रसृतोऽप्यविलोल एव युष्मत्परिचर्याचतुरः सदा भवेयम्॥२५॥

manasi svarasena yatra tatra
pracaratyapyahamasya gocareṣu ।
prasṛto 'pyavilola eva yuṣmat-
paricaryācaturaḥ sadā bhaveyam ॥25॥

There is one problem. I don't want to control my mind as it is so swift that one cannot control it. It is so swift that it cannot be controlled even by God. If one is watching one's breath, one wouldn't realize the point where the mind would give a slip and escape. It escapes when one is not aware; if there is unawareness even for one hundredth part of a second, before one even realizes, it has escaped hundreds of miles away. One can't watch it, so it is very difficult to control it.

So let it go after the worldly objects, I don't want to control it, it is beyond my power, it is very difficult. (Difficulty is felt by only those who watch it; those who do not watch it do not find any difficulty in controlling the mind!) It is alright if the mind goes after the worldly objects, but I must not be disturbed by its going astray always. Wherever my mind goes, I must adjust my worship of God there. Let it go anywhere, I will worship God because God is everywhere. If it goes anywhere, I will worship God. If it goes to gratify the senses, I will worship God. This strength must be possessed by me, maintained by me.

Without any worry I must become skilful, wise and be always aware in worshipping You in each and every act of my mind because it is not controllable.

भगवन्भवदिच्छयैव दासस्तव जातोऽस्मि परस्य नात्र शक्तिः ।
कथमेष तथापि वक्त्रबिम्बं तव पश्यामि न जातु चित्रमेतत् ॥२६ ॥

bhagavanbhavadicchyaiva dāsa-
stava jāto 'smi parasya nātra śaktiḥ ।
kathameṣa tathāpi vaktrabimbaṁ
tava paśyāmi na jātu citrametat ॥26 ॥

O Lord, by Your own will You have made me Your slave. I did not ask You to put me on Your path. It was Your own free will that You put me on Your path and made me Your slave. Well, if You have made me Your slave it is alright, but then I must see my Master.

No other power could do it — make me Your slave, it is Your own will that I have become Your slave, why then is

Your beautiful face never shown to me? I never see Your face. I have never seen my Master. I have never seen You and that really is surprising. So when I am asked by the people as to whom I am serving, what shall I tell them?

When one engages a servant, one is always around, ordering him or guiding him. But I must be the only servant with the Master never to be seen. This is a wonder to me.

समुत्सुकास्त्वां प्रति ये भवन्तं प्रत्यर्थरूपादवलोकयन्ति।
तेषामहो किं तदुपस्थितं स्यात् किं साधनं वा फलितं भवेत्तत्॥२७॥

samutsukāstvāṁ prati ye bhavantaṁ
pratyartharūpādavalokayanti ।
teṣāmaho kiṁ tadupasthitaṁ syāt
kiṁ sādhanaṁ vā phalitaṁ bhavettat ॥27॥

This is a wonder to me: Those people who are intensely attached to You, who have intense desire to meet You, perceive You in each and every object; from each and every object they get Your presence, they perceive Your presence. How they perceive, what technique they adopt, is a wonder to me. In this matter I am totally lost; I can't understand how it happens.

What technique they have achieved to perceive You in each and every object, I cannot fathom. While they perceive Your presence in each and every object, I can't perceive Your presence in any object in spite of all my efforts. What technique they have possessed, what is there in them, what means have they achieved and what tremendous fruit they get from that achievement, all this is beyond my imagination. I can't visualize.

What unique technique is possessed by them is a miracle that I cannot understand. By possessing that intense desire of meeting You, they perceive You face to face in each and every object. I am lost, I am ruined; there is no sign at all of me perceiving You, while they perceive You in each and every object. That surprises me.

भावा भावतया सन्तु भवद्भावेन मे भव।
तथा न किञ्चिदप्यस्तु न किञ्चिद्भवतोऽन्यथा ॥२८॥

bhāvā bhāvatayā santu
bhavadbhāvena me bhava ।
tathā na kiñcidapyastu
na kiñcidbhavato 'nyathā ॥28॥

O Lord, there is one desire in me. Let the objective world be perceived by me in its existent way, let the non-existent world remain non-existent for me because it is not existing. That world which is not one with You is not existing. That world which is one with You is existing. It is philosophy. That world, which exists, is one with You and the world which does not exist, is away from Your God-consciousness. Let these two worlds remain as they are. Let the existent world be perceived by me as it is because it is one with You and let the non-existent world be perceived by me as non-existent because it is away from You.

If you go into the depth of understanding then that non-existent world is also one with the Lord. But anything which is not one with the Lord is not there, does not exist. Things like "milk of a bird" or "son of a barren woman" also exist. In *mahāvyāpti* that is also existing. Non-existent is that world which is not that way also; non-existent world is what you can't imagine, which is beyond your imagination. Saying two plus two equals three is also existing, because it can be imagined, it can be said. Even it can also be said that ten plus two equals one. As long as it is said and as long as it can be imagined, it exists. That thing, which is not imagined, is non-existent. Even that non-existing thing also exists in God-consciousness. So it is beyond that. This is discussed in *pratyabhijñā* in *mahāvyāpti*.

यन्न किञ्चिदपि तन्न किञ्चिदप्यस्तु किञ्चिदपि किञ्चिदेव मे।
सर्वथा भवतु तावता भवान् सर्वतो भवति लब्धपूजितः ॥२९॥

yanna kiñcidapi tanna kiñcid-
apyastu kiñcidapi kiñcideva me ।
sarvathā bhavatu tāvatā bhavān
sarvato bhavati labdhapūjitaḥ ॥29॥

Whatever doesn't exist in God-consciousness doesn't exist and whatever exists in God-consciousness that alone exists. So let me perceive this objective world that way. That object which is not existing does not exist and that object which exists is existing. When I would come to this concluded perception, that way I would achieve You and I would worship You always in every state. This is my only desire.

By this kind of perception, I would find You everywhere and I would worship You everywhere, O Lord.

॥ इति श्रीमदुत्पलदेवाचार्यविरचिते श्रीशिवस्तोत्रावल्यां
रहस्यनिर्देशनाम द्वादशं स्तोत्रम् ॥

॥ *iti śrīmadutpaladevācāryaviracite śrīśivastotrāvalyāṁ*
rahasyanirdeśanāma dvādaśaṁ stotram ॥

13

संग्रहस्तोत्रनाम त्रयोदशं स्तोत्रम्

Saṁgraha Stotra

In Summing Up

संग्रहेण सुखदुःखलक्षणं मां प्रति स्थितमिदं शृणु प्रभो ।
सौख्यमेष भवता समागमः स्वामिना विरह एव दुःखिता ॥१॥

saṁgraheṇa sukhaduḥkhalakṣaṇaṁ
māṁ prati sthitamidaṁ śṛṇu prabho ।
saukhyameṣa bhavatā samāgamaḥ
svāminā viraha eva duḥkhitā ॥1॥

O LORD, I will in brief give You the definitions of my pain and pleasure. In a nu'tshell, I will tell You what pain is and what pleasure is for me. To meet You is pleasure for me and to be away from You is pain for me.

अन्तरप्यतितरामणीयसी या त्वदप्रथनकालिकास्ति मे ।
तामपीश परिमृज्य सर्वतः स्वं स्वरूपममलं प्रकाशय ॥२॥

antarapyatitarāmaṇīyasī
yā tvadaprathanakālikāsti me ।
tāmapīśa parimṛjya sarvataḥ
svaṁ svarūpamamalaṁ prakāśaya ॥2॥

O Lord, there is a very minute impurity of *āṇava-mala* in my mind because of which I cannot perceive You. That dirt resides in the internal state of my mind. Inside there is that impurity which keeps your perception away and disturbs me. The outside states of my mind are quite clear and pure; I have got rid of *māyīya-mala* and *kārma-mala*. O Lord Śiva, please remove that impurity also from all sides in my mind and let Your pure form and pure presence be revealed to me.

तावके वपुषि विश्वनिर्भरे चित्सुधारसमये निरत्यये ।
तिष्ठतः सततमर्चतः प्रभुं जीवितं मृतमथान्यदस्तु मे ॥३॥

tāvake vapuṣi viśvanirbhare
citsudhārasamaye niratyaye ।
tiṣṭhataḥ satatamarcataḥ prabhuṁ
jīvitaṁ mṛtamathānyadastu me ॥3॥

O Lord, there is one longing in me. I would like to reside in that body of Yours which is filled with universal consciousness and nectar of absolute and eternal God-consciousness, not just to rest or relax but to work there to the extent of exhaustion. That work consists in worshipping You day and night without any rest or break. This is my desire.

If I am granted this kind of exertion of constantly worshipping You, who is filled with both universal consciousness and the nectar of transcendental bliss, I would like to reside in that body and worship You constantly. After that let me live in this universe or let me not live in this universe, let me die or let me have liberation from the cycle of repeated births and deaths. I have not thought about it. Let me go to hell, let me go to heaven or let me go to *mokṣadhāma*, I do not care.

ईश्वरोऽहमहमेव रूपवान् पण्डितोऽस्मि सुभगोऽस्मि कोऽपरः ।
मत्समोऽस्ति जगतीति शोभते मानिता त्वदनुरागिणः परम् ॥४॥

īśvaro 'hamahameva rūpavān
paṇḍito 'smi subhago 'smi ko 'paraḥ ।
matsamo 'sti jagatīti śobhate
mānitā tvadanurāgiṇaḥ param ॥4॥

"I am the Lord, I am beautiful, I am charming, I am learned, I am a scholar, I am liked by everyone, who else is parallel to me in this world?" This kind of ego shines and is appropriate to possess for those who are in love with You and who are attached to You. The love for the Lord makes them charming and beautiful irrespective of their physical appearance. Everything about those people is beautiful. On the other hand, those detached from You are ugly even if they are physically beautiful.

देवदेव भवदद्वयामृताख्यातिसंहरणलब्धजन्मना ।
तद्यथास्थितपदार्थसंविदा मां कुरुष्व चरणार्चनोचितम् ॥५॥

devadeva bhavadadvayāmṛtā-
khyātisaṁharaṇalabdhajanmanā ।
tadyathāsthitapadārthasaṁvidā
māṁ kuruṣva caraṇārcanocitam ॥5॥

O Lord of lords, whatever is seen or perceived through the five organic perceptions of *śabda, sparśa, rasa, rūpa* and *gandha,* is old, stale and boring. I am not capable of worshipping You with these organic perceptions in their present form. These organic perceptions must get a new life that is possible only when they are nectarized by Your God-consciousness. By that nectar of non-duality, the perceptions of *śabda, sparśa, rasa, rūpa* and *gandha* will be born anew, revealing direct God-consciousness in them. Let me become capable and worthy of worshipping You always that way. Afterwards I have nothing else to do except worshipping You.

ध्यायते तदनु दृश्यते ततः स्पृश्यते च परमेश्वरः स्वयम् ।
यत्र पूजनमहोत्सवः स मे सर्वदास्तु भवतोऽनुभावतः ॥६॥

dhyāyate tadanu dṛśyate tataḥ
spṛśyate ca parameśvaraḥ svayam ।
yatra pūjanamahotsavaḥ sa me
sarvadāstu bhavato 'nubhāvataḥ ॥6॥

There is a point where Parameśvara, Lord Śiva is meditated upon not through effort but automatically, then perceived automatically and then is embraced automatically. That is the greatest festival of worshipping the Lord. It is due to *anugraha* and not one's own effort.

O Lord, let that greatest festival of worshipping Thee be attained by me each moment every day. I want to remain in that festival always. I know I have no claim to it. You may say no as I am not worthy of it, I know. Still let this happen to me by Your grace.

Normally a festival is observed only on a fixed day like the festival of my birthday comes in the month of April, but he wants to have that festival of worshipping the Lord every moment, every day.

यद्यथास्थितपदार्थदर्शनं युष्मदर्चनमहोत्सवश्च यः ।
युग्ममेतदितरेतराश्रयं भक्तिशालिषु सदा विजृम्भते ॥७ ॥

yadyathāsthitapadārthadarśanaṁ
yuṣmadarcanamahotsavaśca yaḥ ।
yugmametaditaretarāśrayaṁ
bhaktiśāliṣu sadā vijṛmbhate ॥7 ॥

There are two moments of that great festival. One is the normal perception of the organic world through the five cognitive organs of *śabda, sparśa, rasa, rūpa* and *gandha.* Then there is the great festival of worshipping You. No sooner do Your devotees perceive the worldly activities, they get entry into God-consciousness, and as they get entry into God-consciousness, they perceive the universal activity. And not that when they perceive worldly objects and activities are they carried away from God-consciousness.

In Your devotees, worldly activity and God-consciousness are mutually dependent on each other. With Your grace

Your devotees experience both these simultaneously and continuously. It is possible only for Your devotees.

तत्तदिन्द्रियमुखेन सन्ततं युष्मदर्चनरसायनासवम् ।
सर्वभावचषकेषु पूरितेष्वापिबन्नपि भवेयमुन्मदः ॥८ ॥

tattadindriyamukhena santataṁ
yuṣmadarcanarasāyanāsavam ।
sarvabhāvacaṣakeṣu pūrite-
ṣvāpibannapi bhaveyamunmadaḥ ॥8 ॥

O Lord, there is a desire in me. I want always to be completely drunk by drinking continuously the alcohol of the nectar of Thy worship. I would like to worship You continuously. That worship is the nectar.

Like the bar boys place wine glasses on tables, let the cognitive organs of *śabda, sparśa, rasa, rūpa* and *gandha* serve me the wine of Thy worship in the glasses of the collection of objectivity one after the other. I would just go on drinking and get drunk continuously and completely.

अन्यवेद्यमणुमात्रमस्ति न स्वप्रकाशमखिलं विजृम्भते ।
यत्र नाथ भवतः पुरे स्थितिं तत्र मे कुरु सदा तवार्चितुः ॥९ ॥

anyavedyamaṇumātramasti na
svaprakāśamakhilaṁ vijṛmbhate ।
yatra nātha bhavataḥ pure sthitiṁ
tatra me kuru sadā tavārcituḥ ॥9 ॥

O Lord, there is one place, one country in this universe where no object is found other than God-consciousness, where everything is understood as self-evident, self-luminous transcendental God-consciousness and nothing else. Let me reside in that country of Thy world. Let me acquire the capability of entry into that country. I would like to get the visa to be in that country because there is only one desire in me and that is to worship Thee.

दासधाम्नि विनियोजितोऽप्यहं स्वेच्छयैव परमेश्वर त्वया।
दर्शनेन न किमस्मि पात्रितः पादसंवहनकर्मणापि वा ॥१०॥

dāsadhāmni viniyojito 'pyahaṁ
svecchayaiva parmeśvara tvayā ।
darśanena na kimasmi pātritaḥ
pādasaṁvahanakarmaṇāpi vā ॥10॥

O Lord, You have appointed me as Your slave by Your own will. I did not insist that I would like to be Your slave. I never asked for that. You have made me Your slave by Your own will. Now why am I not fit to see You at all? I do not see You now. If You do not like me or if You don't like my presence, still just stretch Your legs and let me massage Your feet, but give me something to do. I am Your slave.

शक्तिपातसमये विचारणं प्राप्तमीश न करोषि कर्हिचित्।
अद्य मां प्रति किमागतं यतः स्वप्रकाशनविधौ विलम्बसे ॥११॥

śaktipātasamaye vicāraṇaṁ
prāptamīśa na karoṣi karhicit ।
adya māṁ prati kimāgataṁ yataḥ
svaprakāśanavidhau vilambase ॥11॥

O Lord, at the time of showering grace on Your devotees, You ought to have considered whether the person was actually worthy of it, whether he was qualified to receive Your grace. But You never think that way. You just shower grace without thinking even for a moment whether the person is fit enough to receive Your grace or not. If Your grace has made me capable, now what has become of me? What has happened to me that You don't come to me?

You are not perceived by me at all. You hesitate in revealing Your nature. You say You would come to me after a few days and after those few days are also gone, You do not show up.

You promise to come tomorrow but that tomorrow never comes. This is Your way of bestowing grace!

Abhinavagupta comments upon this verse in the *Tantrāloka* (13.291-293a) stating that it was appropriate for Thee to think before showering grace on someone but You never do so. Even by mistake also You do not think if the person is worthy of receiving the grace. As a result, it has become very difficult to achieve that because there are no set conditions to be fulfilled which one would strive to accomplish. It is only by Your grace that one achieves it. You have no attachment for anybody. If someone prays to You for twenty-four hours a day for the whole life, You still have no attachment for him. On the contrary, You may shower grace on someone who has never even thought of You. You have no attachment for Your devotees.

In the next two lines of the verse, Ācārya Utpaladeva indicates that through *śaktipāta* He showers grace in many ways. He may appear to you today but will never appear to you until death. He may appear to you today and then after a month, then after two months and then after three months and so on, or He may appear to you and keep appearing to you. Such are the ways and variety of *śaktipāta.* You have to receive it again and again without thinking if you are fit for it. It makes you fit.

Once you have realized this joy even for a second, you are supposed to be a *jīvanamukta;* you are supposed to get liberated at the end. At the time of experiencing God-consciousness, it penetrates you everywhere. It destroys all your bondages. It is such a joy; the imprint in one's brain is there for the whole life. You need this experience just once. It can happen to anyone. There are no suitability conditions.

तत्र तत्र विषये बहिर्विभात्यन्तरे च परमेश्वरीयुतम्।
त्वां जगत्त्रितयनिर्भरं सदा लोकयेय निजपाणिपूजितम् ॥१२॥

tatra tatra viṣaye bahirvibhā-
tyantare ca parameśvarīyutam ।
tvāṁ jagattritayanirbharaṁ sadā
lokayeya nijapāṇipūjitam ॥12॥

O Lord, there is one desire in me. I want to perceive You along with Pārvatī in all my sensual enjoyments, both outside (*śabda, sparśa, rasa, rūpa* and *gandha*) as well as inside (in impressions and in thoughts), not because I want to see You but I would like to feel myself as worshipping You always. When I hear sound, at that time, You must appear to me and I will worship You. That sound would be Your worship. Similarly, sensation of touch will be Your worship. Sensation of perceiving form will be Your worship; worship of both, You as well as Pārvatī.

I would like to perceive that I am already worshipping You with my own hands. Your fullness would appear to me in not only all the three worlds but in all the three states of *jāgrat, svapna* and *suṣupti.*

स्वामिसौधमभिसन्धिमात्रतो निर्विबन्धमधिरुह्य सर्वदा।
स्यां प्रसादपरमामृतासवापानकेलिपरिलब्धनिर्वृतिः ॥१३॥

svāmisaudhamabhisandhimātrato
nirvibandhamadhiruhya sarvadā ।
syāṁ prasādaparamāmṛtāsavā-
pānakeliparilabdhanirvṛtiḥ ॥13॥

O Lord, I have a desire. I would like to ascend the throne of my Master, Lord Śiva. I must ascend that throne of my Master effortlessly but directly without any obstacles and halts, by my own will. I must ascend not tomorrow or weekly or fortnightly but daily, and then You would pat my back with

Your divine hands. That patting of back is Thy *prasāda*, Thy grace that will intoxicate me like Scotch whisky! Thy grace is the absolute nectar and when I am nectarized by that, I would dance with You to my absolute satisfaction and absolute peace. This is my desire.

यत्समस्तसुभगार्थवस्तुषु स्पर्शमात्रविधिना चमत्कृतिम् ।
तां समर्पयति तेन ते वपुः पूजयन्त्यचलभक्तिशालिनः ॥१४॥

yatsamastasubhagārthavastuṣu
sparśamātravidhinā camatkṛtim ।
tāṁ samarpayati tena te vapuḥ
pūjayantyacalabhaktiśālinaḥ ॥14॥

There are some devotees of Thee whose devotion is always unwavering. Whenever they hear a beautiful penetrating and soft sound, they carry that beautiful sound to You and they worship You with that beautiful sound. Whenever they experience an intoxicating touch, or whenever they perceive a beautiful form, or whenever they experience a beautiful fragrance or a beautiful taste, they carry that beautiful sensation and offer that to You, and worship You with that. Those perfect devotees of Thee adore You with all the beautiful sensations of the five senses.

स्फारयस्यखिलमात्मना स्फुरन् विश्वमामृशसि रूपमामृशन् ।
यत्स्वयं निजरसेन घूर्णसे तत्समुल्लसति भावमण्डलम् ॥२५॥

sphārayasyakhilamātmanā sphuran
viśvamāmṛśasi rūpamāmṛśan ।
yatsvayaṁ nijarasena ghūrṇase
tatsamullasati bhāvamaṇḍalam ॥15॥

O Lord, when Your joy knows no bounds, when You are joyously shining, the whole universe shines joyously. When You perceive Your nature, the whole universe is perceived. When You are intoxicated by Your own nectar of God-consciousness, this whole universe comes into its being. Therefore, there is no difference between the universe and Yourself, Your nature. Whenever You are shining, that means the whole world is shining. Whenever You perceive Your nature, it means the whole universe is perceived. Whenever You are intoxicated by Your nectar of God-consciousness, it means the whole universe is intoxicated.

योऽविकल्पमिदमर्थमण्डलं पश्यतीश निखिलं भवद्वपुः ।
स्वात्मपक्षपरिपूरिते जगत्यस्य नित्यसुखिनः कुतो भयम् ॥१६॥

yo 'vikalpamidamarthamaṇḍalaṁ
paśyatīśa nikhilaṁ bhavadvapuḥ ।
svātmapakṣaparipūrite jagat-
yasya nityasukhinaḥ kuto bhayam ॥16॥

O Lord, any person who perceives this whole universe as one with Your nature, he feels that this entire objective world is Your own body. For him this whole universe is filled with God-consciousness everywhere. He is always blissful. There is nothing to fear for such a person.

कण्ठकोणविनिविष्टमीश ते कालकूटमपि मे महामृतम् ।
अप्युपात्तममृतं भवद्वपुर्भेदवृत्ति यदि रोचते न मे ॥१७॥

kaṇṭhakoṇaviniviṣṭamīśa te
kālakūṭamapi me mahāmṛtam ।
apyupāttamamṛtaṁ bhavadvapur-
bhedavṛtti yadi rocate na me ॥17॥

O Lord, I adore that dark coloured throat of Yours which is home to the *kālakūṭa* poison. Please keep me there. In Your presence, even *kālakūṭa* is great nectar for me. I don't mind if I die there. I would prefer to die in You rather than accept nectar from gods while You are away from me.

Kālakūṭa, the tremendous poison was one of the items

thrown up at the time of the churning of the Milky Ocean. Nobody could even touch this poison resulting in a crisis all around heaven. While the *deva*s kept and utilized the nectar to immortalize themselves, Lord Śiva consoled all *deva*s and gods and offered to drink this poison. Lord Śiva swallowed the poison and digested it in His throat that became black. From that day, Lord Śiva came to be called Nīlakaṇṭha.

त्वत्प्रलापमयरक्तगीतिकानित्ययुक्तवदनोपशोभितः।
स्यामथापि भवदर्चनक्रिया प्रेयसीपरिगताशयः सदा ॥१८॥

tvatpralāpamayaraktagītikā-
nityayuktavadanopaśobhitaḥ ।
syāmathāpi bhavadarcanakriyā-
preyasīparigatāśayaḥ sadā ॥18॥

O Lord, everybody is fond of a song and a beautiful girl. I too want the same thing but in a different manner. I like songs connected with Thy devotion. I would like to have my mouth beautified and nectarized by the song of Thy devotion. I would like to always embrace that beautiful girl of Thy worship, be wedded to and always united with that beautiful girl of Your worship.

ईहितं न बत पारमेश्वरं शक्यते गणयितुं तथा च मे।
दत्तमप्यमृतनिर्भरं वपुः स्वं न पातुमनुमन्यते तथा ॥१९॥

īhitaṁ na bata pārameśvaraṁ
śakyate gaṇayituṁ tathā ca me ।
dattamapyamṛtanirbharaṁ vapuḥ
svaṁ na pātumanumanyate tathā ॥19॥

O devotees, come and hear from me the latest news. I have found Lord Śiva to be a first class hypocrite, a first class fraud. You cannot imagine the extent of His fraud! I will prove it to you. He has bestowed on me that supreme nectar of God-consciousness but He does not allow me to drink it. Is it not a fraud to give but not permit to drink? He has bestowed on me that *svarūpa* filled with nectar but he does not permit me to drink it according to my choice. He says He would let me know when I could drink it, which is equivalent to giving nothing. Is it not a fraud?

त्वामगाधमविकल्पमद्वयं स्वं स्वरूपमखिलार्थघस्मरम् ।
आविशन्नहमुमेश सर्वदा पूजयेयमभिसंस्तुवीय च ॥२० ॥

tvāmagādhamavikalpamadvayaṁ
svaṁ svarūpamakhilārthaghasmaram ।
āviśannahamumeśa sarvadā
pūjayeyamabhisaṁstuvīya ca ॥20 ॥

O Lord, leave aside that talk of being a fraud. I did not mean that. I said that in a fit of agitation. (A devotee cannot afford to offend Lord Śiva, so he has again come to apologise!)

O Lord, You are infinite. You are unique. You are always without duality and You are the nature of everybody. You are fond of taking all dualistic cognition in Your own nature.

O Pārvatī's husband, there is one desire in me. I would like to enter into You not with the intention of being one with that God-consciousness, that blissful state but to facilitate the fulfilment of my chief desire of adoring You. I would adore You and sing Your glory.

॥ इति श्रीमदुत्पलदेवाचार्यविरचिते श्रीशिवस्तोत्रावल्यां
संग्रहस्तोत्रनाम त्रयोदशं स्तोत्रम् ॥

॥ *iti śrīmadutpaladevācāryaviracite śrīśivastotrāvalyāṁ*
saṁgrahastotranāma trayodaśaṁ stotram ॥

14

जयस्तोत्रनाम चतुर्दशं स्तोत्रम्

Jaya Stotra

Hymn of Glorification

IN *Jaya Stotra,* Ācārya Utpaladeva reveals the history of the Lord and glorifies Him. In the madness of his love for the Lord, he visualizes the Lord in physical form of a normal human being. He wishes Him prosperity, health and long life. In his love for the Lord, he does not mind misfortunes befalling him but derives consolation in seeing his Master happy and shining beautifully eternally. He is not interested in his own life. He wants his Master to live eternally. This is the real love for the Lord. He has used a wide variety of vocatives to invoke the Lord.

जयलक्ष्मीनिधानस्य निजस्य स्वामिनः पुरः ।
जयोद्घोषणपीयूषरसमास्वादये क्षणम् ॥१॥

jayalakṣmīnidhānasya nijasya svāminaḥ puraḥ ।
jayodghoṣaṇapīyūṣarasamāsvādaye kṣaṇam ॥1॥

My Master is the only treasure house of all glory. He is not anybody's Master, He is my Master. He is not owned by anybody, He is owned by me alone. There is a desire in me; before my Lord, my own Master, I would like to taste the nectar of making this announcement repeatedly:

O Lord,
Glory be to Thee! Glory be to Thee!

Glory be to Thee! Glory be to Thee!

I do not want glory for myself; I want it just for You. You should be glorified. I will pray for Your long life. I do not require my life. I want to give up my span of life also for You. May You always be glorified everywhere.

जयैकरुद्रैकशिव महादेव महेश्वर ।
पार्वतीप्रणयिञ्शर्व सर्वगीर्वाणपूर्वज ॥२॥

jayaikarudraikaśiva mahādeva maheśvara ।
pārvatīpraṇayiñśarva sarvagīrvāṇapūrvaja ॥2॥

O Lord, You are the only Rudra; You are the only Śiva; You are the only Mahādeva, the beloved of Pārvatī; You are the destroyer of the dualistic world; You are the source of all gods.

Glory be to Thee!

May You live for hundreds of millions of years for me. I will die but be born again and be blessed with You as my Master. You must live on.

Glory be to Thee!

जय त्रैलोक्यनाथैकलाञ्छनालिकलोचन ।
जय पीतार्तलोकार्तिकालकूटाङ्ककन्धर ॥३॥

jaya trailokyanāthaikalāñchanālikalocana ।
jaya pītārtalokārtikālakūṭāṅkakandhara ॥3॥

O Lord, the third eye on Your forehead is an indication to the fact that You are the only Master of all the three worlds.

Glory be to Thee! May You live forever.

Emergence of the *kālakūṭa* poison during the churning of the Milky Ocean had put all the gods into crisis. To their relief You drank the poison that left a dark mark on Your throat. You thus relieved everyone of the crisis and torture.

Glory be to Thee! May You live forever.

जय मूर्तत्रिशक्त्यात्मशितशूलोल्लसत्कर ।
जयेच्छामात्रसिद्धार्थपूजार्हचरणाम्बुज ॥४ ॥

jaya mūrtatriśaktyātmaśitaśūlollasatkara ।
jayecchāmātrasiddhārthapūjārhacaraṇāmbuja ॥4 ॥

You are holding the sharp *triśūla* in Your hand, which is indicative of the three great energies that You possess, namely *parā, parāparā* and *aparā.*

Glory be Thee!

Your lotus feet are worthy of being worshipped by the devotees and these bestow *siddhi*s and fulfilment of all ambitions effortlessly, only for the asking. These bestow all the power and the fulfilment of worldly enjoyments as well as spiritual aspirations merely by desire.

Glory be to Thee! May You live forever.

जय शोभाशतस्यन्दिलोकोत्तरवपुर्धर ।
जयैकजटिकाक्षीणगङ्गाकृत्यात्तभस्मक ॥५ ॥

jaya śobhāśatasyandilokottaravapurdhara ।
jayaikajaṭikākṣīṇagaṅgākṛtyāttabhasmaka ॥5 ॥

You have possessed a spiritual body and form which is supernatural. There cannot be any comparison with anybody anywhere. The only beautiful and the best body is possessed by Lord Śiva. One cannot imagine how beautiful, glorious and shining He is. He glorifies and beautifies everybody near Him. Any trace of ugliness vanishes; everything becomes divine and beautiful.

Glory be to Thee! May You live forever.

The Ganges has flown out from just one twisted matted lock of Yours. Not only is the water white but You have also applied ash on Your face just to conceal Your beauty which is perfect.

Glory be to Thee! May you live forever.

जय क्षीरोदपर्यस्तज्योत्स्नाच्छायानुलेपन ।
जयेश्वराङ्गसङ्गोत्थरत्नकान्ताहिमण्डन ॥६ ॥

jaya kṣīrodaparyastajyotsnācchāyānulepana ।
jayeśvarāṅgasaṅgottharatnakāntāhimaṇḍana ॥6 ॥

O Lord, on Your forehead You sport the moon that has emerged from the Milky Ocean. You shine like the bright reflection of the radiant moonlight from the surface of that Milky Ocean.

Glory be to Thee!

It is mentioned in the Purāṇas that those great snakes around Your neck and arms like Śeṣa, Vāsuki and others have developed jewellery in their body by virtue of the mere touch of Lord Śiva. You have decorated Your body with those great snakes and they have thus become beautiful.

Glory be to Thee! May You live forever.

जयाक्षयैकशीतांशुकलासदृशसंश्रय ।
जय गङ्गासदारब्धविश्वैश्वर्याभिषेचन ॥७ ॥

jayākṣayaikaśītāṁśukalāsadṛśasaṁśraya ।
jaya gaṅgāsadārabdhaviśvaiśvaryābhiṣecana ॥7 ॥

The *amākalā* of the moon is exactly like You. You are immortal and so is the *amākalā*. Your forehead is thus the basis for the *amākalā*.[1]

Glory be to Thee!

1. The moon has sixteen *kalās*. In the dark fortnight, the fifteen *kalās* wane one by one. The sixteenth *kalā* namely *amākalā* never vanishes. Lord Śiva sports the sixteenth *kalā* on His forehead.

You bestow glory and prosperity on the whole universe through the Ganges which You sport on Your head.

Glory be to Thee! May You live forever.

जयाधराङ्गसंस्पर्शपावनीकृतगोकुल ।
जय भक्तिमदाबद्धगोष्ठीनियतसन्निधे ॥८ ॥

jayādharāṅgasaṁsparśapāvanīkṛtagokula ।
jaya bhaktimadābaddhagoṣṭhīniyatasannidhe ॥8 ॥

You have made the bull Your transport. With the mere touch of Your feet the entire species of the bulls and cows is supposed to have become pure and divine. Everybody holds the species in high esteem. (Our mothers take care of us till we grow up, but the mother cow serves us for the whole life.)

Glory be to Thee!

Whenever Your devotees gather at a place and think of You, discuss matters regarding You, definitely You are always present there in disguise.

Glory be to Thee! May You live forever.

जय स्वेच्छातपोवेशविप्रलम्भितबालिश ।
जय गौरीपरिष्वङ्गयोग्यसौभाग्यभाजन ॥९ ॥

jaya svecchātapoveśavipralambhitabāliśa ।
jaya gaurīpariṣvaṅgayogyasaubhāgyabhājana ॥9 ॥

By Your own will and for Your own recreation, You made Yourself in the guise of performing penance. Some pictures depict Lord Śiva sitting in *padmāsana*, eyes closed, turning beads, meditating. Meditating on whom, that is yet to be known! This misleads some fools to believe that for Lord Śiva there is some other God as he is seen reciting *mantras*. This *rūpa* of Yours projecting Yourself as a devotee of some other Lord carries away those fools who do not understand Your trick. You have purposely misdirected those people.

Glory be to Thee!

You have embraced Pārvatī. You are very fortunate to have her in Your arms. This fortune is only befitting You. She is fortunate because of You and You are fortunate because of Her. You are both fortunate for being the best combination. Pārvatī's being in Your arms is befitting and Your embracing Pārvatī is befitting.

Glory be to Thee! May You live forever.

जय भक्तिरसार्द्रार्द्रभावोपायनलम्पट ।
जय भक्तिमदोद्दामभक्तवाङ्नृत्ततोषित ॥१० ॥

jaya bhaktirasārdrārdrabhāvopāyanalampaṭa ।
jaya bhaktimadoddāmabhaktavāṅnṛttatoṣita ॥10 ॥

You are fond of the presents flowing with *bhakti rasa* kept before You by Your devotees with great love and devotion. They offer You whatever they like, such as fruits, good flowers, etcetera. You are so fond of their offerings that You always earnestly look forward to these offerings. Your dreams come true when You receive those offerings from those devotees. You are craving for them.

Glory be to Thee! May You live long.

Whenever You hear even a single call of "O Lord Śiva" from a devotee filled with the intoxication of Your devotion and attachment, You dance with happiness. You are pleased and satisfied whenever You hear such calls from those devotees.

Glory be to Thee!

जय ब्रह्मादिदेवेशप्रभावप्रभवव्यय ।
जयलोकेश्वरश्रेणीशिरोविधृतशासन ॥११ ॥

jaya brahmādideveśaprabhāvaprabhavavyaya ।
jayalokeśvaraśreṇīśirovidhṛtaśāsana ॥11 ॥

The glory of Brahmā is to create this universe, the glory of Viṣṇu is to protect this universe and the glory of Rudra is to destroy this universe. You are the creator of that glory, You can withdraw that glory. You create that glory in them and You may withdraw that glory from them. You have got that power. They hold their glory at Your pleasure. You have bestowed this glory onto them.

O Lord Śiva, Glory be to Thee!

There are ten *lokapāla*s who govern this universe and protect it from ten directions. Those *lokapāla*s have accepted Your order. They accept Your authority and sovereignty.

O Lord Śiva, Glory be to Thee!

जय सर्वजगन्न्यस्तस्वमुद्राव्यक्तवैभव ।
जयात्मदानपर्यन्तविश्वेश्वर महेश्वर ॥१२॥

jaya sarvajagannyastasvamudrāvyaktavaibhava ।
jayātmadānaparyantaviśveśvara maheśvara ॥12॥

O Lord, You have put Your spiritual stamp on each and every act of this universe. It may be a creative act, it may be a protective act or it may be a destructive act. You have put Your stamp on each of these acts so that it is not touched or utilized by anybody except when You break that seal. You have put this seal so that there is no further handling except when You order it to be utilized. Only then would it be handled or utilized. So Your glory is not revealed to anyone. Nobody has perceived Your glory.

O Lord Śiva, this whole universe is handled by Yourself alone. There is no authority with anyone else to handle it. Only with Your orders will Brahmā create, only with Your orders will Viṣṇu protect and with Your orders alone will Rudra destroy it. You have kept Your glory absolutely under Your stamp.

Glory be to Thee!

At the same time, on the contrary, You are so generous that You bestow even Your own self to Your devotees. You become slave to Your devotees. This is Your greatness. You don't become the master of Your devotees. You give to them everything You have. This is Your greatness. Your generosity is so great that You bestow Your everything, even Your own self also to Your devotees, and Your devotees handle You as if You are their slave.

Glory be to Thee!

जय त्रैलोक्यसर्गेच्छावसरासद्द्वितीयक ।
जयैश्वर्यभरोद्वाहदेवीमात्रसहायक ॥१३ ॥

jaya trailokyasargecchāvasarāsaddvitīyaka ।
jayaiśvaryabharodvāhadevīmātrasahāyaka ॥13 ॥

At the time of creating this whole universe, You do not take anybody's help. You do not need anybody's assistance at that moment. You just create it by Your own will.

Glory be to Thee!

At the same time the intensity of glory You have accomplished by virtue of creating this universe has been possible with the help of Pārvatī. Pārvatī is the only instrument to glorify You. Nobody knew Lord Śiva when he was not married to Pārvatī. He was transcendental and nobody knew Him. He was known to the whole universe only when Pārvatī joined Him. Pārvatī refers to the world of *upāya*s, the means. Pārvatī is the revealer of Lord Śiva.

Glory be to Thee!

जयाक्रमसमाक्रान्तसमस्तभुवनत्रय ।
जयाविगीतमाबालगीयमानेश्वरध्वने ॥१४ ॥

jayākramasamākrāntasamastabhuvanatraya ।
jayāvigītamābālagīyamāneśvaradhvane ॥14 ॥

O Lord Śiva, You have pervaded all these three worlds simultaneously. The pervasion of the three worlds by You takes place simultaneously and not in succession.

Glory be to Thee!

From Rudra right to the innocent child everybody sings Your glory. Everybody knows Your glory. That is why whenever there is a crisis like earthquake, etcetera; everybody automatically chants *namaḥ śivāya, namaḥ śivāya.*

Glory be to Thee!

जयानुकम्पादिगुणानपेक्षसहजोन्नते ।
जय भीष्ममहामृत्युघटनापूर्वभैरव ॥१५॥

jayānukampādiguṇānapekṣasahajonnate ।
jaya bhīṣmamahāmṛtyughaṭanāpūrvabhairava ॥15 ॥

A man in possession of all qualifications is worthy of receiving grace from gods. If one has the requisite qualifications, one will receive grace from Brahmā, Nārāyaṇa and Rudra. If one is qualified and devoted one will receive grace from one's Master. But this case is not attributed to You sir. Your greatness of bestowing grace is not dependent on all these qualifications. Without qualifications, You spontaneously bestow grace on people.

Glory be to Thee! May You live for one hundred billion years.

You have conquered the frightful great lord of death who is not conquered by anyone in this world. Whom the whole world dreads, You have destroyed.

O Lord Śiva, O destroyer of that frightful lord of death, glory be to Thee!

He has destroyed the lord of death also. So there is no worry of his dying. Just for our satisfaction we pray for His long life. He is otherwise always young.

जय विश्वक्षयोच्चण्डक्रियानिष्परिपन्थिक ।
जय श्रेयःशतगुणानुगनामानुकीर्तन ॥१६ ॥

jaya viśvakṣayoccaṇḍakriyāniṣparipanthika ।
jaya śreyaḥśataguṇānuganāmānukīrtana ॥16 ॥

When You destroy the whole universe, when You adopt that frightful action of destruction, there is no cry; there is no impeding or offensive movement from the other side. There is no complaint from anybody from any corner, everything freezes. There is no one to complain at that moment.

Glory be to Thee! May You live forever.

Whenever anybody remembers You, whenever anybody recites Your name, *namaḥ śivāya, namaḥ śivāya* . . . hundreds of thousands of glories are followed upon it. Hundreds and thousands of glories are going to come in the wake of reciting Your name.

Glory be to Thee!

जय हेलावितीर्णैतदमृताकरसागर ।
जय विश्वक्षयाक्षेपिक्षणकोपाशुशुक्षणे ॥१७ ॥

jaya helāvitīrṇaitadamṛtākarasāgara ।
jaya viśvakṣayākṣepikṣaṇakopāśuśukṣaṇe ॥17 ॥

Once gods and *asura*s went to Lord Śiva who is the owner of *Kṣīra Sāgara* the Milky Ocean, and requested Him to permit them to churn the Milky Ocean and have whatever emerged. Lord Śiva vehemently declined permission and sent them away. The gods nominated Nārāyaṇa to plead with and convince Lord Śiva. Bowing to Lord Śiva in salutation, Nārāyaṇa brought out that they wanted to churn the Milky Ocean with the aim of getting some nectar out of it to make them immortal in order to overcome the *asuras*. With great difficulty, Lord Śiva permitted them to churn it.

Upamanyu was a devotee of Lord Śiva who was so pleased with him that He bestowed upon him *Kṣīra Sāgara*, the Milky Ocean stating "from this day *Kṣīra Sāgara* will belong to you and I have got nothing to do with it anymore." Such is the greatness and generosity of Lord Śiva.

Glory be to Thee!

Whenever the fire of wrath rises in Lord Śiva, even for a second, that is the end of this universe. So if there is wrath in Lord Śiva, it is an indication of the impending destruction of the whole universe.

Glory be to Thee!

जय मोहान्धकारान्धजीवलोकैकदीपक ।
जय प्रसुप्तजगतीजागरूकाधिपूरुष ॥१८ ॥

jaya mohāndhakārāndhajīvalokaikadīpaka ।
jaya prasuptajagatījāgarūkādhipūruṣa ॥18 ॥

This mortal world is absolutely blind with illusion and ignorance, being away from God-consciousness. In this blind mortal world, You are the only torch to show the way.

Glory be to Thee!

This whole universe is dead asleep in ignorance. In this deadened insensitive universe, You are the only one who is always wakeful, always aware. You are the only Supreme Being who is ever awake, all others are asleep.

Glory be to Thee!

जय देहाद्रिकुञ्जान्तर्निकूजज्जीवजीवक ।
जय सन्मानसव्योमविलासिवरसारस ॥१९॥

jaya dehādrikuñjāntarnikūjañjīvajīvaka ।
jaya sanmānasavyomavilāsivarasārasa ॥19॥

This worldly body is just like a mountain. In this mountain of the body there is a cave; the cave of the heart wherein there is a bird. The individual is a bird. That universal Lord Śiva has become an individual bird there in everybody's heart. That cuckoo makes the sound of *kū kū* all by *śabda, sparśa, rasa, rūpa* and *gandha*; all these five senses he talks and produces sound.

O Lord Śiva, You are that bird, You have become that individual in that cave of each and every individual.

Glory be to Thee!

You are that *rājahaṁsa*, the glorified swan who is playing in the lake of the minds of Your devotees. In the minds of devotees, You are shining, You are playing always. You are that swan.

Glory be to Thee!

जय जाम्बूनदोदग्रधातूद्भवगिरीश्वर ।
जय पापिषु निन्दोल्कापातनोत्पातचन्द्रमः ॥२०॥

jaya jāmbūnadodagradhātūdbhavagirīśvara ।
jaya pāpiṣu nindolkāpātanotpātacandramaḥ ॥20॥

The great Sumeru mount is formed of only precious minerals like gold. It is a golden mount made up of gold, pearls, etcetera. There is no ordinary stone there. You have become that Sumeru-Parvata, *Giri-rāja* the king of mountains possessing all those valuable and precious minerals.

Glory be to Thee!

You have become *ulkā,* that moon of crisis for those who

are sinners, to annihilate them.[2] All those who are away from God-consciousness, who don't love You, who are detached from You, who are away from You, who neglect Your presence, are liable to be destroyed. They must be destroyed because they are the actual sinners. For those sinners You have taken the place of that moon that is the indicator of the impending total destruction.

Glory be to Thee!

जय कष्टतपःक्लिष्टमुनिदेवदुरासद ।
जय सर्वदशारूढभक्तिमल्लोकलोकित ॥२१ ॥

jaya kaṣṭatapaḥkliṣṭamunidevadurāsada ।
jaya sarvadaśārūḍhabhaktimallokalokita ॥21 ॥

All *munis*, *ṛṣis* and gods adopt severe penance for thousands and thousands of years to attain You but they do not find You even after adopting severe penance, severe *tapas*, and severe recitation. You are absolutely absent for them.

Glory be to Thee!

Those devotees of Thee, who enjoy all worldly actions but are attached to You internally and love You internally, find You there. They indulge in all worldly activities, still they are with You and You are with them.

Glory be to Thee!

जय स्वसम्पत्प्रसरपात्रीकृतनिजाश्रित ।
जय प्रपन्नजनतालालनैकप्रयोजन ॥२२ ॥

jaya svasampatprasarapātrīkṛtanijāśrita ।
jaya prapannajanatālālanaikaprayojana ॥22 ॥

2. *ulkā* is a fiery phenomenon in the sky when the moon shines but spits blood and fire. The moon of crisis is indicative of the destruction of the world that is to follow. It is said that one such occasion was the day Rāvaṇa was to be killed by Lord Rāma. Finally, on the day of Dussehra, Lord Rāma achieved victory over Rāvaṇa.

Anybody who takes refuge in Thee, You make him capable and worthy of receiving all Your glories. All glories are digested in him; that capacity grows in him by taking refuge in You.

Glory be to Thee!

Your only work day and night is to fondle those persons who have surrendered to You, taken refuge in You or just bowed down before You. You have accepted only that type of work and forgotten about all other work. You are fond of fondling Your devotees.

Glory be to Thee!

जय सर्गस्थितिध्वंसकारणैकावदानक ।
जय भक्तिमदालोललीलोत्पलमहोत्सव ॥२३॥

jaya sargasthitidhvaṁsakāraṇaikāvadānaka ।
jaya bhaktimadālolalīlotpalamahotsava ॥23॥

In the act of creating this universe, in the act of protecting this universe and in the act of destroying this universe, You are the only glorified actor. Brahmā is not the glorified actor in creating; Brahmā is only an ordinary actor in creating this universe. That is only his job but You are the glorified actor. If he does not act according to Your wishes, Brahmā will no more be Brahmā. While Nārāyaṇa is the actor of protecting this universe, You are the glorified actor in protecting this universe. When Narayaṇa does not protect it according to Your choice, he loses his job and You will take his seat. You are the only glorified actor in creating, protecting and destroying this universe.

Glory be to Thee!

Utpaladeva is given to play of swinging, intoxicated by devotion. Utpaladeva is always swinging in that intoxication just to please You, just to kiss You, just to embrace You. He has nothing else to do. He himself says that You are his only festival.

Glory be to Thee!

जय जयभाजन जय जितजन्म-
जरामरण जय जगज्ज्येष्ठ ।
जय जय जय जय जय जय जय
जय जय जय जय जय जय त्र्यक्ष ॥२४ ॥

jaya jayabhājana jaya jitajanma-
jarāmaraṇa jaya jagajjyeṣṭha ।
jaya jaya jaya jaya jaya jaya jaya
jaya jaya jaya jaya jaya jaya tryakṣa ॥24 ॥

You are worthy of glory. You have conquered birth, ageing and death. Being eternal, You are elder to the whole universe. You are superior to all; You are the Supreme Being.

Glory be to Thee!
Glory be to Thee!
Glory be to Thee!
Glory be to Thee, O Possessor of the third eye.
Endless glory be to Thee!
Glory be to Thee!
Glory be to Thee!
Glory be to Thee!
Glory be to Thee!

॥ इति श्रीमदुत्पलदेवाचार्यविरचिते श्रीशिवस्तोत्रावल्यां
जयस्तोत्रनाम चतुर्दशं स्तोत्रम् ॥

॥ *iti śrīmadutpaladevācāryaviracite śrīśivastotrāvalyāṁ*
jayastotranāma caturdaśaṁ stotram ॥

15

भक्तिस्तोत्रनाम पञ्चदशं स्तोत्रम्

Bhakti Stotra

The Song of Devotion

त्रिमलक्षालिनो ग्रन्थाः सन्ति तत्पारगास्तथा ।
योगिनः पण्डिताः स्वस्थास्त्वद्भक्ता एव तत्त्वतः ॥१॥

trimalakṣālino granthāḥ santi tatpāragāstathā ।
yoginaḥ paṇḍitāḥ svasthāstvadbhaktā eva tattvataḥ ॥1॥

In this world Śāstras are available that help remove the three impurities, namely *āṇava-mala, māyīya-mala* and *kārma-mala.* Also available are those *paṇḍit*s, learned scholars and *yogī*s who are absolutely informed on these Śāstras. However, Your devotees only are appeased. They are really appeased in their mind. Their mind is calm. Those books that remove all the three *mala*s are already agitated and those scholars who are informed on these Śāstras are also agitated. Those *paṇḍit*s and scholars are also agitated because You are agitated with those books. However, only Your devotees hold an unagitated position.

मायीयकालनियतिरागाद्याहारतर्पिताः ।
चरन्ति सुखिनो नाथ भक्तिमन्तो जगत्तटे ॥२॥

māyīyakālaniyatirāgādyāhāratarpitāḥ ।
caranti sukhino nātha bhaktimanto jagattaṭe ॥2॥

O Lord, Your devotees are filled and satisfied by consuming

the *māyā*-related elementary worlds of *kāla, niyati* and *rāga* into their nature. They happily roam the shores of the ocean of the universe without going into it and getting drowned. They stay on the shores.

रुदन्तो वा हसन्तो वा त्वामुच्चैः प्रलपन्त्यमी ।
भक्ताः स्तुतिपदोच्चारोपचाराः पृथगेव ते ॥३॥

rudanto vā hasanto vā tvāmuccaiḥ pralapantyamī ।
bhaktāḥ stutipadoccāropacārāḥ pṛthageva te ॥3 ॥

O Lord, Your devotees are absolutely unique for they always crave for You. Whether in pain or pleasure, they are always engrossed in You. They always cry for You; they also laugh at the same time. Those devotees of Yours are actually worthy of being adored by everybody. They are special and unique people without parallel.

न विरक्तो न चापीशो मोक्षाकाङ्क्षी त्वदर्चकः ।
भवेयमपि तूद्रिक्तभक्त्यासवरसोन्मदः ॥४॥

na virakto na cāpīśo mokṣākāṅkṣī tvadarcakaḥ ।
bhaveyamapi tūdriktabhaktyāsavarasonmadaḥ ॥4 ॥

O Lord, I do not want to be detached from this universe nor do I want to govern this universe. I do not want to desire liberation. I do not want to become Your worshipper. I do not worship You. I want to become mad with the intensity of Thy devotion. All I want is that madness. I want to become mad with the intensity of Your love.

बाह्यं हृदय एवान्तरभिहृत्यैव योऽर्चति ।
त्वामीश भक्तिपीयूषरसपूरैर्नमामि तम् ॥५॥

bāhyaṁ hṛdaya evāntarabhihṛtyaiva yo 'rcati ।
tvāmīśa bhaktipīyūṣarasapūrairnamāmi tam ॥5 ॥

O Lord, I bow to that person who is capable of worshipping

You with all the outward objective world by first diverting it and gathering it in his heart and then offering You this objectivity with the floods of the streams of the nectar of Thy devotion. Worshipping You with the *rasa* of Thy supreme devotion, with the objective world after gathering it from the outside world and putting it into one's own heart and then offer this objectivity to You along with the stream of *rasa*, the essence of nectar of Thy devotion, is the real worship. I bow to that person who is capable of worshipping You like that.

धर्माधर्मात्मनोरन्तः क्रिययोर्ज्ञानयोस्तथा ।
सुखदुःखात्मनोर्भक्ताः किमप्यास्वादयन्त्यहो ॥६ ॥

dharmādharmātmanorantaḥ kriyayorjñānayostathā ।
sukhaduḥkhātmanorbhaktāḥ kimapyāsvādayantyaho ॥6 ॥

O Lord, there are such devotees of Thee who not only in the ecstasy of God-consciousness enjoy that absolute joy, but do so even in the middle of the pairs of opposites like right and wrong, pleasure and pain, etcetera. They taste the divine nectar of God-consciousness in between two actions, two knowledges, two cognitions.

चराचरपितः स्वामिन् अप्यन्धा अपि कुष्ठिनः ।
शोभन्ते परमुद्दामभवद्भक्तिविभूषणाः ॥७ ॥

carācarapitaḥ svāmin apyandhā api kuṣṭhinaḥ ।
śobhante paramuddāmabhavadbhaktivibhūṣaṇāḥ ॥7 ॥

O father of the animate and inanimate objects, even people who are blind or suffering from leprosy or otherwise condemned by the society, are glorified in their way if they are ornamented with the supreme devotion of Thee. Outwardly, they may be in such a position that nobody wants to go near them or touch them. Your devotion is their ornament and they are glorified in that. They are divine. They are filled with divinity although they may be suffering from these diseases. Nobody cares to look after them, nobody wants to go near them but still in their own way, they are shining.

शिलोञ्छपिच्छकशिपुविच्छायाङ्गा अपि प्रभो ।
भवद्भक्तिमहोष्माणो राजराजमपीशते ॥८ ॥

śiloñchapicchakaśipuvicchāyāṅgā api prabho ।
bhavadbhaktimahoṣmāṇo rājarājamapīśate ॥8 ॥

O my Master, even the extremely poor people who feed on the grains left over on the fields after reaping the harvest, who can only afford to cover their bodies with banana leaves; who have turned pale but whose hearts are full with the warmth of Your devotion, rule over the kings of kings even in this state. They do not have time for kings. They turn away the influential. They do not care for the rich.[1]

सुधार्द्रायां भवद्भक्तौ लुठताप्यारुरुक्षुणा ।
चेतसैव विभोऽर्चन्ति केचित्त्वामभितः स्थिताः ॥९ ॥

sudhārdrāyāṁ bhavadbhaktau luṭhatāpyārurukṣuṇā ।
cetasaiva vibho 'rcanti kecittvāmabhitaḥ sthitāḥ ॥9 ॥

O omnipresent Lord, there are two classes of Your devotees. The first one comprises those who want to get liberated from the cycle of repeated births and deaths. These devotees who want to get released from the repeated births and deaths don't get firmly established in the nectar of Your devotion. They stumble and slip every now and then. The other class on the other hand comprises those devotees who see You, perceive You and worship You everywhere. They worship You in their own hearts and perceive You everywhere.

---

1. Swamiji cited here the example of Rājāṇaka Gopāl Rāzdān, a great Śaivite of Kashmir, who addressed the king of Kashmir as a poor beggar.

रक्षणीयं वर्धनीयं बहुमान्यमिदं प्रभो ।
संसारदुर्गतिहरं भवद्भक्तिमहाधनम् ॥१० ॥

rakṣaṇīyaṁ vardhanīyaṁ bahumānyamidaṁ prabho ।
saṁsāradurgatiharaṁ bhavadbhaktimahādhanam ॥10 ॥

O Lord, the supreme treasure of Your devotion has to be protected all around. It is worth protecting, it is worth enhancing, it is worth respecting because it removes the poverty of differentiated perception. The poverty of differentiated perception is removed by the supreme treasure of Your devotion. Therefore, it alone is to be protected, to be kept and owned; not the materialistic bank balance, let that go to dogs.

नाथ ते भक्तजनता यद्यपि त्वयि रागिणी ।
तथापीर्ष्यां विहायास्यास्तुष्टास्तु स्वामिनी सदा ॥११ ॥

nātha te bhaktajanatā yadyapi tvayi rāgiṇī ।
tathāpīrṣyāṁ vihāyāsyāstuṣṭāstu svāminī sadā ॥11 ॥

O my dear Lord, there are two wives who have owned You. One is Pārvatī and the other girl is my devotion for You. I want to be devotedly devoted to You. That devotion is another girl who is fond of You. Although she is attached to You Pārvatī hates her. (It is clear; the first wife becomes jealous when the second wife comes!) You cannot disown her (my devotion). She also wants to be with You but there is Pārvatī with You. I would request You to grant me one wish. Pārvatī should not develop envy for this second girl. She should help her and give her a chance to meet You and be with You. This is my request.

भवद्भावः पुरो भावी प्राप्ते त्वद्भक्तिसम्भवे ।
लब्धे दुग्धमहाकुम्भे हता दधनि गृध्नुता ॥१२ ॥

bhavadbhāvaḥ puro bhāvī prāpte tvadbhaktisambhave ।
labdhe dugdhamahākumbhe hatā dadhani
gr̥dhnutā ॥12॥

O Lord, if Thy devotion is owned, You are owned. In other words, You are owned altogether. If Thy devotion is there, You are there. Like when a big jar of milk is available, the greed for curds is finished. So if Thy devotion is there, You are there.

किमियं न सिद्धिरतुला
किं वा मुख्यं न सौख्यमास्रवति ।
भक्तिरुपचीयमाना
येयं शम्भोः सदातनी भवति ॥१३॥

kimiyaṁ na siddhiratulā
kiṁ vā mukhyaṁ na saukhyamāsravati ।
bhaktirupacīyamānā
yeyaṁ śambhoḥ sadātanī bhavati ॥13॥

O Lord, if there is eternal devotion for Thee in the form of ever-increasing movement of accumulation; it is like achieving that unparalleled yogic power, that state where from this predominant beatitude of ultimate reality flows. This is that predominant source of ultimate beatitude.

मनसि मलिने मदीये
मग्ना त्वद्भक्तिमणिलता कष्टम् ।
न निजानपि तनुते तान्
अपौरुषेयान्स्वसम्पदुल्लासान् ॥१४॥

manasi maline madīye
magnā tvadbhaktimaṇilatā kaṣṭam ।
na nijānapi tanute tān
apauruṣeyānsvasampadullāsān ॥14॥

O Lord, my mind is absolutely impure all-round, and in the

mud of that mind the pearl bearing creeper of Thy devotion has sunk. It has submerged into that mud of my impure mind. In my mind, it ought to have grown and borne fruit, but the problem is that this creeper of jewel-like fruits of Thy devotion is sunk in the mud of my impure mind. It does not grow. Its fruit, flowers and branches do not expand. It is stuck.

भक्तिर्भगवति भवति
त्रिलोकनाथे ननूत्तमा सिद्धिः ।
किन्त्वणिमादिकविरहात्
सैव न पूर्णेति चिन्ता मे ॥१५॥

bhaktirbhagavati bhavati
trilokanāthe nanūttamā siddhiḥ ।
kintvaṇimādikavirahāt
saiva na pūrṇeti cintā me ॥15॥

O Master, it is a fact that Your devotion and attachment is the real and supreme yogic power already attained. Yet the eight yogic internal powers (*siddhis*) are not found in that devotion. Hence that devotion is not complete. This is the worry knocking in the background of my mind. It is absolutely correct that if there is devotion and attachment for Thee, that is the highest yogic power one can attain, but it is not complete in the absence of the eight internal yogic powers (*siddhis*).

बाह्यतोऽन्तरपि चोत्कटोन्मिष-
त्त्र्यम्बकस्तवकसौरभाः शुभाः ।
वासयन्त्यपि विरुद्धवासनान्
योगिनो निकटवासिनोऽखिलान् ॥१६॥

bāhyato 'ntarapi cotkaṭonmiṣat-
tryambakastavakasaurabhāḥ śubhāḥ ।
vāsayantyapi viruddhavāsanān
yogino nikaṭavāsino 'khilān ॥16॥

Singing the glory of Lord Śiva is actually like a bunch of fragrant flowers with such intense, such dense fragrance that is circulated inside and outside everywhere. Those *yogīs* who hold that bunch of flowers in their divine hands, singing the glory of the Lord, make fragrant all those living near them. Anybody whoever comes near that *yogī* is also flooded by that fragrance. That fragrance passes through their minds also. Such is the greatness of this bunch of flowers of Thy devotion.

ज्योतिरस्ति कथयापि न किंचि-
द्विश्वमप्यतिसुषुप्तमशेषम्
यत्र नाथ शिवरात्रिपदेऽस्मिन्
नित्यमर्चयति भक्तजनस्त्वाम् ॥१७॥

jyotirasti kathayāpi na kiñci-
dviśvamapyatisuṣuptamaśeṣam ।
yatra nātha śivarātripade 'smin
nityamarcayati bhaktajanastvām ॥17॥

O Lord, there is a place where Śivarātri is being celebrated; Śivarātri, the night when the marriage of Lord Śiva and Pārvatī took place, is being celebrated. That night there is no other light found; no light of the sun, no light of the moon and no light of fire. That night the whole universe has fallen asleep; that night only Your devotees are wakeful and they celebrate Thy devotion wholeheartedly.

सत्त्वं सत्यगुणे शिवे भगवति स्फारीभवत्वर्चने
चूडायां विलसन्तु शङ्करपदप्रोद्यद्रजःसञ्चयाः ।
रागादिस्मृतिवासनामपि समुच्छेत्तुं तमो जृम्भतां
शम्भो मे भवतात्त्वदात्मविलये त्रैगुण्यवर्गोऽथवा ॥१८॥

sattvaṁ satyaguṇe śive bhagavati
sphārībhavatvarcane cūḍāyāṁ vilasantu
śaṅkarapadaprodyadrajaḥsañcayāḥ ।

rāgādismṛtivāsanāmapi samucchettuṁ tamo
jṛmbhatāṁ śambho me bhavatāttvadātmavilaye
traiguṇyavargo 'thavā ॥18॥

O Lord Śiva, I don't want to get rid of the three *guṇas*, namely, *sattva-guṇa, rajo-guṇa* and *tamo-guṇa*. Let the *sattva-guṇa* in me grow to be utilized in worshipping Lord Śiva who is qualified with the true and real divine qualifications. I want that *sattva-guṇa* in me to grow to adore You. Let the collection of dust (*rajo-guṇa*) from the feet of Lord Śiva remain and shine on the top of my forehead. (*Rajo-guṇa* means those qualifications in a person which get him entangled in worldly pleasures. In other words *rajo-guṇa* is also called dust.)

Let that *tamo-guṇa* also shine in me, so that even the impressions of *kāma, krodha, lobha, moha, mada* and *ahaṁkāra* vanish. All traces of these impressions should be removed and absolutely washed away by that darkness.

He wants to convert all these into divinity. *Tamas* in the gross sense means *tamo-guṇa* which is dullness, sluggishness, laziness, forgetfulness and darkness.

O Lord Śiva, let the class of the three *guṇas* governing my mind just get appeased in Your God-consciousness, in Your Supreme Self.

संसाराध्वा सुदूरः खरतरविविधव्याधिदग्धाङ्गयष्टिः
भोगा नैवोपभुक्ता यदपि सुखमभूज्जातु तन्नो चिराय ।
इत्थं व्यर्थोऽस्मि जातः शशिधरचरणाक्रान्तिकान्तोत्तमाङ्ग-
स्त्वद्भक्तश्चेति तन्मे कुरु सपदि महासम्पदो दीर्घदीर्घाः ॥१९॥

saṁsārādhvā sudūraḥ kharataravividha-
vyādhidagdhāṅgayaṣṭiḥ bhogā
naivopabhuktā yadapi sukhamabhūjjātu tanno cirāya ।
itthaṁ vyartho 'smi jātaḥ

śaśidharacaraṇākrāntikāntottamāṅga-
stvadbhaktaśceti tanme kuru
sapadi mahāsampado dīrghadīrghāḥ ॥19॥

O Lord, O governor of the universe, the path of this universe is endless. At the same time, it is not a clear path so that one could tread on it, walk on it and travel without fear. There is fear all-round; at each step there is fear that something might happen. All limbs and organs of one's body are almost burnt by numerous fearful diseases, pains, sadness, sorrows, tortures and crises. It is not easy at all with so many tortures on the way.

In this universe, whatever pleasures, whatever joy I acquired in the enjoyment of worldly pleasures, proved to be impermanent. So there is no fun in coming into and living in this universe. I have got a feeling that I have come for nothing. I have not covered the pathway that as such is endless and filled with torture. All the worldly pleasures I enjoyed have also faded away. I have had no chance of enjoying divine pleasures.

Although I have come uselessly here, there is only one qualification in me. I have held the feet of Lord Śiva, who sports the crescent moon on his forehead and have kept those divine feet on my head. I have always been Your devotee. This is the only way out of this tortured universe. You have to help me quickly and make me unite with those eternal glories of Thee, so that I too am glorified with those everlasting glories.

॥ इति श्रीमदुत्पलदेवाचार्यविरचिते श्रीशिवस्तोत्रावल्यां
भक्तिस्तोत्रनाम पञ्चदशं स्तोत्रम् ॥

॥ *iti śrīmadutpaladevācāryaviracite śrīśivastotrāvalyāṁ*
bhaktistotranāma pañcadaśaṁ stotram ॥

16

पाशानुद्भेदनाम षोडशं स्तोत्रम्

Pāśānudbheda Stotra

Breaking the Fetters

न किञ्चिदेव लोकानां भवदावरणं प्रति ।
न किञ्चिदेव भक्तानां भवदावरणं प्रति ॥१॥

na kiñcideva lokānāṁ bhavadāvaraṇaṁ prati ।
na kiñcideva bhaktānāṁ bhavadāvaraṇaṁ prati ॥1॥

THERE are two classes of people found in this universe; one class comprises the ordinary worldly people and the other class is composed of people who are Thy devotees. For the worldly people, everything is an impediment and comes in their path because these people are away from Thy consciousness. Their meditating on You also takes them away from You. Their love for You has also become a means to take them away from Your God-consciousness. Everything in this world is an obstacle for them in Your path. They have no clearance at all.

On the other hand, for Thy devotees, there are no obstacles. Those obstacles which are obstacles for worldly people show the devotees Your way. Thy devotees experience no obstacles. Nothing for them is a hindrance in perceiving You. Any hindrance itself reveals to them Your nature. Such is the wonderful result of Your devotion.

अप्युपायक्रमप्राप्यः सङ्कुलोऽपि विशेषणैः ।
भक्तिभाजां भवानात्मा सकृच्छुद्धोऽवभासते ॥२॥

apyupāyakramaprāpyaḥ saṅkulo 'pi viśeṣaṇaiḥ ।
bhaktibhājāṁ bhavānātmā
sakr̥cchuddho 'vabhāsate ॥2॥

You are attained by the successive means of *śāmbhavopāya*, *śāktopāya* and *āṇavopāya*, and Your nature is dense with Your countless qualifications, like You are all-knowing, all-pervading, divine, omnipresent, etcetera. But for Your devotees, You are revealed to them once for all and not in a successive manner. They do not perceive Your nature in succession, in a limited way of understanding. When they find You, they find You altogether. This is the greatness of Thy devotees.

जयन्तोऽपि हसन्त्येते जिता अपि हसन्ति च ।
भवद्भक्तिसुधापानमत्ताः केऽप्येव ये प्रभो ॥३॥

jayanto 'pi hasantyete jitā api hasanti ca ।
bhavadbhaktisudhāpānamattāḥ ke 'pyeva ye prabho ॥3॥

O Lord, Your devotees have tasted the liquor of the nectar of Thy devotion and have become mad; they have lost their senses. Whenever they conquer anybody, they smile and whenever they are conquered, they smile. There is no distinctive feeling in them. Whenever they conquer anybody, they smile. That is good. That is only natural. When they are conquered, they still smile. They are actually mad.

शुष्ककं मैव सिद्धेय मैव मुच्येय वापि तु ।
स्वादिष्ठपरकाष्ठाप्तत्वद्भक्तिरसनिर्भरः ॥४॥

śuṣkakaṁ maiva siddheya maiva mucyeya vāpi tu ।
svādiṣṭhaparakāṣṭhāptatvadbhaktirasanirbharaḥ ॥4॥

I do not want to achieve those great yogic powers in a dry way if I am kept away from the moistness of Thy devotion.

What use are those yogic powers if there is dryness in my heart. I do not want that liberation when I am dry inside. I want to get filled with that divine, tasteful, limitless attachment for You. I don't want liberation or those yogic powers in that dry way. I want to become filled with that tasteful, divine, limitless devotion of Thee.

यथैवाज्ञातपूर्वोऽयं भवद्भक्तिरसो मम ।
घटितस्तद्वदीशान स एव परिपुष्यतु ॥५॥

yathaivājñātapūrvo 'yaṁ bhavadbhaktiraso mama ।
ghaṭitastadvadīśāna sa eva paripuṣyatu ॥5॥

O Lord Śiva, this taste of Thy devotion I have achieved but I do not know how I achieved it. You know it. I didn't know the ways and the regulations of meditation. How I have achieved that devotion of Thee, You know it. It was not known to me earlier. The way to achieve that devotion You already knew and that devotion is now with me. In the same way O Lord Śiva, I want this devotion to get denser, it must get strengthened. I do not know how to develop it, how to strengthen it, You know it. So please do that for me.

सत्येन भगवन्नान्यः प्रार्थनाप्रसरोऽस्ति मे ।
केवलं स तथा कोऽपि भक्त्यावेशोऽस्तु मे सदा ॥६॥

satyena bhagavannānyaḥ prārthanāprasaro 'sti me ।
kevalaṁ sa tathā ko 'pi bhaktyāveśo 'stu me sadā ॥6॥

O Lord Śiva, I am telling You the truth, I have no other desire except the one tickling in my mind and that is to get merged in the greatness of Thy devotion. That is my only desire: getting entry into that indescribable blissful devotion of Thee.

भक्तिक्षीवोऽपि कुप्येयं भवायानुशयीय च ।
तथा हसेयं रुद्यां च रटेयं च शिवेत्यलम् ॥७॥

bhaktikṣīvo 'pi kupyeyaṁ bhavāyānuśayīya ca ।
tathā haseyaṁ rudyāṁ ca raṭeyaṁ ca śivetyalam ॥7 ॥

O Lord, let me get intoxicated with Thy devotion, then I will get annoyed with this universe. I will take pity on the poor worldly people who are ruining their lives for nothing, wasting time running after the materialistic world. When I am intoxicated with Thy devotion I will do that. At the same time, I would laugh, I would weep, I would cry for You, O Śiva, O Śiva. . . .

विषमस्थोऽपि स्वस्थोऽपि रुदन्नपि हसन्नपि ।
गम्भीरोऽपि विचित्तोऽपि भवेयं भक्तितः प्रभो ॥८ ॥

viṣamastho 'pi svastho 'pi rudannapi hasannapi ।
gambhīro 'pi vicitto 'pi bhaveyaṁ bhaktitaḥ prabho ॥8 ॥

O my Master, by the intensity of Thy devotion, I do not mind whether I am in crises throughout my life or I am peaceful. If my life is peaceful let me remain peaceful. If my life is altogether miserable, let it remain like that. If I am bent upon weeping all through day and night, let me remain like that. If I laugh for the whole life let it be like that. If I am grave and solemn let me remain grave and solemn. If I am not reserved and am indiscreet, putting forth all secrets and reveal whatever is not to be revealed to people, let it be so. Such a position I shall attain only by the intensity of Thy devotion.

भक्तानां नास्ति संवेद्यं त्वदन्तर्यदि वा बहिः ।
चिद्धर्मा यत्र न भवान्निर्विकल्पः स्थितः स्वयम् ॥९ ॥

bhaktānāṁ nāsti saṁvedyaṁ tvadantaryadi vā bahiḥ ।
ciddharmā yatra na bhavānnirvikalpaḥ sthitaḥ svayam ॥9 ॥

Really, for Thy devotee nothing else is known to them inside Your *svarūpa* or outside Your *svarūpa* where Thyself, who is filled with consciousness and who is without thought, is not present. Therefore, they feel Your presence everywhere inside and outside the world.

भक्ता निन्दानुकारेऽपि तवामृतकणैरिव ।
हृष्यन्त्येवान्तराविद्धास्तीक्ष्णरोमाञ्चसूचिभिः ॥१० ॥

bhaktā nindānukāre 'pi tavāmṛtakaṇairiva ।
hṛṣyantyevāntarāviddhāstīkṣṇaromāñcasūcibhiḥ ॥10 ॥

Thy devotees, when they are seated in the company of those people who deny Your existence and who call You names, outwardly pose as if they agree with those atheists. They do not argue with them or confront them. Since the topic is Yours, even though against You, they are filled with joy. By hearing Your name, they are filled with joy even if it may be against Your consciousness. Then they have to agree with the conclusion of the atheists that God does not exist, God is treacherous and thus should not be revered. By that feeling, they get horripilation in every pore of the hair on their body. Outwardly they laugh and pose to agree with those atheists but internally they weep. This is the position of Thy devotees.

दुःखापि वेदना भक्तिमतां भोगाय कल्पते ।
येषां सुधार्द्रा सर्वैव संवित्त्वच्चन्द्रिकामयी ॥११ ॥

duḥkhāpi vedanā bhaktimatāṁ bhogāya kalpate ।
yeṣāṁ sudhārdrā sarvaiva saṁvittvaccandrikāmayī ॥11 ॥

For those devotees who possess Thy knowledge, that enlightening knowledge of the light of Your consciousness; if they get tortured, if they are in crisis, if they have pain, that pain also carries them to the great enjoyment of God-consciousness.

यत्र तत्रोपरुद्धानां भक्तानां बहिरन्तरे ।
निर्व्याजं त्वद्वपुःस्पर्शरसास्वादसुखं समम् ॥१२ ॥

yatra tatroparuddhānāṁ bhaktānāṁ bahirantare ।
nirvyājaṁ tvadvapuḥsparśarasāsvādasukhaṁ
samam ॥12 ॥

Thy devotees wherever they are seated, internally or externally, they feel the nearness of Your divine touch and the joy that comes from that divine touch. They feel that divine touch to the same extent without obstruction, whether they are in Your presence or absence.

तवेश भक्तेरर्चायां दैन्यांशं द्वयसंश्रयम् ।
विलुप्यास्वादयन्त्येके वपुरच्छं सुधामयम् ॥१३ ॥

taveśa bhakterarcāyāṁ dainyāṁśaṁ
dvayasaṁśrayam ।
vilupyāsvādayantyeke vapuracchaṁ sudhāmayam ॥13 ॥

O Lord, when Thy devotees worship You, their pitiable condition arising out of their dualistic differentiated perception is removed in that worship. Then they enjoy the pure and clean existence of Your presence which is filled with nectar.

भ्रान्तास्तीर्थदृशो भिन्ना भ्रान्तेरेव हि भिन्नता ।
निष्प्रतिद्वन्द्वि वस्त्वेकं भक्तानां त्वं तु राजसे ॥१४ ॥

bhrāntāstīrthadṛśo bhinnā bhrāntereva hi bhinnatā ।
niṣpratidvandvi vastvekaṁ bhaktānāṁ tvaṁ tu
rājase ॥14 ॥

The viewpoints of various Śāstras differ from one another. The viewpoint of Śaivism is different from the viewpoint of Vedānta. They are away from Your consciousness because to be separated from You is illusion. However, Your devotees see the oneness of Your consciousness and that always shines in them everywhere.

Śaivism is not Śaivism alone. Śaivism encompasses each

and every theory. Even the theory of atheists is also Śaivism from one point of view, because atheism is also God-consciousness. When you deny God that is the existence of God. While denying God, you only prove God.

मानावमानरागादिनिष्पाकविमलं मनः ।
यस्यासौ भक्तिमांल्लोकतुल्यशीलः कथं भवेत् ॥१५॥

mānāvamānarāgādiniṣpākavimalaṁ manaḥ ।
yasyāsau bhaktimāṁllokatulyaśīlaḥ kathaṁ bhavet ॥15॥

That devotee of Thee whose mind is purified by the ripening or vanishing of the pairs of opposites; for instance to be respected and to be disrespected, to be attached and to be detached, etcetera, cannot be compared with ordinary worldly people. He is beyond any comparison. He is above the situation of ordinary people.

रागद्वेषान्धकारोऽपि येषां भक्तित्विषा जितः ।
तेषां महीयसामग्रे कतमे ज्ञानशालिनः ॥१६॥

rāgadveṣāndhakāro 'pi yeṣāṁ bhaktitviṣā jitaḥ ।
teṣāṁ mahīyasāmagre katame jñānaśālinaḥ ॥16॥

Those who have conquered the darkness of attachment and detachment; those who have removed the darkness from their minds by the light of Your devotion, by the light of being attached to You, are great people, honoured kings. People who are filled with knowledge (*jñāna*) are nothing in front of them. In other words devotion is far superior to knowledge.

यस्य भक्तिसुधास्नानपानादिविधिसाधनम् ।
तस्य प्रारब्धमध्यान्तदशासूच्चैः सुखासिका ॥१७॥

yasya bhaktisudhāsnānapānādividhisādhanam ।
tasya prārabdhamadhyāntadaśāsūccaiḥ sukhāsikā ॥17॥

Those devotees who possess the technique of bathing with

the nectar of devotion and who have the technique of drinking the nectar of devotion; for them, in the beginning, in the centre and in the end the bliss of God-consciousness shines everywhere.

कीर्त्यश्चिन्तापदं मृग्यः पूज्यो येन त्वमेव तत् ।
भवद्भक्तिमतां श्लाघ्या लोकयात्रा भवन्मयी ॥१८ ॥

kīrtyaścintāpadaṁ mṛgyaḥ pūjyo yena tvameva tat ।
bhavadbhaktimatāṁ ślāghyā lokayātrā bhavanmayī ॥18 ॥

For those who are Your devotees You are the only one who is being sung by them, You are thought by them, You are searched by them, You are worshipped by them. So the journey of those devotees in this universe is respectable. It is a great journey. Singing of the Lord, thinking of the Lord, searching for the Lord and worshipping the Lord makes their journey in this universe divine. This is their greatest journey in this universe.

मुक्तिसंज्ञा विपक्वाया भक्तेरेव त्वयि प्रभो ।
तस्यामाद्यदशारूढा मुक्तकल्पा वयं ततः ॥१९ ॥

muktisaṁjñā vipakvāyā bhaktereva tvayi prabho ।
tasyāmādyadaśārūḍhā muktakalpā vayaṁ tataḥ ॥19 ॥

O Lord, O my Master, this is a fact that when Thy devotion ripens, that is liberation. In other words, that is to get liberated in this world. As we have stepped in that state of Your devotion, we are liberated already. We have no worry of getting liberated, we are already liberated.

दुःखागमोऽपि भूयान्मे त्वद्भक्तिभरितात्मनः ।
त्वत्पराची विभो मा भूदपि सौख्यपरम्परा ॥२० ॥

duḥkhāgamo 'pi bhūyānme
tvadbhaktibharitātmanaḥ ।
tvatparācī vibho mā bhūdapi
saukhyaparamparā ॥20 ॥

I welcome the continuity of pain and sadness in this world, I welcome that suffering — but only in case I am filled with Thy devotion. When I am filled with Your devotion, I welcome that pain. Let that pain destroy me, let that pain shatter me to pieces but there must be Thy devotion. In the absence of Your devotion, I will not accept even being flooded with pleasures, joy and happiness.

त्वं भक्त्या प्रीयसे भक्तिः प्रीते त्वयि च नाथ यत्।
तदन्योन्याश्रयं युक्तं यथा वेत्थ त्वमेव तत्॥२१॥

tvaṁ bhaktyā prīyase bhaktiḥ prīte tvayi ca nātha yat ।
tadanyonyāśrayaṁ yuktaṁ yathā vettha tvameva tat ॥21॥

There is a problem with this theory of devotion; it is a fact that You are pleased when we are devoted to You. However, that devotion comes when You are pleased. So this is a mutually dependent cycle. There must be *bhakti* then You will be pleased, and You must be pleased then there will be *bhakti*. You alone can solve this theory of mutually dependent cycle, this fallacy, the logical error. How You solve it, You must be knowing it, we don't know. You can solve the defect in this logical theory because it is a fact that when we are devoted to You, then only You are pleased with us, and this is also a fact that when You are pleased with us then the devotion will come. How can it be solved, You know that, we do not know.

साकारो वा निराकारो वान्तर्वा बहिरेव वा।
भक्तिमत्तात्मनां नाथ सर्वथासि सुधामयः॥२२॥

sākāro vā nirākāro vāntarvā bahireva vā ।
bhaktimattātmanāṁ nātha sarvathāsi sudhāmayaḥ ॥22॥

O Master, You may appear with form or You may appear formless; You may appear in our mind or You may appear outside our mind; but for those who are mad in Your devotion, who are maddened by Your devotion, You are sweet everywhere. You are sweet when You are with any form and You are sweet to them when You are formless. You are sweet when You appear to them internally. You are sweet to them when You appear to them externally. You are sweet everywhere for those who are devoted to Thee.

अस्मिन्नेव जगत्यन्तर्भवद्भक्तिमतः प्रति ।
हर्षप्रकाशनफलमन्यदेव जगत्स्थितम् ॥२३॥

asminneva jagatyantarbhavadbhaktimataḥ prati ।
harṣaprakāśanaphalamanyadeva jagatsthitam ॥23॥

This universe is full of torture, sadness and crisis. However, for Your devotees it appears as divine. The sorrows of this universe do not touch them as they are not attached to anything. They are in an entirely different world that is full of bliss. I have seen that.

गुह्ये भक्तिः परे भक्तिर्भक्तिर्विश्वमहेश्वरे ।
त्वयि शम्भौ शिवे देव भक्तिर्नाम किमप्यहो ॥२६॥

guhye bhaktiḥ pare bhaktirbhaktirviśvamaheśvare ।
tvayi śambhau śive deva bhaktirnāma kimapyaho ॥24॥

I want Thy devotion secretly. I want devotion for the supreme Lord. I want devotion for the ruler of this universe. I want devotion for Thee. I want devotion for Lord Śiva. I want devotion.

भक्तिर्भक्तिः परे भक्तिर्भक्तिर्नाम समुत्कटा ।
तारं विरौमि यत्तीव्रा भक्तिर्मेऽस्तु परं त्वयि ॥२५॥

bhaktirbhaktiḥ pare bhaktirbhaktirnāma samutkaṭā ।
tāraṁ viraumi yattīvrā bhaktirme 'stu paraṁ
tvayi ॥25॥

I want only devotion, Thy devotion, supreme devotion, that

intense devotion. I will weep, I will cry loudly. I beseech You let me possess that real intense devotion.

यतोऽसि सर्वशोभानां प्रसवावनिरीश तत्।
त्वयि लग्नमनर्घं स्याद्रत्नं वा यदि वा तृणम्॥२६॥

yato 'si sarvaśobhānāṁ prasavāvanirīśa tat ।
tvayi lagnamanarghaṁ syādratnaṁ vā yadi
vā tṛṇam ॥26॥

O Lord, it is a fact that You are the abode of all the glories in this universe. All the glories originate from You. As a result when anything is attached to You, whether it be a jewel or just a blade of grass, it becomes priceless.

आवेदकादा च वेद्याद्येषां संवेदनाध्वनि।
भवता न वियोगोऽस्ति ते जयन्ति भवज्जुषः॥२७॥

āvedakādā ca vedyādyeṣāṁ saṁvedanādhvani ।
bhavatā na viyogo 'sti te jayanti bhavajjuṣaḥ ॥27॥

Those who are Thy devotees, they are glorified in this world because on the path of knowledge, right from the subjective consciousness to the objective field, they are never separated from Thy consciousness. They are glorified in this universe.

संसारसदसो बाह्ये कैश्चित्त्वं परिरभ्यसे।
स्वामिन्परैस्तु तत्रैव ताम्यद्भिस्त्यक्तयन्त्रणैः॥२८॥

saṁsārasadaso bāhye kaiścittvaṁ parirabhyase ।
svāminparaistu tatraiva tāmyadbhistyaktayantraṇaiḥ ॥28॥

O my Master, there are some devotees of Yours who embrace You after leaving aside all the worldly affairs. They take to the caves in the Himalayas and then they embrace You there. O Lord, there however are a few devotees who embrace You in the activities of this universe. They are not bound by any rules and regulations or any restrictions for embracing You.

They may embrace a prostitute; during that activity also they are embracing You only. They are such devotees because they feel Your presence everywhere.

पानाशनप्रसाधनसम्भुक्तसमस्तविश्वया शिवया।
प्रलयोत्सवसरभसया दृढमुपगूढं शिवं वन्दे ॥२९॥

pānāśanaprasādhana-
sambhuktasamastaviśvayā śivayā ।
pralayotsavasarabhasayā
dṛḍhamupagūḍhaṁ śivaṁ vande ॥29 ॥

I bow to that Lord Śiva who is tightly embraced by Pārvatī. What is the position of Pārvatī who embraces You? She drinks, she eats sweet dishes; she adjusts fine make-up on her body; she enjoys all the enjoyment of senses. She enjoys the festival of universal destruction and she tightly embraces You at that time. I bow to that Lord Śiva who is embraced by Pārvatī in such a way.

परमेश्वरता जयत्यपूर्वा
तव विश्वेश यदीशितव्यशून्या।
अपरापि तथैव ते ययेदं
जगदाभाति यथा तथा न भाति॥३०॥

parameśvaratā jayatyapūrvā
tava viśveśa yadīśitavyaśūnyā ।
aparāpi tathaiva te yayedaṁ
jagadābhāti yathā tathā na bhāti ॥30 ॥

O Lord, there are two glories of Thee existing in this universe. One glory of Lord Śiva is grace, that is *anugraha,* which is not governed by any other agency. There is another divinity of Thee, which is also not governed by any one else, and that is concealing Your nature. Concealing Your nature and revealing Your nature both are handled by You alone. These two kinds of Lordship are glorified.

One Lordship is where You feel like revealing Your nature, revealing the nature of God-consciousness. Another Lordship is when that nature is concealed totally. It is also not governed by any other agency; You handle it Yourself. One's own effort cannot touch it. It is beyond one's own effort.

॥ इति श्रीमदुत्पलदेवाचार्यविरचिते श्रीशिवस्तोत्रावल्यां
पाशानुद्भेदनाम षोडशं स्तोत्रम् ॥

॥ *iti śrīmadutpaladevācāryaviracite śrīśivastotrāvalyāṁ*
pāśānudbhedanāma ṣoḍaśaṁ stotram ॥

17

दिव्यक्रीडाबहुमाननाम सप्तदशं स्तोत्रम्

Divyakrīḍābahumāna Stotra

Celebrating the Divine Play

अहो कोऽपि जयत्येष स्वादुः पूजामहोत्सवः।
यतोऽमृतरसास्वादमश्रूण्यपि ददत्यलम् ॥१॥

aho ko 'pi jayatyeṣa svāduḥ pūjāmahotsavaḥ I
yato 'mṛtarasāsvādamaśrūṇyapi dadatyalam II1 II

IT is a wonderful thing; that sweet unique festival of Thy devotion, the festival of Your worship is glorified all-round. As a result of that festival even a few drops of tears also carry a person to the great joy of that blissful festival.

व्यापाराः सिद्धिदाः सर्वे ये त्वत्पूजापुरःसराः।
भक्तानां त्वन्मयाः सर्वे स्वयं सिद्धय एव ते ॥२॥

vyāpārāḥ siddhidāḥ sarve ye tvatpūjāpuraḥsarāḥ I
bhaktānāṁ tvanmayāḥ sarve svayaṁ siddhaya eva te II2 II

All those activities which are concerned and connected with Thy devotion, bestow upon people those powers of achievements (*siddhis*). But for Thy devotees all those activities in this universe become powers themselves, these activities are powers themselves. These are not the bestower of powers; these are the powers themselves. For ordinary people these bestow power, but for Thy devotees these are powers themselves, these shine as powers. For Thy devotees, there is no difference between the objective and the means of attaining it; the worship and the worshipped.

सर्वदा सर्वभावेषु युगपत्सर्वरूपिणम् ।
त्वामर्चयन्त्यविश्रान्तं ये ममैतेऽधिदेवताः ॥३॥

sarvadā sarvabhāveṣu yugapatsarvarūpiṇam ।
tvāmarcayantyaviśrāntaṁ ye mamaite 'dhidevatāḥ ॥3॥

Those devotees of Thee who adore You simultaneously in each and every object, always and without a break, they are my presiding gods. They have to rule over me. They have to take care of me. They are my gods. You are not my God. They are my gods, who worship You like this.

ध्यानायासतिरस्कारसिद्धस्त्वस्पर्शनोत्सवः ।
पूजाविधिरिति ख्यातो भक्तानां स सदास्तु मे ॥४॥

dhyānāyāsatiraskārasiddhastvatsparśanotsavaḥ ।
pūjāvidhiriti khyāto bhaktānāṁ sa sadāstu me ॥4॥

The festival of Your touch is a great festival. Those devotees of Thee get this festival of Your touch without having to meditate through the techniques of *āṇavopāya*, *śāktopāya* or *śāmbhavopāya* or *anupāya*, without adopting any of these techniques. This is the real technique of worshipping You, this is the technique owned by Your devotees, and I want to possess that technique.

भक्तानां समतासारविषुवत्समयः सदा ।
त्वद्भावरसपीयूषरसेनैषां सदार्चनम् ॥५॥

bhaktānāṁ samatāsāraviṣuvatsamayaḥ sadā ।
tvadbhāvarasapīyūṣarasenaiṣāṁ sadārcanam ॥5॥

Thy devotees have possessed always the sacred moment of equinox when day and night are equal, and they worship You with the nectar of that love for Thee. Thy devotees are absorbed in worshipping You every moment. For them, there is no particular time assigned to Your worship. They have the equinox every moment.[1]

यस्यानारम्भपर्यन्तौ न च कालक्रमः प्रभो।
पूजात्मासौ क्रिया तस्याः कर्तारस्त्वज्जुषः परम् ॥६॥

yasyānārambhaparyantau na ca kālakramaḥ prabho ।
pūjātmāsau kriyā tasyāḥ kartārastvajjuṣaḥ param ॥6॥

For Thy devotees there is no restriction of time for Your worship. There is no beginning of that worship, there is no end to that, nor is there a track of time in between. This is the real act of worship and such worshippers alone are Your real devotees. They worship You every moment. They don't sport a wristwatch to keep a track of the time for Your devotion. Every time they meditate.

ब्रह्मादीनामपीशास्ते ते च सौभाग्यभागिनः।
येषां स्वप्नेऽपि मोहेऽपि स्थितस्त्वपूजनोत्सवः ॥७॥

brahmādīnāmapīśāste te ca saubhāgyabhāginaḥ ।
yeṣāṁ svapne 'pi mohe 'pi sthitastvatpūjanotsavaḥ ॥7॥

Those for whom the festival of Your worship is existing in dreaming state as well as in illusion are really the rulers of the great gods namely Brahmā, Viṣṇu and Rudra; they rule over those three great Lords who are the creator, the protector and the destroyer of this universe. They are the actual rulers of those three Lords. They are the real fortunate people for whom the festival of Your worship exists in all the three states,

1. When the sun appears to cross the celestial equator, it is called equinox, day and night become of equal duration. The *viṣuvat-kāla* as it is called occurs twice a year on sixth day of the month of *Caitra* when it crosses south to north and sixth day of the month of *Aśvin* when it crosses north to south. It is considered to be very auspicious and one should particularly worship at that time.

namely the wakeful, the dreaming and the dreamless states.

जपतां जुह्वतां स्नातां ध्यायतां न च केवलम् ।
भक्तानां भवदभ्यर्चामहो यावद्यदा तदा ॥८ ॥

japatāṁ juhvatāṁ snātāṁ dhyāyatāṁ na ca kevalam ।
bhaktānāṁ bhavadabhyarcāmaho yāvadyadā tadā ॥8 ॥

Thy devotees always possess the festival of Your worship, whether they are reciting Your name, or performing sacrifice, or bathing, or meditating on You; not only in these states but Your devotees always possess the festival of Thy worship. Not only in the state of reciting Your name, not only in the state of offering various offerings in the sacred fire, not only in the state of bathing, not only in the state of meditation, but those devotees possess the festival of Your devotion always and everywhere and not only in these sacred states.

भवत्पूजासुधास्वादसम्भोगसुखिनः सदा ।
इन्द्रादीनामथ ब्रह्ममुख्यानामस्ति कः समः ॥९ ॥

bhavatpūjāsudhāsvādasambhogasukhinaḥ sadā ।
indrādīnāmatha brahmamukhyānāmasti kaḥ samaḥ ॥9 ॥

Those devotees, who have always possessed the enjoyment of the joy of tasting the nectar of Your devotion, cannot be matched even by any of the gods. Even Indra, the governor of the kingdom of heaven, Brahmā the creator, Viṣṇu the protector and Īśvara the destroyer of this universe cannot compare with that devotee who is always immersed in Thy worship and who is always enjoying that divine nectar of that worship. There is no comparison with those great Lords of divinity.

जगत्क्षोभैकजनके भवत्पूजामहोत्सवे ।
यत्प्राप्यं प्राप्यते किंचिद्भक्ता एव विदन्ति तत् ॥१० ॥

jagatkṣobhaikajanake bhavatpūjāmahotsave ।
yatprāpyaṁ prāpyate kiñcidbhaktā eva vidanti tat ॥10 ॥

The greatest festival of Your worship is only that worship which destroys the agitation of the universe. The great festival of Thy worship destroys differentiated consciousness. What is achieved in that worship is not known to anybody; only Your devotees know that. Only those devotees know what is achieved in that festival. It is unknown to all others.

त्वद्धाम्नि चिन्मये स्थित्वा षट्त्रिंशत्तत्त्वकर्मभिः ।
कायवाक्चित्तचेष्टाद्यैरर्चये त्वां सदा विभो ॥११ ॥

tvaddhāmni cinmaye sthitvā ṣaṭtriṁśattattvakarmabhiḥ ।
kāyavākcittaceṣṭādyairarcaye tvāṁ sadā vibho ॥11 ॥

O Lord there is one desire in me. I want to worship You always. I would like to worship You always with body, with speech, with mind and with action. I want to worship You always but I don't want to worship You from a distance. I want to worship You after entering into Your body. I want to worship You not only with flowers but with all the thirty-six elements of the universe right from earth to Śiva.

भवत्पूजामयासङ्गसम्भोगसुखिनो मम ।
प्रयातु कालः सकलोऽप्यनन्तोऽपीयदर्थये ॥१२ ॥

bhavatpūjāmayāsaṅgasambhogasukhino mama ।
prayātu kālaḥ sakalo 'pyananto 'pīyadarthaye ॥12 ॥

I am peaceful only when I am enjoying the nearness of Your worship, that moment alone I remain peaceful. I crave for only one thing; this is the only desire in me that all the time I must worship You. I don't want to die, I don't want to live, I don't want anything, I just want that all my time should pass in the act of worshipping You because I am peaceful only in worshipping You and nothing else can give me any peace.

भवत्पूजामृतरसाभोगलम्पटता विभो।
विवर्धतामनुदिनं सदा च फलतां मम ॥१३॥

bhavatpūjāmṛtarasābhogalampaṭatā vibho ।
vivardhatāmanudinaṁ sadā ca phalatāṁ mama ॥13॥

O Lord, I want this passion for enjoying the taste of the nectar of devotion of Your worship to grow each day and it must always culminate in bearing a fruit also, and that fruit is Your nearness.

जगद्विलयसञ्जातसुधैकरसनिर्भरे।
त्वदब्धौ त्वां महात्मानमर्चन्नासीय सर्वदा ॥१४॥

jagadvilayasañjātasudhaikarasanirbhare ।
tvadabdhau tvāṁ mahātmānamarcannāsīya sarvadā ॥14॥

You are an unlimited ocean that is filled with the greatest nectar that has appeared by the destruction of the differentiated cognition, the differentiated knowledge of the universe. The destruction of the differentiated knowledge of the universe has created the taste of that nectar that is filled in the ocean of Thy being. That nectar is filled in Thy being. You are that great being. I wish I would devote all my time to Your worship; that is my only craving.

अशेषवासनाग्रन्थिविच्छेदसरलं सदा।
मनो निवेद्यते भक्तैः स्वादु पूजाविधौ तव ॥१५॥

aśeṣavāsanāgranthivicchedasaralaṁ sadā ।
mano nivedyate bhaktaiḥ svādu pūjāvidhau tava ॥15॥

There are devotees of Thee who offer to Thee their sweet minds which are not disturbed or filled with those worldly affairs, just to adore You. They always offer You their sweet minds, which are straightforward, those minds without the knots of the impressions of the cravings for worldly enjoyments. Those knots, those impressions are always removed from their minds. They always offer You those sweet and straightforward minds.

अधिष्ठायैव विषयानिमाः करणवृत्तयः ।
भक्तानां प्रेषयन्ति त्वत्पूजार्थममृतासवम् ॥१६ ॥

adhiṣṭhāyaiva viṣayānimāḥ karaṇavṛttayaḥ ।
bhaktānāṁ preṣayanti tvatpūjārthamamṛtāsavam ॥16 ॥

These very senses of cognition and these very senses of action carry the greatest, highest, and priceless liquor of Thy worship to those devotees of Thee. They carry that liquor and place that before Thy devotees not keeping away the enjoyment of senses. In the very enjoyment of senses, these carry that liquor to them for Thy worship.

For ordinary people these sense-organs become hurdles and great distractions; on the other hand these assist Thy devotees in their spiritual path. Such is the distinguished effect of Your devotion.

भक्तानां भक्तिसंवेगमहोष्मविवशात्मनाम् ।
कोऽन्यो निर्वाणहेतुः स्यात्त्वत्पूजामृतमज्जनात् ॥१७ ॥

bhaktānāṁ bhaktisaṁvegamahoṣmavivaśātmanām ।
ko 'nyo nirvāṇahetuḥ syāttvatpūjāmṛtamajjanāt ॥17 ॥

There are some devotees whose mind has become beyond control; they have become mad by the fire of Thy attachment. This attachment to You is a kind of fire that makes them mad for You. And that madness is beyond any control. Nothing can stop that madness in them; those are such devotees. They are never freed from that madness unless they are totally drowned in the nectar of Thy worship.

सततं त्वत्पदाभ्यर्चासुधापानमहोत्सवः ।
त्वत्प्रसादैकसम्प्राप्तिहेतुर्मे नाथ कल्पताम् ॥१८ ॥

satataṁ tvatpadābhyarcāsudhāpānamahotsavaḥ ।
tvatprasādaikasamprāptiheturme nātha kalpatām ॥18 ॥

This great festival of tasting the nectar of the devotion of Thy feet can be owned not by our actions and efforts but only through Your grace. Let me continuously have that festival.

अनुभूयासमीशान प्रतिकर्म क्षणात्क्षणम् ।
भवत्पूजामृतापानमदास्वादमहामुदम् ॥१९ ॥

anubhūyāsamīśāna pratikarma kṣaṇātkṣaṇam ।
bhavatpūjāmṛtāpānamadāsvādamahāmudam ॥19 ॥

O Lord, will that day ever come when I would experience in each and every action of mine and from moment to moment, the great enjoyment of becoming mad by tasting the nectar of Thy worship? Will that day ever come?

दृष्टार्थ एव भक्तानां भवत्पूजामहोद्यमः ।
तदैव यदसम्भाव्यं सुखमास्वादयन्ति ते ॥२० ॥

dṛṣṭārtha eva bhaktānāṁ bhavatpūjāmahodyamaḥ ।
tadaiva yadasambhāvyaṁ sukhamāsvādayanti te ॥20 ॥

Now You will say: "No it is very difficult to achieve, it will come by and by; you will achieve it by and by." But I have seen such people who have experienced this great enthusiasm of worshipping You. They have enthusiasm to worship You and by that enthusiasm only they are carried to Your God-consciousness. They don't worship You at all. There is no time taken by them; only enthusiasm and they are carried to God-consciousness. I have seen such people with my own eyes. But then why not me; why am I deprived of this?

यावन्न लब्धस्त्वत्पूजासुधास्वादमहोत्सवः ।
तावन्नास्वादितो मन्ये लवोऽपि सुखसम्पदः ॥२१ ॥

yāvanna labdhastvatpūjāsudhāsvādamahotsavaḥ ।
tāvannāsvādito manye lavo 'pi sukhasampadaḥ ॥21 ॥

O my Lord, this is my belief that, until this great festival of tasting the nectar of Thy devotion is achieved, one has not achieved anything; one has achieved nothing. Although one may have achieved everything else in this universe, yet one has not achieved anything. Without achieving this, one is a naught because this is the achievement to be achieved, just tasting the nectar of Thy devotion. So let me taste it.

भक्तानां विषयान्वेषाभासायासाद्विनैव सा ।
अयत्नसिद्धं त्वद्धामस्थितिः पूजासु जायते ॥२२॥

bhaktānāṁ viṣayānveṣābhāsāyāsādvinaiva sā ।
ayatnasiddhaṁ tvaddhāmasthitiḥ pūjāsu jāyate ॥22॥

O Lord, there are such devotees of Yours, who have not to collect the usual substances of worship; they do not have to collect the items used in worship like *dhūpa, dīpa, ghī*, fruits, flowers, incense, etcetera. The celebration of their worship takes place automatically without collecting those substances. Thy worship takes place in them without collecting all these things.

न प्राप्यमस्ति भक्तानां नाप्येषामस्ति दुर्लभम् ।
केवलं विचरन्त्येते भवत्पूजामदोन्मदाः ॥२३॥

na prāpyamasti bhaktānāṁ nāpyeṣāmasti durlabham ।
kevalaṁ vicarantyete bhavatpūjāmadonmadāḥ ॥23॥

For Thy devotees there is nothing to be achieved and for Thy devotees there is nothing difficult to achieve. They are mad with the intoxication of Thy worship. They roam around peacefully here and there but they are maddened with Thy devotion.

अहो भक्तिभरोदारचेतसां वरद त्वयि ।
श्लाघ्यः पूजाविधिः कोऽपि यो न याच्ञाकलंकितः ॥२४॥

aho bhaktibharodāracetasāṁ varada tvayi ।
ślāghyaḥ pūjāvidhiḥ ko 'pi yo na yācñākalaṅkitaḥ ॥24 ॥

O bestower of boons, it is amazing, this is a great wonder to me that those devotees of Thee have a very broad mind and their way of worshipping You is supreme, wonderful as they do not ask for anything from You. They just worship You, they don't ask for any boons from You. This is their greatness. So great is their way of worship that they do not want to blemish it by asking for something.

का न शोभा न को ह्लादः का समृद्धिर्न वापरा ।
को वा न मोक्षः कोऽप्येष महादेवो यदर्च्यते ॥२५ ॥

kā na śobhā na ko hlādaḥ kā samṛddhir na vāparā ।
ko vā na mokṣaḥ ko 'pyeṣa mahādevo yadarcyate ॥25 ॥

Where the worship of Lord Śiva takes place that is the real glory; that is the ecstasy; that is the joy, the highest joy. That is the real rise, the real liberation, and that is everything where Lord Śiva is worshipped. Lord Śiva's worship is everything. That is the glory, the supreme bliss.

अन्तरुल्लसदच्छाच्छभक्तिपीयूषपोषितम् ।
भवत्पूजोपयोगाय शरीरमिदमस्तु मे ॥२६ ॥

antarullasadacchācchabhaktipīyūṣapoṣitam ।
bhavatpūjopayogāya śarīramidamastu me ॥26 ॥

O Lord, I have one request for You and that is I want my body to be meant only for Your worship. Let my body be worthy of only worshipping You and nothing else because this body of mine is nourished by the nectar of Thy devotion that is very pure and which rises from the core of my heart. So I want this body of mine to exist just for the purpose of Thy devotion alone and nothing else.

त्वत्पादपूजासम्भोगपरतन्त्रः सदा विभो ॥
भूयासं जगतामीश एकः स्वच्छन्दचेष्टितः ॥२७ ॥

tvatpādapūjāsambhogaparatantraḥ sadā vibho ।
bhūyāsaṁ jagatāmīśa ekaḥ svacchandaceṣṭitaḥ ॥27 ॥

O Lord, O all-pervading Lord, O ruler of all the three worlds, I would like to be dependent only in tasting the nectar of Thy worship. I want to be dependent on the enjoyment of that nectar of Thy worship. But at the same time, side-by-side, in other activities of the outward world, I want to be absolutely independent. In the outside world I would like to be independent, fully independent, not agreeing with any other thing in this world; but where there is Your worship, I would like to be dependent on that worship always and independent everywhere else.

त्वद्ध्यानदर्शनस्पर्शतृषि केषामपि प्रभो ।
जायते शीतलस्वादु भवत्पूजामहासरः ॥२८ ॥

tvaddhyānadarśanasparśatṛṣi keṣāmapi prabho ।
jāyate śītalasvādu bhavatpūjāmahāsaraḥ ॥28 ॥

O Lord, there are some unique devotees of Thee who have got the thirst of meditating on You and embracing You (*dhyāna* and *sparśa*) at the same time. Their thirst is quenched by the adoration of Thee, which is a dive in the great lake of Thy worship that is very cool and very sweet. When they dive into the cool and sweet water of that lake of Thy devotion, Thy worship, that thirst is quenched.

यथा त्वमेव जगतः पूजासम्भोगभाजनम् ।
तथेश भक्तिमानेव पूजासम्भोगभाजनम् ॥२९ ॥

yathā tvameva jagataḥ pūjāsambhogabhājanam ।
tatheśa bhaktimāneva pūjāsambhogabhājanam ॥29 ॥

O Lord, just as You are the only being worthy of enjoying the nectar of worship, in the same way, Thy devotee is also worthy of enjoying the nectar of Thy worship. So there are only two beings who have to enjoy the nectar of Thy devotion. You are enjoying the nectar of Thy worship and in the same way Your devotee also enjoys the nectar of Your worship.

कोऽप्यसौ जयति स्वामिन्भवत्पूजामहोत्सवः ।
षट्त्रिंशतोऽपि तत्त्वानां क्षोभो यत्रोल्लसत्यलम् ॥३० ॥

ko 'pyasau jayati svāminbhavatpūjāmahotsavaḥ ।
ṣaṭtriṁśato 'pi tattvānāṁ kṣobho yatrollasatyalam ॥30 ॥

O my Master, that unique great festival of Thy worship is always glorified, where all those thirty-six elements are absorbed in nothingness, only Śiva remains.

नमस्तेभ्यो विभो येषां भक्तिपीयूषवारिणा ।
पूज्यान्येव भवन्ति त्वत्पूजोपकरणान्यपि ॥३१ ॥

namastebhyo vibho yeṣāṁ bhaktipīyūṣavāriṇā ।
pūjyānyeva bhavanti tvatpūjopakaraṇānyapi ॥31 ॥

O Lord, I adore those devotees of Thee, who first adore all those substances like flowers, fruits, incense, etcetera they have gathered for Thy devotion before offering these to Your image. They don't offer these substances directly to You; they first adore these substances because they feel as these are going to be offered to Lord Śiva, so these substances are worth worshipping, and that they must worship these substances first. I bow to those devotees who worship these substances also with the water of the nectar of devotion.

पूजारम्भे विभो ध्यात्वा मन्त्राधेयां त्वदात्मताम् ।
स्वात्मन्येव परे भक्ता मान्ति हर्षेण न क्वचित् ॥३२ ॥

pūjārambhe vibho dhyātvā mantrādheyāṁ tvadātmatām ।
svātmanyeva pare bhaktā mānti harṣeṇa na kvacit ॥32 ॥

O Lord, at the beginning of Thy worship, Thy devotees first meditate on Thy nature, to whom the worship is to be offered and then they meditate on You who is to be worshipped and accomplished through all these *mantras*. This way their joy knows no bounds and they don't worship You at all. They just sink in that ecstasy in meditating on You and the rest of the worship does not take place.

राज्यलाभादिवोत्फुल्लैः कैश्चित्पूजामहोत्सवे ।
सुधासवेन सकला जगती संविभज्यते ॥३३॥

rājyalābhādivotphullaiḥ kaiścitpūjāmahotsave ।
sudhāsavena sakalā jagatī saṁvibhajyate ॥33॥

Those devotees of Thee are elated when this great festival of Thy worship occurs to them. They get blossomed just as one gets elated on achieving the great honour of a great kingdom. They become blossomed in celebrating Your worship and are so overjoyed that they do not know how to handle this joy of the nectar of Thy devotion. They distribute that nectar to each and every being in this world. They distribute this liquor of worship everywhere. They want to share it.

पूजामृतापानमयो येषां भोगः प्रतिक्षणम् ।
किं देवा उत मुक्तास्ते किं वा केऽप्येव ते जनाः ॥३४॥

pūjāmṛtāpānamayo yeṣāṁ bhogaḥ pratikṣaṇam ।
kiṁ devā uta muktāste kiṁ vā ke 'pyeva te janāḥ ॥34॥

Those devotees who taste the enjoyment of drinking the nectar of Thy worship each and every second; in whom this enjoyment takes place each and every moment, I can't understand who they are. Are they gods? Are they liberated? Are they some unique beings? I can't understand. They are beyond my imagination. They are so great that I can't explain their greatness. So glorious are those wonderful devotees of

Thee who enjoy the nectar of Thy devotion each and every moment in this world that words cannot describe them.

पूजोपकरणीभूतविश्वावेशेन गौरवम् ।
अहो किमपि भक्तानां किमप्येव च लाघवम् ॥३५॥

pūjopakaraṇībhūtaviśvāveśena gauravam ।
aho kimapi bhaktānāṁ kimapyeva ca lāghavam ॥35॥

This is a wonder to me that those devotees of Thee, on one side they are reserved because they get entry, they get merged in the substances utilized for Your worship; when they handle flowers, they get merged into those flowers. They don't worship You, the worship has yet to take place but they have already got merged into those substances of Thy worship; and it does not take place with flowers and all these limited substances alone, but with this entire universe. They feel that this whole universe is meant for offering to Lord Śiva. On the other hand they expose everything to everybody and nothing remains within them. They expose all the secrets of Thy worship to everybody. They don't expose anything as long as they are merged in that substance of this universal Being. This universe seems to them to be meant for Thy worship. So they are reserved. This is their reservation, and they expose that secret to everybody, this is their shallowness. They cannot keep these things to themselves.

पूजामयाक्षविक्षेपक्षोभादेवामृतोद्गमः ।
भक्तानां क्षीरजलधिक्षोभादिव दिवौकसाम् ॥३६॥

pūjāmayākṣavikṣepakṣobhādevāmṛtodgamaḥ ।
bhaktānāṁ kṣīrajaladhikṣobhādiva divaukasām ॥36॥

Thy devotees, when they operate their organic functions of *śabda, sparśa, rasa, rūpa* and *gandha,* all these organic functions appear to them as if they are worshipping Lord Śiva; when they see anything it seems to them they are worshipping Lord

Śiva, when they eat, it appears to them as if they are worshipping Lord Śiva; when they indulge in sensual gratification, they feel they are worshipping Lord Śiva. The agitation of this organic field is just like worship to them. So with the agitation of these organic sensations, the rise of supreme nectar takes place in them like the supreme nectar which rose from the agitation of the eyes of that great snake Vāsuki during the churning of the Milky Ocean. In the same way when Thy devotees are agitated in their organic field, by the mere agitation of the organic field, the rise of nectar of God-consciousness takes place in them. This is *śāmbhavopāya*.[2]

पूजां केचन मन्यन्ते धेनुं कामदुघामिव ।
सुधाधाराधिकरसां धयन्त्यन्तर्मुखाः परे ॥३७॥

pūjāṁ kecana manyante dhenuṁ kāmadughāmiva ।
sudhādhārādhikarasāṁ dhayantyantarmukhāḥ pare ॥37॥

There are two sections of Thy devotees. One section comprises those who believe that Thy worship is just like Kāmadhenu, the cow of heaven that bestows boons to everybody. They consider that Thy worship bestows boons to everybody.

The other class of devotees of Thee just drink the nectar of Thy worship, they taste that worship. They don't wait to ponder over the glories that Your worship is going to bestow on them. They just drink that worship and absorb that in their nature. They don't care for explaining and investigating Thy worship. What kind of worship is this, what is the quality of

2. During the churning of Kṣīra Sāgara the Milky Ocean, Vāsuki was utilized as the churning rope; Mandhāra-Parvata was the churning stick, his eyes would sometimes look this way and sometimes that way. At that time his eyes were agitated and vomited blood due to the pressure. That is *ākāśā vikṣepa* and by that, the rise of nectar took place afterwards from Kṣīra Sāgara, the Milky Ocean.

Thy worship, they just drink that worship; they just don't care for explanation. (The first section is commercial and the second is spiritual!)

भक्तानामक्षविक्षेपोऽप्येष संसारसंमतः।
उपनीय किमप्यन्तः पुष्णात्यर्चामहोत्सवम् ॥३८॥

bhaktānāmakṣavikṣepo 'pyeṣa saṁsārasaṁmataḥ ।
upanīya kimapyantaḥ puṣṇātyarcāmahotsavam ॥38॥

The agitation of the organic field is really admitted to be the only cause of entangling oneself in the cycle of repeated births and deaths. When one's mind, intellect, eyes, your ego and other organs are agitated that is the state of *saṁsāra*, which is believed to be the only cause of carrying and entangling oneself in the wheel of repeated births and deaths. But for Thy devotees, O Lord, such is not the case. This agitation of the organic field for Thy devotees carries and directs them internally and gets them entry in the great celebration, the great festival of Thy devotion. So this agitation of the organic field is just Thy devotion for them.

भक्तिक्षोभवशादीश स्वात्मभूतेऽर्चनं त्वयि।
चित्रं दैन्याय नो यावद्दीनतायाः परं फलम् ॥३९॥

bhaktikṣobhavaśādīśa svātmabhūte 'rcanaṁ tvayi ।
citraṁ dainyāya no yāvaddīnatāyāḥ paraṁ phalam ॥39॥

O Lord, it is by the flood of devotion that Thy worship takes place, which is essentially one's own worship. Thy worship is just the worship of one's own nature. By the flood of Thy devotion when that worship takes place; this is a wonder to me that it is not to seek some boon or beg forgiveness. It is not like that. It is just the establishment in God-consciousness. It is that state which establishes one in God-consciousness.

उपचारपदं पूजा केषांचित्त्वत्पदाप्तये।
भक्तानां भवदैकात्म्यनिर्वृत्तिप्रसरस्तु सः ॥४०॥

upacārapadaṁ pūjā keṣāñcittvatpadāptaye ।
bhaktānāṁ bhavadaikātmyanirvṛttiprasarastu saḥ ॥40 ॥

There are some devotees for whom Thy worship, which takes place in collecting those substances of Your worship, is meant to carry them to God-consciousness. They believe that this worship of Lord Śiva is just the means to carry them to God-consciousness. But there are some devotees, some unique devotees who believe that just worshipping You is God-consciousness and after worshipping there is no next step. This is the real existence of God-consciousness.

अप्यसम्बद्धरूपार्चा भक्त्युन्मादनिरर्गलैः ।
वितन्यमाना लभते प्रतिष्ठां त्वयि कामपि ॥४१ ॥

apyasambaddharūpārcā bhaktyunmādanirargalaiḥ ।
vitanyamānā labhate pratiṣṭhāṁ tvayi kāmapi ॥41 ॥

There are some devotees who have no bondages, no limitations of Thy worship because of their madness of Thy devotion. They have achieved the madness of Thy devotion and as they are mad, they don't know the rules and regulations of Your worship. The worship by Thy devotees does not follow the conventional rules or any set sequence. They will first send Him away: This is Your *visarjana*, go! and then adopt the worship after He is gone because they are mad. They don't know how to handle this system of Thy worship. But those mad people know the reality of Lord Śiva that He is all-pervading. Where will He come from and where will He go? He is already here. They achieve that great establishment in Thy nature through that devotion.[3]

3. The sequence and rules of worship dictate first *āvāhana* — just calling Lord Śiva and when Lord Śiva appears then *sthāpanā* i.e. offer Him a seat, and after He is seated on that for seat for being worshipped, then offer *arghyam, pādyam, ācamanīyam, puṣpam, dhūpam, dīpam, naivedyam, tāmbūlam,* and *āratī.* Afterwords when the worship is over, *visarjanam* — You may go now, and come later.

स्वादुभक्तिरसास्वादस्तब्धीभूतमनश्च्युताम् ।
शम्भो त्वमेव ललितः पूजानां किल भाजनम् ॥४२॥

svādubhaktirasāsvādastabdhībhūtamanaścyutām ।
śambho evameva lalitaḥ pūjānāṁ kila bhājanam ॥42 ॥

O Lord Śiva, those ways of Thy worship are very sweet and are filled with the nectar of Thy devotion. This worship of Thee is produced by the mind that is unminded and one-pointed by the fullness of the nectar of Thy devotion. Those ways of worship are absorbed and conceived by You only. You alone are worthy of such worship and You are all-round sweet, all-round best and all-round tasty.

परिपूर्णानि शुद्धानि भक्तिमन्ति स्थिराणि च ।
भवत्पूजाविधौ नाथ साधनानि भवन्तु मे ॥४३॥

paripūrṇāni śuddhāni bhaktimanti sthirāṇi ca ।
bhavatpūjāvidhau nātha sādhanāni bhavantu me ॥43 ॥

O Lord, there is only one request I want to place before You. I want these ways of Thy worship to always become fulfilled in me; whenever I worship You, it must get fulfilled. I must get its fruit then and there. This worship must be absolutely pure without any fraud, and this worship must be filled with the taste of Thy love. This worship must be continuous and lasting. Please bestow on me such ways of worship, this is my request.

अशेषपूजासत्कोशे त्वत्पूजाकर्मणि प्रभो ।
अहो करणवृन्दस्य कापि लक्ष्मीर्विजृम्भते ॥४४॥

aśeṣapūjāsatkośe tvatpūjākarmaṇi prabho ।
aho karaṇavṛndasya kāpi lakṣmīrvijṛmbhate ॥44 ॥

O Lord Śiva, O my Master, when Thy adoration is functioned, that adoration is the treasure of all worships. Oh, this is a wonder, there in that treasure, all my organic field is glorified with that great wealth of liberation, great wealth of devotion.

एषा पेशलिमा नाथ तवैव किल दृश्यते ।
विश्वेश्वरोऽपि भृत्यैर्यदर्च्यसे यश्च लभ्यसे ॥४५॥

eṣā peśalimā nātha tavaiva kila dṛśyate ।
viśveśvaro 'pi bhṛtyairyadarcyase yaśca labhyase ॥45॥

O my Master, You bestow everything to Your devotees and do not hold back anything. This generosity is found only in You. Although You are always full and possess the whole kingdom of spiritual wealth, yet You are so generous that You bestow everything to Your slaves. Whenever Your slaves worship You, that very moment they achieve whatever they desire. This softness is found only in Your hands and not in anyone else's hands. You only give.

सदा मूर्त्तादमूर्त्ताद्वा भावाद्यद्वाप्यभावतः ।
उत्थेयान्मे प्रशस्तस्य भवत्पूजामहोत्सवः ॥४६॥

sadā mūrttādamūrttādvā bhāvādyadvāpyabhāvataḥ ।
uttheyānme praśastasya bhavatpūjāmahotsavaḥ ॥46॥

This is my desire that the great festival of Thy worship should just rise in me as I am always glorified because I have this intense desire to worship You. I am glorified, I am fortunate so this festival of Thy devotion, Thy worship should rise in me always from anything solid or anything subtle, any existing object or any non-existent object. Everywhere the festival of Thy worship should rise in me because I am glorified with Thy devotion. Everything in this universe should help me attain that great festival of Thy worship.

कामक्रोधाभिमानैस्त्वामुपहारीकृतैः सदा ।
येऽर्चयन्ति नमस्तेभ्यस्तेषां तुष्टोऽसि तत्त्वतः ॥४७॥

kāmakrodhābhimānaistvāmupahārīkṛtaiḥ sadā ।
ye 'rcayanti namastebhyasteṣāṁ tuṣṭo 'si tattvataḥ ॥47 ॥

There are some devotees of Thee who offer You their lust, their anger and their ego. They just offer You whatever lust they have, whatever anger they possess, whatever ego they possess because they have earned only these three things in their whole lifetime. I adore those devotees of Thee who offer You their *kāma, krodha* and *abhimāna.* I adore those devotees, I don't adore You. I don't want to bow before You, I want to bow before those devotees who adore You by offering You their *kāma, krodha* and *abhimāna,* because in reality You are pleased with them, You are really happy with them.

जयत्येष भवद्भक्तिभाजां पूजाविधिः परः ।
यस्तृणैः क्रियमाणोऽपि रत्नैरेवोपकल्पते ॥४८ ॥

jayatyeṣa bhavadbhaktibhājāṁ pūjāvidhiḥ paraḥ ।
yastṛṇaiḥ kriyamāṇo 'pi ratnairevopakalpate ॥48 ॥

Thy devotees have possessed that supreme way of adoring You which is always glorified. They adore You with blades of grass and that adoration done with the blades of grass becomes the producer of jewels and diamonds. It culminates into the priceless jewel of liberation.

॥ इति श्रीमदुत्पलदेवाचार्यविरचिते श्रीशिवस्तोत्रावल्यां
दिव्यक्रीडाबहुमाननाम सप्तदशं स्तोत्रम् ॥

॥ *iti śrīmadutpaladevācāryaviracite śrīśivastotrāvalyāṁ*
divyakrīḍābahumānanāma saptadaśaṁ stotram ॥

18

आविष्कारनाम अष्टादशं स्तोत्रम्

Āviṣkāra Stotra

Revealing Hymn

जगतोऽन्तरतो भवन्तमाप्त्वा पुनरेतद्भवतोऽन्तराल्लभन्ते ।
जगदीश तवैव भक्तिभाजो न हि तेषामिह दूरतोऽस्ति किञ्चित् ॥१ ॥

jagato 'ntarato bhavantamāptvā
punaretadbhavato 'ntarāllabhante ।
jagadīśa tavaiva bhaktibhājo
na hi teṣāmiha dūrato 'sti kiñcit ॥1 ॥

O Lord of one hundred and eighteen worlds, those are Your real devotees who find You amidst the universal state. They first achieve You in the centre of the universe and after they find You, they find the universe in You. They first find You in the universe, and afterwards they find the universe in Your body. This is the way of understanding of Your devotees. There is nothing far away from their understanding. They understand the universe and You as one. So for them it is one and the same thing, be it the universe or be it You.

क्वचिदेव भवान् क्वचिद्भवानी सकलार्थक्रमगर्भिणी प्रधाना ।
परमार्थपदे तु नैव देव्या भवतो नापि जगत्त्रयस्य भेदः ॥२ ॥

kvacideva bhavān kvacidbhavānī
sakalārthakramagarbhiṇī pradhānā ।
paramārthapade tu naiva devyā
bhavato nāpi jagattrayasya bhedaḥ ॥2 ॥

At some places, from one point of view, it seems that You are the only person existing in this universe. From another point of view, it seems that the universe alone exists (Bhavānī, Pārvatī). But in the real sense of understanding there is no differentiation between You, Pārvatī, or this universe. This all is one and the same thing.

नो जानते सुभगमप्यवलेपवन्तो लोकाः प्रयत्नसुभगा निखिला हि भावाः।
चेतः पुनर्यदिदमुद्यतमप्यवैति नैवात्मरूपमिह हा तदहो हतोऽस्मि ॥३॥

no jānate subhagamapyavalepavanto
lokāḥ prayatnasubhagā nikhilā hi bhāvāḥ ।
cetaḥ punaryadidamudyatamapyavaiti
naivātmarūpamiha hā tadaho hato 'smi ॥3॥

People having impurity in their minds do not understand, do not experience that sweet and wonderful nature of God. This whole collection of universal objects becomes refined and sweet only through the effort of meditation. When we meditate they appear divine. When we do not meditate on these worldly objects, they become deprived of divinity and give pain, crisis, torture, sorrow, etcetera. Otherwise when we put in that effort, they appear divine. There is a problem in me. My mind is just bent upon finding out the truth of this objective world, to realize the divinity and the real nature of this objective world, but if it does not achieve that, where will I go? I am ruined really. I am completely lost.

This whole universe is divine in the real sense but it does not seem divine to everybody. This divinity appears only when one puts effort of meditation on it. Meditate upon Lord Śiva and then this world becomes *jagad-ānanda*, it will be merged in *jagad-ānanda*. Then it will appear divine. But the author apprehends, "in my case, I have put in all my effort to find it as divine, it does not happen. I am lost, I am ruined altogether. Where will I go?"

भवन्मयस्वात्मनिवासलब्धसम्पद्भराभ्यर्चितयुष्मदङ्घ्रिः ।
न भोजनाच्छादनमप्यजस्रमपेक्षते यस्तमहं नतोऽस्मि ॥४ ॥

bhavanmayasvātmanivāsalabdha-
sampadbharābhyarcitayuṣmadaṅghriḥ ।
na bhojanācchādanamapyajasram-
apekṣate yastamahaṁ nato 'smi ॥4 ॥

There are such devotees in this universe, who have achieved the position of residing in their own nature which is essentially one with Your nature, the nature of Lord Śiva. Such a devotee of Thee, who has achieved the highest glory by residing in Your own nature and by that glory always adores Your lotus-like feet, does not even feel the need to cover his body or eat anything. I bow to such a person; I truly am a slave of such a person.

सदा भवद्देहनिवासस्वस्थोऽप्यन्तः परं दह्यत एष लोकः ।
तवेच्छया तत्कुरु मे यथात्र त्वदर्चनानन्दमयो भवेयम् ॥५ ॥

sadā bhavaddehanivāsasvastho-
'pyantaḥ paraṁ dahyata eṣa lokaḥ ।
tavecchayā tatkuru me yathātra
tvadarcanānandamayo bhaveyam ॥5 ॥

In reality everybody is residing in the nature of Lord Śiva. This worldly ignorant class of people by virtue of residing in Your nature has actually achieved a peaceful state, but internally is tortured, sentenced to sadness and crisis. This is Your will. This does not take place according to their *karma*s. This takes place according to Your sweet will. But I want Your sweet will in another way. Please act in such a way for me in this universe so that I am merged in worshipping You always and everywhere. I want only this much in this universe. Otherwise being already situated in You does not mean anything to me, and if I am away from You and do not realize that I am residing in You, that too does not mean anything to me. I want to worship You always and everywhere.

स्वरसोदितयुष्मदङ्घ्रिपद्मद्वयपूजामृतपानसक्तचित्तः ।
सकलार्थचयेष्वहं भवेयम् सुखसंस्पर्शनमात्रलोकयात्रः ॥६ ॥

svarasoditayuṣmadaṅghripadma-
dvayapūjāmṛtapānasaktacittaḥ ।
sakalārthacayeṣvahaṁ bhaveyam
sukhsaṁsparśanamātralokayātraḥ ॥6 ॥

My Lord, there is one desire in me: my mind should be directed towards tasting the nectar of worshipping Your lotus feet, and Your lotus feet should appear to me without putting in any effort to achieve them, and I would like to taste the nectar of the worship of Your lotus feet. By drinking the nectar of the worship of Your lotus feet, with one-pointed devotion, I should be effortlessly carried to God-consciousness in all my worldly actions without having to adopt any means (*śāmbhavopāya, śāktopāya* or *āṇavopāya*). All my worldly activities should lead me to that blissful state of Thy worship.

सकलव्यवहारगोचरे स्फुटमन्तः स्फुरति त्वयि प्रभो ।
उपयान्त्यपयान्ति चानिशम् मम वस्तूनि विभान्तु सर्वदा ॥७ ॥

sakalavyavahāragocare
sphuṭamantaḥ sphurati tvayi prabho ।
upayāntyapayānti cāniśam
mama vastūni vibhāntu sarvadā ॥7 ॥

O my Master, in all the agitation of my sense-organs, You alone are shining. I must always get to taste the nectar of Your worship during creation or destruction of anything in this world. In the creation or destruction of anything in this universe I must see You.

सततमेव तवैव पुरेऽथवाप्यरहितो विचरेयमहं त्वया ।
क्षणलवोऽप्यथमा स्म भवेत् स मे न विजये ननु यत्र भवन्मयः ॥८ ॥

satatameva tavaiva pure 'thavā-
pyarahito vicareyamahaṁ tvayā ।
kṣaṇalavo 'pyathamā sma bhavet sa me
na vijaye nanu yatra bhavanmayaḥ ॥8 ॥

O Lord, I have a request. I would like to roam about with You whether in Your city of bliss or outside it. There should not be even a moment when I am not glorified with the festival of Your worship. For not even a fraction of a moment should I be away from You. Let there not be even a moment when I am not able to perceive You.

भवदङ्गपरिस्रवत्सुशीतामृतपूरैर्भरिते समन्ततोऽपि ।
भवदर्चनसम्पदेह भक्तास्तव संसारसरोऽन्तरे चरन्ति ॥९॥

bhavadaṅgaparisravatsuśītā-
mṛtapūrairbharite samantato 'pi ।
bhavadarcanasampadeha bhaktā-
stava saṁsārasaro 'ntare caranti ॥9 ॥

Your devotees, wearing the ornaments of Your worship roam about the ocean of this universe that is filled from all sides by the streams of very cool nectar flowing from Your body. The heat of the fire of their sorrows has been calmed down by that nectar.

महामन्त्रतरुच्छायाशीतले त्वन्महावने ।
निजात्मनि सदा नाथ वसेयं तव पूजकः ॥१०॥

mahāmantratarucchāyāśītale tvanmahāvane ।
nijātmani sadā nātha vaseyaṁ tava pūjakaḥ ॥10 ॥

O Lord, this is my ardent desire; I would like to worship You always in my own nature, in the cool shade of the beautiful shady tree of I-consciousness. It has become cool with the removal of the torture of the differentiated perception. I-consciousness is compared to the shady trees in the dense forest of God-consciousness. In that dense forest which is my own self, I would always like to reside there just adoring You.

प्रतिवस्तु समस्तजीवतः प्रतिभासि प्रतिभामयो यथा ।
मम नाथ तथा पुरः प्रथां व्रज नेत्रत्रयशूलशोभितः ॥११ ॥

prativastu samastajīvataḥ
pratibhāsi pratibhāmayo yathā ।
mama nātha tathā puraḥ prathāṁ
vraja netratrayaśūlaśobhitaḥ ॥11 ॥

O Master, it is a fact that, to each and every being, You appear in each and every object in the form of knowledge. I do not want to have such knowledge. My desire is something else. I want You to appear before me with a physical body having three eyes, with a *triśūla* in Your hand. That is my desire. I do not want to have this knowledge (*jñāna*). Let the knowledge be possessed by those people who like it. I just want You to appear before me in physical form with three eyes and a *triśūla* in Your hand.

अभिमानचरूपहारतो ममताभक्तिभरेण कल्पितात् ।
परितोषगतः कदा भवान् मम सर्वत्र भवेद् दृशः पदम् ॥१२ ॥

abhimānacarūpahārato
mamatābhaktibhareṇa kalpitāt ।
paritoṣagataḥ kadā bhavān
mama sarvatra bhaved dṛśaḥ padam ॥12 ॥

I have got something that I want to offer to You. My offering for You is the sweet cake of the ego in me that I have acquired all through my life. I want to offer that ego in me at Your feet, I want You to be pleased with me by the intensity of my attachment to You, and I would like You to appear to me in each and every act of Yours. I would like to offer this ego to

You first and then I would create that *mamatā*, that devotional attachment for You.

The devotional attachment for God, that God is only mine, I have possessed God, this is the universal *mamatā*, unlike the crude *mamatā*, which is the individual *māyīya-mala*.

निवसन्परमामृताब्धिमध्ये भवदर्चाविधिमात्रमग्नचित्तः ।
सकलं जनवृत्तमाचरेयं रसयन्सर्वत एव किञ्चनापि ॥१३॥

nivasanparamāmṛtābdhimadhye
bhavadarcāvidhimātramagnacittaḥ ।
sakalaṁ janavṛttamācareyaṁ
rasayansarvata eva kiñcanāpi ॥13॥

There is another problem in me. I would like to reside in the centre of the ocean of Thy supreme nectar and my mind should be attached only in worshipping You, adoring You. I would like to continue to indulge in each and every worldly activity pertaining to the sense-organs, namely *śabda, sparśa, rūpa, rasa* and *gandha*, but not like the ordinary people do. All those worldly things I would function, but with a difference; whenever I would hear sound, I would hear something else; I would experience some supreme enjoyment. Whenever I would taste the enjoyment of sensual pleasures through *śabda, sparśa, rūpa, rasa* and *gandha*, I would enjoy something else, some supreme enjoyment. This is the mission of my life.

भवदीयमिहास्तु वस्तु तत्त्वं विवरीतुं क इवात्र पात्रमर्थे ।
इदमेव हि नामरूपचेष्टाद्यसमं ते हरते हरोऽसि यस्मात् ॥१४॥

bhavadīyamihāstu vastu tattvaṁ
vivarītuṁ ka ivātra pātramarthe ।
idameva hi nāmarūpaceṣṭā-
dyasamaṁ te harate haro 'si yasmāt ॥14॥

Let Thy Reality reside where it is because who can define

Your Reality? It is so great that it cannot be defined by anybody. Your name, Your form, or Your actions are also not understood. Your name is Lord Śiva, why Your name is Lord Śiva, cannot be explained. What *Śivabhāva* is there cannot be explained. Your *rūpa*, Your form, whenever You appear to Your devotees, cannot be perceived by them; they perceive nothing, they just cannot. Your action is unparalleled; there is no parallel to it because Your name itself is Hara (One who takes away all instinctive and intellective understanding from a person). No one can understand You. So let Your reality remain where it is. I don't want to define it. It can't be defined.

If Lord Śiva appears to me, I won't be able to see Him because my sphere of senses is so limited that it cannot calculate the formation of Lord Śiva. First I will perceive only light everywhere and no form but then when I persist again and again to be there, to find what it is, then slowly and slowly that formation of Lord Śiva is developed. His shining body is so great and joyous.

शान्तये न सुखलिप्सुता मनाक् भक्तिसम्भृतमदेषु तैः प्रभोः।
मोक्षमार्गणफलापि नार्थना स्मर्यते हृदयहारिणः पुरः ॥१५॥

śāntaye na sukhalipsutā manāk-
bhaktisambhṛtamadeṣu taiḥ prabhoḥ ।
mokṣamārgaphalāpi nārthanā
smaryate hṛdayahāriṇaḥ puraḥ ॥15॥

Now take the example of Your devotees. Before Your devotees are situated face to face with You, they have a programme drawn up in their minds, that as soon as You would appear to them, they would ask You for this boon to grant them peace, absolute peace, absolute joy and absolute freedom, liberation. They make a wish list of the things they have to ask You; and when You finally appear before them, they forget everything.

They are so wonderstruck. They just keep on looking at You. The intoxication of that *bhakti* is so intense and grown that they absolutely forget everything that they had decided to ask You for. That memory also vanishes from their minds; the memory that they had to ask You to liberate them from the cycle of repeated births and deaths. They cannot remember anything as they are so full of joy. You have absolutely captivated their hearts, how can they think?

जागरेतरदशाथवा परा यापि काचन मनागवस्थितेः।
भक्तिभाजनजनस्य साखिला त्वत्सनाथमनसो महोत्सवः ॥१६॥

jāgaretaradaśāthavā parā
yāpi kācana manāgavasthiteḥ ।
bhaktibhājanajanasya sākhilā
tvatsanāthamanaso mahotsavaḥ ॥16॥

Let it be the state of wakefulness, let it be the dreaming state or let it be the dreamless state; whatever state is there of the mind, for Thy devotees all these three states of the mind become the greatest festival of the world. They enjoy that festival as they find Your existence in the wakeful state, the dreaming state and the dreamless state. In the state of *turīya*, You are already there as it is.

आमनोऽक्षवलयस्य वृत्तयः सर्वतः शिथिलवृत्तयोऽपि ताः।
त्वामवाप्य दृढदीर्घसंविदो नाथ भक्तिधनसोष्मणां कथम्॥१७॥

āmano 'kṣavalayasya vṛttayaḥ
sarvataḥ śithilavṛttayo 'pi tāḥ ।
tvāmavāpya dṛḍhadīrghasaṁvido
nātha bhaktidhanasoṣmaṇāṁ katham ॥17॥

O my Master, all the actions of senses including the mind, by nature are seen flickering everywhere, always wavering and are not stable at all. But when You are achieved, the state of all the senses becomes still and steady; these are established in continuous flow of God-consciousness. I really wonder as to how these become one with God-consciousness. How this flickering state of senses takes the form of God-consciousness in Thy devotees when You are achieved, is astonishing. I cannot understand the background of this.

न च विभिन्नमसृज्यत किञ्चिदस्त्यथ सुखेतरदत्र न निर्मितम्।
अथ च दुःखि च भेदि च सर्वथाप्यसमविस्मयधाम नमोऽस्तु ते ॥१८॥

na ca vibhinnamasṛjyata kiñcid-
astyatha sukhetaradatra na nirmitam ।
atha ca duḥkhi ca bhedi ca sarvathā-
pyasamavismayadhāma namo 'stu te ॥18॥

There is great sadness, great torture in my mind about this universe that You have created. You have not created this world away from Your God-consciousness, or away from Your spiritual state. You have created this world as Your own nature. Nor does this universe exist away from You. You have not created pain in this universe. You have created only God-consciousness, super joy and supreme bliss in this universe. You have created this universe as supreme God-consciousness, as supreme joy and supreme bliss. But for me this is a great torture, I find pain everywhere in this universe, I don't find any joy in this universe. I find this universe always differentiated, away from Your nature. Your act of being is really uncontrollable and astonishing. I cannot understand You. I bow to Thee.

खरनिषेधखदामृतपूरणोच्छलितधौतविकल्पमलस्य मे।
दलितदुर्जयसंशयवैरिणस्त्वदवलोकनमस्तु निरन्तरम्॥१९॥

kharaniṣedhakhadāmṛtapūraṇo-
cchalitadhautavikalpamalasya me ।

dalitadurjayasaṁśayavairiṇa-
stvadavalokanamastu nirantaram ॥19 ॥

There is one desire in me; I would like to clean the impurity of my mind. That impurity of being away from You is a terrifying ditch that cannot be filled with anything except with the nectar of God-consciousness; otherwise this abyss will remain as it is. It will always be a torture as I would fall into that abyss every now and then, at each and every point in this universe. When that terrifying abyss of not knowing You, of being away from You, is filled by the flood of the nectar of God-consciousness, I would at the same time, on the sidelines, wash the impurity of my mind with that flood of the nectar of God-consciousness and I would be freed from the enemy of doubt, of doubting Your existence in this universe. I would like to perceive You universally, in continuity, always and everywhere.

स्फुटमाविश मामथाविशेयं सततं नाथ भवन्तमस्मि यस्मात्।
रभसेन वपुस्तवैव साक्षात्परमासत्तिगतः समर्चयेयम्॥२०॥

sphuṭamāviśa māmathāviśeyaṁ
satataṁ nātha bhavantamasmi yasmāt ।
rabhasena vapaustavaiva sākṣāt-
paramāsattigataḥ samarcayeyam ॥20 ॥

O Lord, could You do one thing for me and that is to get entry into my body? Then, after You enter my body, I would enter in You and this course must function each moment, each second, each day. Now You will ask why? What is the fun in that? What is the purpose of that? I am Yours, I am a particle of Yours. Just as a ray is one with the sun, in the same way I must be one with You. So You get entry into my body and I will get entry into Your body and vice versa. And this course of functioning of entry into each other must take place with a great zeal and with great hurry. During the course of the function of this mutual entry, I would like to worship You; I would worship You while You enter my body and I would worship You while I enter Your body. I would worship You always. This is my desire.

त्वयि न स्तुतिशक्तिरस्ति कस्याप्यथवास्त्येव यतोऽतिसुन्दरोऽसि ।
सततं पुनरर्थितं ममैतद्यदविश्रान्ति विलोकयेयमीशम् ॥२१ ॥

tvayi na stutiśaktirasti kasyā-
pyathavāstyeva yato 'tisundaro 'si ।
satataṁ punararthitaṁ mamaita-
dyadaviśrānti vilokayeyamīśam ॥21 ॥

Nobody has the power, the capacity to sing Your glory. Nobody can sing Your glory because You are absolutely away from this limited sphere of the universe. But everybody has the right to sing Your glory. Why? Because You are very beautiful. You are the most beautiful person in this universe, in all the hundred and eighteen worlds. This is Your greatness that in spite of not being capable of singing Your glory because You are so great, everybody sings Your glory because You are so beautiful, and so attractive. Everybody gets attached to You so everybody sings Your glory from his or her level of thinking. But my problem is that I just want to look at You without pause till I live in this universe. I do not want to eat; I do not want to drink; I do not want to go anywhere, I just want to keep looking at You continuously.

॥ इति श्रीमदुत्पलदेवाचार्यविरचिते श्रीशिवस्तोत्रावल्यां
आविष्कारनाम अष्टादशं स्तोत्रम् ॥

॥ *iti śrīmadutpaladevācāryaviracite śrīśivastotrāvalyāṁ*
āviṣkāranāma aṣṭādaśaṁ stotram ॥

19

उद्योतनाभिधानम्
एकोनविंशं स्तोत्रम्
Udyotanābhidhāna Stotra
The Meaning Revealed

प्रार्थनाभूमिकातीतविचित्रफलदायकः ।
जयत्यपूर्ववृत्तान्तः शिवः सत्कल्पपादपः ॥१॥

prārthanābhūmikātītavicitraphaladāyakaḥ ।
jayatyapūrvavṛttāntaḥ śivaḥ satkalpapādapaḥ ॥1॥

In this verse the author has compared Lord Śiva to the *kalpa-vṛkṣa,* that unique and special tree of heaven which bestows boons and grants wishes. It gives one everything that one asks for.

Glory be to Lord Śiva who is like a supreme *kalpa-vṛkṣa*. While the *kalpa-pādapa* of heaven grants one all one's wishes just for the asking, the supreme *kalpa-vṛkṣa* of Lord Śiva without even asking gives you fruit in all respects. It gives you everything without even asking for. Everything is bestowed by that tree but you don't know what that everything could be because your vision of understanding is always limited. The vision of an individual being will always remain limited. The *kalpa-vṛkṣa* tree can only grant you whatever you wish for whereas Lord Śiva grants those things also what one cannot even think of, leave alone asking. So this supreme tree of Lord Śiva is glorified.

सर्ववस्तुनिचयैकनिधानात्स्वात्मनस्त्वदखिलं किल लभ्यम्।
अस्य मे पुनरसौ निज आत्मा न त्वमेव घटसे परमास्ताम्॥२॥

sarvavastunicayaikanidhānāt-
svātmanastvadakhilaṁ kila labhyam ।
asya me punarasau nija ātmā
na tvameva ghaṭase paramāstām ॥2॥

O Lord, this is a fact that You are the treasure of all universal things, animate and inanimate, both. Undoubtedly You can bestow anything and everything. That is also true. But my problem is that I cannot perceive You in my worldly activities, what to talk of achieving *siddhis*, those great yogic powers.

ज्ञानकर्ममयचिद्वपुरात्मा सर्वथैष परमेश्वर एव।
स्याद्वपुस्तु निखिलेषु पदार्थेष्वेषु नाम न भवेत्किमुतान्यत्॥३॥

jñānakarmamayacidvapurātmā
sarvathaiṣa parameśvara eva ।
syādvapustu nikhileṣu padārtheṣveṣu
nāma na bhavetkimutānyat ॥3॥

O Lord, You are full of *jñāna-śakti* and *kriyā-śakti* and have pervaded the entire objective world in the form of *ātman* that is Your own *svarūpa*. In fact, this whole objective world is the extension of Your own body. If it was not so, it would not have existed.

विषमार्तिमुषानेन फलेन त्वद्दृगात्मना।
अभिलीय पथा नाथ ममास्तु त्वन्मयी गतिः॥४॥

viṣamārtimuṣānena phalena tvaddṛgātmanā ।
abhilīya pathā nātha mamāstu tvanmayī gatiḥ ॥4॥

O Lord, let me be dissolved on the path that removes all the tortures and the sorrows of this world and leads to Your abode. At the moment of understanding You I would like not to understand You at all. I would like only Your existence.

My individuality would be shattered on my journey on this path. For instance an individual is travelling on that path and all his limbs, all his faculties, all his ego, everything is gone and at the end only the residence of Lord Śiva remains. I want to be like that. I want to dissolve myself, dissolve my individuality on that path so that nothing of me remains except You and I merge into You.

भवदमलचरणचिन्तारत्नलतालङ्कृता कदा सिद्धिः।
सिद्धजनमानसानां विस्मयजननी घटेत मम भवतः ॥५॥

bhavadamalacaraṇacintāratnalatā-
laṅkṛtā kadā siddhiḥ ।
siddhajanamānasānāṁ vismayajananī
ghaṭeta mama bhavataḥ ॥5॥

O Lord, the memory of Thy pure lotus feet is just like a fine and beautiful creeper of *cintāmaṇi* jewels. When shall I achieve from that *cintāmaṇi* creeper that great power, the *siddhi* of continuous memory of Thy lotus feet in my mind? I want only the achievement of that power, the power to always remember You in continuity. When shall I attain that power which produces wonders in those great Masters (*siddha yogīs*)? When shall that power be achieved by me? Not by my credentials, but by Your grace. Not because it is due to me. I know it is not due to me. It must come to me only by Your grace, not by my qualifications.[1]

कर्हि नाथ विमलं मुखबिम्बं तावकं समवलोकयितास्मि।
यत्स्रवत्यमृतपूरमपूर्वं यो निमज्जयति विश्वमशेषम् ॥६॥

1. *Cintāmaṇi-latā* is a creeper existing in the heaven that also is like *kalpa-vṛkṣa*. It fulfils all the desires one has. He doesn't want that creeper of heaven; he only wants the continuous memory of the lotus feet of the Lord that he has likened to the wish-fulfilling *cintāmaṇi* creeper of heaven.

karhi nātha vimalaṁ mukhabimbaṁ
tāvakaṁ samavalokayitāsmi ।
yatsravatyamṛtapūramapūrvaṁ
yo nimajjayati viśvamaśeṣam ॥6 ॥

O my Master, when shall that day come when I would see Your pure face, I would perceive Your pure face? That perceiving of Your face would release a flood of supreme and unique nectar and that flood would sink all the differentiated perception of the universe.

ध्यातमात्रमुदितं तव रूपं कर्हि नाथ परमामृतपूरैः ।
पूरयेत्त्वदविभेदविमोक्षाख्यातिदूरविवराणि सदा मे ॥७ ॥

dhyātamātramuditaṁ tava rūpaṁ
karhi nātha paramāmṛtapūraiḥ ।
pūrayettvadavibhedavimokṣā-
khyātidūravivarāṇi sadā me ॥7 ॥

O my Lord, I have created in my mind some trouble which is due to being deprived of oneness with You. Being kept away from God-consciousness and being deprived of oneness with You has created a great disease of an incurable deep wound in my mind. This deep wound can be cured by only one medicine and that is Your state of being, Your state of God-consciousness. That supreme divine nectar of God-consciousness should fill that fissure and clear it. Then alone would I be relieved of this disease. When shall that cure appear to me? Dawning of God-consciousness should take place at once and not in successive steps. I must get that no sooner I would just think of You and not by practising morning and evening, day and night. By just remembering You, I must enter into that God-consciousness.

O Lord, the worldly desires often exercise so much influence over my mind and deprive it of that unique joy. So it is my ardent longing that God-consciousness should dawn on me the moment I think of You and it should wash away all those desires.

त्वदीयानुत्तररसासङ्गसन्त्यक्तचापलम् ।
नाद्यापि मे मानो नाथ कर्हि स्यादस्तु शीघ्रतः ॥८॥

tvadīyānuttararasāsaṅgasantyaktacāpalam ।
nādyāpi me māno nātha karhi syādastu śīghrataḥ ॥8॥

O my Master, my mind has not yet removed the instability from its nature even by being near to the taste of Your supreme nectar of God-consciousness. It has not become steady even now. When shall my mind become absolutely stable? Couldn't it have happened to me now? When shall my mind for ever overcome the separation from You. Let it happen quickly. Let it happen now.

मा शुष्ककटुकान्येव परं सर्वाणि सर्वदा ।
तवोपहृत्य लब्धानि द्वन्द्वान्यप्यापतन्तु मे ॥९॥

mā śuṣkakaṭukānyeva paraṁ sarvāṇi sarvadā ।
tavopahṛtya labdhāni dvandvānyapyāpatantu me ॥9॥

I do not want to discard these pairs of opposites (heat and cold; pleasure and pain, etcetera). But when these appear to me, these must not appear to me dry or in the bitter way as everybody else experiences these. I must feel God-consciousness in these. Let these things happen to me, let pain and pleasure come to me, let joy and sorrow come to me, I welcome these pairs of opposites. Let everything come to me accompanied by You, along with You.

नाथ साम्मुख्यमायान्तु विशुद्धास्तव रश्मयः ।
यावत्कायमनस्तापतमोभिः परिलुप्यताम् ॥१०॥

nātha sāmmukhyamāyāntu viśuddhāstava raśmayaḥ ।
yāvatkāyamanastāpatamobhiḥ parilupyatām ॥10॥

O my Master, let Thy rays always shine on me till the darkness and sadness of my mind and body is totally gone. Let Thy pure energies brighten Thy path for me till the darkness of the physical and mental torture is completely removed.

देव प्रसीद यावन्मे त्वन्मार्गपरिपन्थिकाः ।
परमार्थमुषो वश्या भूयासुर्गुणतस्कराः ॥११ ॥

deva prasīda yāvanme tvanmārgaparipanthikāḥ ।
paramārthamuṣo vaśyā bhūyāsurguṇataskarāḥ ॥11 ॥

O Lord, I am looted by these thieves of sense-organs. These sense-organs are great thieves and they have looted all the wealth of my spirituality. They not only obstruct, misguide and divert me from Thy path but also steal the wealth of God-consciousness.

O Lord, there is a request to You from my side. You have to be there on my side with a helping hand until these come under my control. Please do me that favour. I will be ruined otherwise.

त्वद्भक्तिसुधासारैर्मानसमापूर्यतां ममाशु विभो ।
यावदिमा उह्यन्तां निःशेषासारवासनाः प्लुत्वा ॥१२ ॥

tvadbhaktisudhāsārair-
mānasamāpūryatāṁ mamāśu vibho ।
yāvadimā uhyantāṁ
niḥśeṣāsāravāsanāḥ plutvā ॥12 ॥

O Lord, let the dry lake of my mind be quickly filled with the streams of the nectar of Thy devotion so that the insignificant birds of the limited worldly desires fly away from the fear of getting drowned and make room for Thee, the swan. With the dawning of God-consciousness, all the desires will melt away.

The author has likened the limited desires existing in individuals, for instance, "I want a child, I want a car, I want a good job," etcetera to the ordinary birds roaming uselessly about the bed of a lake without water. In the rainy season, as the lake gets filled, there is no room for the ordinary birds which are forced to fly away making way for the swans that move into the lake and add to its splendour.

मोक्षदशायां भक्तिस्त्वयि कुत इव मर्त्यधर्मिणोऽपि न सा।
राजति ततोऽनुरूपामारोपय सिद्धिभूमिकामज माम्॥१३॥

mokṣadaśāyāṁ bhaktistvayi kuta
iva martyadharmiṇo 'pi na sā ।
rājati tato 'nurūpāmāropaya
siddhibhūmikāmaja mām ॥13॥

Just to achieve the state of liberation means Thy devotion. How can that devotion be achieved by an individual? Thy devotion is so unlimited and the devotion of individual is very limited. How will that devotion rise in a limited being? I don't want such devotion which is limited.

O Lord, You are so great and my devotion is so low, how can that devotion carry me to that state of Your being. Take me up to that level so that my devotion also becomes divine. This is my request.

There are such devotees found in this universe who devote only one hour of meditation and get entry in *samādhi,* and there are such devotees also who devote their whole lifetime but never enter into *samādhi*. That devotion is no devotion at all. So that supreme devotion does not suit that limited being. So let me become unlimited being. Let me ascend onto the supreme universal state of life and then I can assign my time to Your devotion. That devotion will shine.

सिद्धिलवलाभलुब्धं मामवलेपेन मा विभो संस्थाः ।
क्षामस्त्वद्भक्तिमुखे प्रोल्लसदणिमादिपक्षतो मोक्षः ॥१४ ॥

siddhilavalābhalubdhaṁ
māmavalepena mā vibho saṁsthāḥ ।
kṣāmastvadbhaktimukhe
prollasadaṇimādipakṣato mokṣaḥ ॥14 ॥

O Lord Śiva, let me not get attached to these limited yogic powers (*siddhis*). Let me not ever get lured by those yogic powers. Achievement of the yogic powers in comparison to Your devotion is inferior thus not worthwhile. So let me not get entangled in those yogic powers. Attaining of liberation through achievement of yogic powers is a very inferior way of achieving liberation. Liberation without even touching the field of these yogic powers is the divine achievement of liberation.

दासस्य मे प्रसीदतु भगवानेतावदेव ननु याचे ।
दाता त्रिभुवननाथो यस्य न तन्मादृशां दृशो विषयः ॥१५ ॥

dāsasya me prasīdatu
bhagavānetāvadeva nanu yāce ।
dātā tribhuvananātho
yasya na tanmādṛśāṁ dṛśo viṣayaḥ ॥15 ॥

O Lord, let Thee become pleased with me who is Thy slave. You are the giver; You are the bestower of everything. You are the ruler of all the three worlds and You are my Master. But so far I have not seen You. It is a great wonder to me. You take care of me; You are the giver of the luxury of all the three worlds but You are not perceived by me. I crave only for this achievement, just be pleased with me.

त्वद्वपुःस्मृतिसुधारसपूर्णे मानसे तव पदाम्बुजयुग्मम् ।
मामके विकसदस्तु सदैव प्रस्रवन्मधु किमप्यतिलोकम् ॥१६ ॥

tvadvapuḥsmṛtisudhārasapūrṇe
mānase tava padāmbujayugmam ।
māmake vikasadastu sadaiva
prasravanmadhu kimapyatilokam ॥16 ॥

There is one desire in me. My mind is always filled with the nectar of Thy memory. My mind has already become divine by Your constant remembrance. But there is one problem in my mind. In a lake one usually finds lotuses, but there is not even one lotus in this lake of my mind, nothing is growing there. There should be at least two lotuses in that lake and that is Your two divine feet. Let Thy two lotus feet grow in the lake of my mind and let those lotuses always drip that supreme nectar of God-consciousness on the surface of my mind.

अस्ति मे प्रभुरसौ जनकोऽथ त्र्यम्बकोऽथ जननी च भवानी।
न द्वितीय इह कोऽपि ममास्तीत्येव निर्वृततमो विचरेयम्॥१७॥

asti me prabhurasau janako 'tha
tryambako 'tha jananī ca bhavānī ।
na dvitīya iha ko 'pi mamāstī-
tyeva nirvṛtatamo vicareyam ॥17 ॥

There is one desire in me and that is the last desire. I want You as my Master and as my father and Pārvatī as my mother. No one else is my father and no one else is my mother. Only Lord Śiva is my father and Pārvatī my mother. In this way let me roam about this world filled with satisfaction, the highest satisfaction.

॥ इति श्रीमदुत्पलदेवाचार्यविरचिते श्रीशिवस्तोत्रावल्यां
उद्योतनाभिधानं एकोनविंशं स्तोत्रम्॥

॥ *iti śrīmadutpaladevācāryaviracite śrīśivastotrāvalyāṁ*
udyotanābhidhānaṁ ekonaviṁśaṁ stotram ॥

20

चर्वणाभिधानं विंशं स्तोत्रम्

Carvaṇābhidhāna Stotra

Savouring the Meaning

THE last chapter is nominated as *Carvaṇābhidhāna; carvaṇā* means tasting the real taste inside, and *abhidhānam* means speaking out.

नाथं त्रिभुवननाथं भूतिसितं त्रिनयनं त्रिशूलधरम् ।
उपवीतीकृतभोगिनमिन्दुकलाशेखरं वन्दे ॥१॥

nāthaṁ tribhuvananāthaṁ bhūtisitaṁ trinayanaṁ triśūladharam ।
upavītīkṛtabhoginamindukalāśekharaṁ vande ॥1॥

I bow to my Master who is the Master of all the three worlds, white with the smearing of ash, who has three eyes, who carries a trident, who wears Vāsukī and other snakes as the sacred thread and who sports the crescent moon on His forehead.

नौमि निजतनुविनिस्सरदंशुकपरिवेषधवलपरिधानम् ।
विलसत्कपालमालाकल्पितनृत्तोत्सवाकल्पम् ॥२॥

naumi nijatanuvinissaradaṁśukapariveṣadhavalaparidhānam ।
vilasatkapālamālākalpitanṛttotsavākalpam ॥2॥

I bow to that Lord Śiva, who by His own nature is absolutely shining, donning the robes of a bright sparkling halo; who decorates Himself with the glittering garland of skulls at the time of the festival of *tāṇḍava-nṛtya.*

वन्दे तान् दैवतं येषां हरश्चेष्टा हरोचिताः ।
हरैकप्रवणाः प्राणाः सदा सौभाग्यसद्मनाम् ॥३॥

vande tān daivataṁ yeṣāṁ haraścesṭā harocitāḥ ।
haraikapravaṇā prāṇāḥ sadā saubhāgyasadmanām ॥3॥

I always bow to those devotees of Lord Śiva who are fortunate to have received the highest glory; whose all endeavours, actions and desires are directed towards the attainment of Lord Śiva and whose entire lifetime is spent in the devotion of Lord Śiva.

क्रीडितं तव महेश्वरतायाः पृष्ठतोऽन्यदिदमेव यथैतत् ।
इष्टमात्रघटितेष्ववदानेष्वात्मना परमुपायमुपैमि ॥४॥

krīḍitaṁ tava maheśvaratāyāḥ pṛṣṭhato 'nyadidameva yathaitat ।
iṣṭamātraghaṭiteṣvavadāneṣvātmanā paramupāyamupaimi ॥4॥

O Lord, You are the supreme ruler of this universe. The other aspect of Your pastime is that with Your grace, after getting absorbed in Your God-consciousness, even I, if I just wish, can spontaneously perform those five classes of activities like You do. With Your grace, even I find myself capable of performing those fivefold activities which are normally Your jurisdiction; five divine actions of *sṛṣṭi, sthiti, saṁhāra, tirobhava* and *anugraha.*

त्वद्धाम्नि विश्ववन्द्येऽस्मिन्नियति क्रीडने सति ।
तव नाथ कियान् भूयान्नानन्दरससम्भवः ॥५॥

tvaddhāmni viśvavandye 'sminniyati krīḍane sati ।
tava nātha kiyān bhūyānnānandarasasambhavaḥ ॥5॥

O Lord, You are the only being worth worshipping in this universe; You are the only one capable of being worshipped in this entire universe. In Your abode of God-consciousness, the creation of this universe is just a matter of play for You. What can be said of the greatness of the nectar of the unique bliss created by Your entire *svarūpa*? It is incomprehensible. How beautiful will be the manifestation of the unparalleled joy through the perception of Your complete *svarūpa*? It will indeed be wonderful.

कथं स सुभगो मा भूद्यो गौर्या वल्लभो हरः ।
हरोऽपि मा भूदथ किं गौर्याः परमवल्लभः ॥६ ॥

kathaṁ sa subhago mā bhūdyo gauryā vallabho haraḥ ।
haro 'pi mā bhūdatha kiṁ gauryāḥ paramavallabhaḥ ॥6 ॥

Lord Śiva is most fortunate because He is embraced by such a great lady like Pārvatī. But who else could have taken Her in arms except Lord Śiva. Lord Śiva is the only right person to take Her into His arms. Lord Śiva is lucky as He is the beloved of Pārvatī. He is so beautiful that He enchants everyone and He is desired by everyone.

ध्यानामृतमयं यस्य स्वात्ममूलमनश्वरम् ।
संविल्लतास्तथारूपास्तस्य कस्यापि सत्तरोः ॥७ ॥

dhyānāmṛtamayaṁ yasya svātmamūlamanaśvaram ।
saṁvillatāstathārūpāstasya kasyāpi sattaroḥ ॥7 ॥

The devotee of Lord Śiva is like a beautiful glorious tree whose roots are soaked with the nectar of Thy meditation, because those devotees always meditate on Your form, Your being. So the roots of that tree are always soaked with the nectar of meditation. The branches, fruits and whatever that tree later bears, are also soaked with that nectar. Knowledge pertaining to those devotees is also like that supreme nectar of meditation.

भक्तिकण्डूसमुल्लासावसरे परमेश्वर ।
महानिकषपाषाणस्थूणा पूजैव जायते ॥८ ॥

bhaktikaṇḍūsamullāsāvasare parameśvara ।
mahānikaṣapāṣāṇasthūṇā pūjaiva jāyate ॥8 ॥

O Lord Śiva, when a devotee of Thee has created the itching sensation of Thy devotion, Your presence alone can subside and relieve that. Whenever the itch of devotion rises in Thy devotees, whenever the pitch of this urge rises, the worship of Lord Śiva becomes the pillar of whetting stone to rub against and calm down that itch. That itching sensation will never be removed unless the worship of Lord Śiva takes place. *Samāveśa* is the only solution to the enhanced pitch of the itch of devotion. The severity of the sensation of itching calms down by rubbing against a pillar. In a similar manner only when the devotion for Lord Śiva reaches that pitch, does the devotee qualify for the worship of Lord Śiva; *samāveśa.*

सदा सृष्टिविनोदाय सदा स्थितिसुखासिने ।
सदा त्रिभुवनाहारतृप्ताय स्वामिने नमः ॥९ ॥

sadā sṛṣṭivinodāya sadā sthitisukhāsine ।
sadā tribhuvanāhāratṛptāya svāmine namaḥ ॥9 ॥

I bow to my Master who always enjoys the act of creating this whole universe, who is always absorbed in protecting it and who is always bent upon destroying it. This is a great satisfaction to Lord Śiva that He creates, then He protects and then He destroys. Then He creates afresh. So destruction is a must. There is no loss of energy. He is only vibrating in His own nature.

Without destruction freshness won't be there. For instance I am in my seventies, bodily I feel weak though internally I am not weak. I am just like Lord Śiva, filled with energy. So that energy will be again charged when this body is destroyed and one would be again energetic like a young boy. So energy is never lost.

न क्वापि गत्वा हित्वापि न किंचिंदिदमेव ये ।
भव्यं त्वद्धाम पश्यन्ति भव्यास्तेभ्यो नमो नमः ॥१० ॥

na kvāpi gatvā hitvāpi na kiñcididameva ye ।
bhavyaṁ tvaddhāma paśyanti bhavyāstebhyo namo namaḥ ॥10 ॥

I bow to those fortunate souls who are Thy devotees. They don't go to forests to maintain their penance; they don't go to woods for seclusion. They don't abandon any pleasure or any worldly enjoyment. Those devotees experience this very world to be filled with great energy of God-consciousness. I bow to those devotees. I don't bow to those devotees who detach themselves from worldly activities and feel this universe to be filled with torture. I bow to those devotees who feel and experience in this very universe itself that it is not torture or crisis, it is not sadness or pain, but that it is filled with actual bliss; and I bow to those devotees who perceive it like that.

भक्तिलक्ष्मीसमृद्धनां किमन्यदुपयाचितम् ।
एतया वा दरिद्राणां किमन्यदुपयाचितम् ॥११ ॥

bhaktilakṣmīsamṛddhānāṁ kimanyadupayācitam ।
etayā vā daridrāṇāṁ kimanyadupayācitam ॥11 ॥

Those who are glorified with the wealth of Thy devotion, what else do they need? They have got everything. Those who have accomplished the wealth of Thy devotion have no longing for anything else. What else is there to ask for? They are glorified with the real wealth. On the contrary, those persons who are deprived of this wealth of Thy devotion, even if they earn billions of dollars, they have earned nothing. They always remain paupers. On the other hand, those who have thy devotion even if they have no money, they are glorified with real wealth.

दुःखान्यपि सुखायन्ते विषमप्यमृतायते ।
मोक्षायते च संसारो यत्र मार्गः स शाङ्करः ॥१२॥

duḥkhānyapi sukhāyante viṣamapyamṛtāyate ।
mokṣāyate ca saṁsāro yatra mārgaḥ sa śāṅkaraḥ ॥12॥

On that path where various pains are transformed into pleasures, where the poison also takes the form of nectar and on that path where this very universe which otherwise is the only cause of getting you entangled in the wheel of repeated births and deaths, becomes the means of liberating you, it liberates you. On that path this very universe becomes the means of attaining *mokṣa*. The universe which was responsible for entangling you in the cycle of repeated births and deaths, liberates you now. That is the path of Śaivism; that is the pathway of Śiva.

मूले मध्येऽवसाने च नास्ति दुःखं भवज्जुषाम् ।
तथापि वयमीशान सीदामः कथमुच्यताम् ॥१३॥

mūle madhye 'vasāne ca nāsti duḥkhaṁ bhavajjuṣām ।
tathāpi vayamīśāna sīdāmaḥ kathamucyatām ॥13॥

O glorified Lord, there is a problem in me. You have announced that Your devotees will never experience pain in the beginning, the middle or the end, and that they would always remain blissful. Your devotees have Your assurance that for them, there is no possibility of pain either in the beginning, the centre or the end. But the problem with me is something else. O Lord, I have experienced only pain in my whole life and am still experiencing pain. Please tell me the cause. I am also Your devotee but I am always tortured by the continuous pain in this world. Why should it happen? Please explain it to me.

ज्ञानयोगादिनान्येषामप्यपेक्षितुर्महति ।
प्रकाशः स्वैरिणामेव भवान् भक्तिमतां प्रभो ॥१४॥

jñānayogādinānyeṣāmapyapekṣiturmahati ।
prakāśaḥ svairiṇāmeva bhavān bhaktimatāṁ prabho ॥14॥

O Lord, for experiencing Your blissful state, *yogī*s have to adopt various means and take the help of *jñāna, yoga,* practice of meditation, discipline, *yama, niyama, āsana, prāṇāyāma, pratyāhāra, dhāraṇā,* etcetera. They have to adopt all limbs of *yoga* and then only they can experience the bliss of Thy nature. This is a fact. But there is an extraordinary thing about Your class of devotees. Without the adjustment of *jñāna, yoga, dhyāna, dhāraṇā, samādhi,* etcetera, they are glorified in possessing that supreme bliss of Your consciousness. They don't have to adopt any means. Even in the course of their routine independent self-willed conduct, they always experience the bliss of Thy consciousness spontaneously. This is the difference between the ordinary *yogī*s and Thy devotees.

भक्तानां नार्तयो नाप्यस्त्याध्यानं स्वात्मनस्तव ।
तथाप्यस्ति शिवेत्येतत्किमप्येषां बहिर्मुखे ॥१५॥

bhaktānāṁ nārtayo nāpyastyādhyānaṁ svātmanastava ।
tathāpyasti śivetyetatkimapyeṣāṁ bahirmukhe ॥15॥

Thy devotees have no problems nor is there any desire in them to search for You. They don't desire to seek You. They already exist in Your consciousness so there is no need to search for You or to achieve You. You are always there. Although this is a fact about Your devotees, yet the sound of 'O Lord, O Lord' leaks automatically from their mouth even during the course of routine activities like moving around here and there. Otherwise there is no problem in them and they are always situated in Your consciousness, still there is an automatic utterance of 'Śiva, Śiva'. . . .

सर्वाभासावभासो यो विमर्शवलितोऽखिलम् ।
अहमेतदिति स्तौमि तां क्रियाशक्तिमीश ते ॥१६॥

sarvābhāsāvabhāso yo vimarśavalito 'khilam ।
ahametaditi staumi tāṁ kriyāśaktimīśa te ॥16 ॥

O Lord Śiva, that supreme I-consciousness which lightens this whole universe, which is the cause of the shining of this whole universe, which illuminates all cognitions, in other words, This I-consciousness is Your *kriyā-śakti*, Your energy of action.

There are five energies of action of Lord Śiva. First energy of action is the energy of creating, the creating act. Second energy of action is the protecting energy, the protecting act. The third energy is the act of destroying this whole universe. The fourth energy is the energy of concealing this universe. The fifth energy is the revealing energy, when He reveals His own nature. The author here refers to the fifth energy. This *kriyā-śakti* is *anugraha-śakti*. That is the act of grace.

In creating He doesn't create this universe for creating, He creates this universe to bestow grace on it. He doesn't protect this universe just to protect it; He protects this universe just to reveal His nature to it. He destroys this universe just to reveal His nature to it. He conceals this universe just to reveal His nature to it and in the end He reveals his nature.

In his commentary of *Parātriṁśikā*, Ācārya Abhinavagupta comments that although He performs five acts, yet He actually functions only the fifth act. It is only *anugraha* that He does. He creates, He destroys, and He punishes just to bestow grace. When He punishes, He doesn't punish for the sake of punishment, He punishes for bestowing grace.

वर्तन्ते जन्तवोऽशेषा अपि ब्रह्मेन्द्रविष्णवः ।
ग्रसमानास्ततो वन्दे देव विश्वं भवन्मयम् ॥१७ ॥

vartante jantavo 'śeṣā api brahmendraviṣṇavaḥ ।
grasamānāstato vande deva viśvaṁ bhavanmayam ॥17 ॥

In fact, this whole universe has not come out from Brahmā. It is not like Brahmā because if it were like Brahmā this whole universe ought to have always been entangled in reproduction activity alone. But it is not so. Similarly if it was like Viṣṇu, it would have been likewise. This universe is like Śiva, just eating, all the time. Everyone is eating, consuming something or the other all the time. Brahmā, Viṣṇu, Indra, all *deva*s and all the individual beings are just bent upon eating. This eating, destroying, taking in, absorbing, etcetera is the sign of Lord Śiva. The act of absorption takes place in this whole universe day and night, in all the senses, all the time.

O Lord, this is why I bow to this whole universe which is just one with You.

(Watch the birds, they are always on the look out for food, and once located, they fly to that point and eat. Look at a baby; it only eats right from the very time of its birth. The baby does not have inclination for reproduction but for eating it has and this is the sign of Lord Śiva.)

सतो विनाशसम्बन्धान्मत्परं निखिलं मृषा ।
एवमेवोद्यते नाथ त्वया संहारलीलया ॥१८ ॥

sato vināśasambandhānmatparaṁ nikhilaṁ mṛṣā ।
evamevodyate nātha tvayā saṁhāralīlayā ॥18 ॥

O my Master, at the time of destroying this whole universe, You actually teach us a lesson and that lesson is "whatever is created will be destroyed in the end, whatever has existed will be destroyed. It is all a dream except Me. Only I am detached from this position because I am not born, I will not die. Whatever is born will die." This is what You teach through Your play of destruction.

ध्यातमात्रमुपतिष्ठत एव त्वद्वपुर्वरद भक्तिधनानाम् ।
अप्यचिन्त्यमखिलाद्भुतचिन्ताकर्तृतां प्रति च ते विजयन्ते ॥१९ ॥

dhyātamātramupatiṣṭhata eva
tvadvapurvarada bhaktidhanānām ।
apyacintyamakhilādbhutacintā-
kartṛtāṁ prati ca te vijayante ॥19 ॥

There are two classes of Your devotees. One class of Your devotees is Śaivite devotees, they are the real devotees; the other class comprises the Vedāntin or Vaiṣṇavite devotees who are not real devotees of Thee. They are Your devotees because anyone who is devoted to Viṣṇu is devoted to Lord Śiva, one who is devoted to Brahmā is devoted to Lord Śiva because Lord Śiva is the glory existing in Viṣṇu and Brahmā. They have no personal glory of their own. Their glory is borrowed from Lord Śiva's glory.

O bestower of boons, O Lord Śiva, those devotees who possess the wealth of Thy devotion, for them Your form, Your *svarūpa* shines not by adopting the means of the system of *yoga, kriyā-yoga* or *dhyāna-yoga* or *bhakti-yoga,* etcetera. They just begin to think of You and get into God-consciousness. At the time of beginning of their meditation, You are just there, spontaneously, not in successive progressive steps. This is true of those devotees of Thee who are Śaivite devotees. For Vaiṣṇavite devotees and Brahmā's devotees, even if they devote their whole lifetime to meditation, still they cannot perceive You, they will still remain away from You.

तावकभक्तिरसासवसेकादिव सुखितमर्ममण्डलस्फुरितैः ।
नृत्यति वीरजनो निशि वेतालकुलैः कृतोत्साहः ॥२० ॥

tāvakabhaktirasāsavasekādiva
sukhitamarmamaṇḍalasphuritaiḥ ।
nṛtyati vīrajano niśi
vetālakulaiḥ kṛtotsāhaḥ ॥20 ॥

O Lord, glorified and shining with the sprinkling of the nectar of Thy devotion; having overcome the multitude of the nooses of the differentiated perception; inspired by the collection of the ghosts of the sense-organs; with the lotuses of their hearts fully bloomed; having conquered the universe; Thy devotees dance in ecstasy in the dark night of the illusion of *māyā* itself. Those heroes drink the alcohol of thy devotion encouraged by those nine ghosts, and they dance in the graveyard.

आरब्धा भवदभिनुतिरमुना येनाङ्गकेन मम शम्भो ।
तेनापर्यन्तमिमं कालं दृढमखिलमेव भविषीष्ट ॥२१ ॥

ārabdhā bhavadabhinutira-
munā yenāṅgakena mama śambho ।
tenāparyantamimaṁ kālaṁ
dṛḍhamakhilameva bhaviṣīṣṭa ॥21 ॥

In the end there is one request before you, O Lord: I have composed these glorious songs, with what ambition have I composed them, that does not have to be known. My only desire and request is that you should bestow me the sensation that I should always sing your glory for my whole lifetime.

॥ इति श्रीमदुत्पलदेवाचार्यविरचिते श्रीशिवस्तोत्रावल्यां
चर्वणाभिधानं विंशं स्तोत्रम् ॥

॥ *iti śrīmadutpaladevācāryaviracite śrīśivastotrāvalyāṁ*
carvaṇābhidhānaṁ viṁśaṁ stotram ॥

॥ इति श्रीमदुत्पलदेवाचार्यविरचिता श्रीशिवस्तोत्रावली समाप्ता ॥

॥ *iti śrīmadutpaladevācāryaviracitā*
śrīśivastotrāvalī samāptā ॥

श्लोकानुक्रमणिका

अ

अग्नीषोमरविब्रह्म 2.1

अणिमादिषु मोक्षान्ते 1.25

अधिष्ठायैव विषयानिमाः 17.16

अनन्तानन्दसरसी 1.9

अनन्तानन्दसिन्धोस्ते 1.6

अनुभूयासमीशान 17.19

अन्तरप्यति 13.2

अन्तरुल्लसदच्छाच्छ 17.26

अन्तर्भक्तिचमत्कार 5.15

अन्यवेद्यमणु 13.9

अन्ये भ्रमन्ति भगवन्नात्म 10.12

अपरिमितरूपमहं 12.19

अपि कदाचन 8.9

अपि भावगणादपीन्द्रिय 12.2

अपि लब्धभवद्भावः 5.16

अपीत्वापि भवद्भक्तिसुधा 10.13

अप्यसम्बद्धरूपार्चा 17.41

अप्युपार्जितमहं त्रिषु लोके 4.23

अप्युपायक्रमप्राप्यः 16.2

अभिमानचरूपहारतो 18.12

अलमाक्रन्दितैरन्यै 3.21

अविभागो भवानेव 10.22

अशेषपूजासत्कोशे 17.44

अशेषभुवनाहारनित्यतृप्तः 5.14

अशेषवासनाग्रन्थि 17.15

अशेष-विश्वखचित 3.3

अशेषविषया 9.14

अस्ति मे प्रभुरसौ 19.17

अस्मिन्नेव जगत्यन्त 16.23

अहमित्यमुतो 12.18

अहो कोऽपि जयत्येष 17.1

अहो भक्तिभरोदारचेतसां 17.24

अहो सुधानिधे स्वामिन् 5.4

आ

आकांक्षणीयमपरं 5.17

आत्मसात्कृत 9.12

आत्मा मम भवद्भक्ति 1.2

आनन्दबाष्पपूर 9.16
आनन्दरसबिन्दुस्ते 10.5
आमनोऽक्षवलयस्य 18.17
आमूलाद् वाग्लता सेयं 1.13
आरब्धा भवदभिनुति 20.21
आवेदकादा व वेद्याद्येषां 16.27
आसतां तावदन्यानि 3.16
आसुरर्षिजनादस्मिन्न 3.2
आस्तां भवत्प्रभावेण 10.10

ई

ईश्वरमभयमुदारं 9.6
ईश्वरोऽहमहमेव 13.4
ईहितं न बत 13.19

उ

उत्तमः पुरुषोऽन्योस्ति 3.14
उपचारपदं पूजा 17.40
उपयान्तु विभो 8.11
उपहासैकसारेऽस्मि 2.18
उल्लङ्घ्य विविधदैवत 4.2

ए

एतन्मम न त्विदमिति 7.2
एषा पेशलिमा नाथ 17.45

ऐ

ऐक्यसंविदमृता 12.17

क

कण्ठकोणविनि 13.17
कथं ते जायेरन्कथमपि च ते 12.3
कथं स सुभगो मा 20.6
कदा कामपि 9.7
कदाचित्क्वापि लभ्योऽसि 1.16
कदा नवरसार्द्रार्द्र 9.1
कदा मे स्याद्विभो 9.5
कर्हि नाथ विमलं 19.6
कां भूमिकां नाधिशेषे 6.9
का न शोभा न को ह्लादः 17.25
कामक्रोधाभिमानै 17.47
कायवाङ्मनसैर्यत्र 6.3
किमपि नाथ कदाचन चेतसि 5.26
किमियं न सिद्धिरतुला 15.13
किमिव च लभ्यते बत न 11.10
किल यदैव शिवाध्वनि तावके 4.21
कीर्त्यश्चिन्तापदं मृग्यः 16.18
केव न स्याद्दशा तेषां 3.10
कोऽपि देव हृदि तेषु तावको 4.11
कोऽप्यसौ जयति 17.30
क्रीडितं तव महेश्वरतायाः 20.4
क्वचिदेव भवान् 18.2
क्व नु रागादिषु रागः 5.20
क्षणमपीह न तावकदासतां 4.18
क्षणमात्रमपीशान 6.1
क्षणमात्रसुखेनापि 10.4

ख

खरनिषेधखदा 18.19

ग

गर्जामि बत नृत्यामि 3.11

गलतु विकल्प 7.3

गाढगाढभवद् 9.20

गाढानुरागवशतो 9.3

गुह्ये भक्तिः परे 16.24

च

चपलमसि यदपि मानस 4.1

चराचरपितः स्वामिन् 15.7

चित्तभूभृद्भुवि विभो 5.6

चित्रं निसर्गतो नाथ 1.26

ज

जगतोऽन्तरतो 18.1

जगत्क्षोभैकजनके 17.10

जगदिदमथ वा 11.1

जगद्विलयसञ्जात 17.14

जडे जगति चिद्रूपः 3.20

जपतां जुह्वतां स्नातां 17.8

जय कष्टतपःक्लिष्टमुनि 14.21

जय क्षीरोदपर्यस्तज्योत्स्ना 14.6

जय जयभाजन 14.24

जय जाम्बूनदोदग्र 14.20

जयत्येष भवद्भक्तिभाजां 17.48

जय त्रैलोक्यनाथैक 14.3

जय त्रैलोक्यसर्गेच्छा 14.13

जय देव नमो नमोऽस्तु ते 2.29

जय देहाद्रिकुञ्जान्त 14.19

जयन्ति ते जगद्वन्द्या 3.15

जयन्ति भक्तिपीयूष 1.5

जयन्तोऽपि हसन्त्येते 16.3

जय ब्रह्मादिदेवेश 14.11

जय भक्तिरसार्द्रार्द्र 14.10

जय मूर्तत्रिशक्त्या 14.4

जय मोहान्धकारान्ध 14.18

जय लक्ष्मीनिधानस्य 14.1

जय विश्वक्षयोच्चण्ड 14.16

जय शोभाशतस्य 14.5

जय सर्गस्थितिध्वंस 14.23

जय सर्वजगन्न्यस्त 14.12

जय स्वसम्पत्प्रसर 14.22

जय स्वेच्छातपोवेश 14.9

जय हेलावितीर्णै 14.17

जयाक्रमसमाक्रान्त 14.14

जयाक्षयैकशीतांशु 14.7

जयाधराङ्गसंस्पर्श 14.8

जयानुकम्पादि 14.15

जयैकरुद्रैकशिव 14.2

जागरेतरदशाथवा 18.16

ज्ञानकर्ममय	19.3	त्वत्कर्णदेशमधिशय्य	11.9
ज्ञानयोगादिनान्येषा	20.14	त्वत्पादपद्मसम्पर्कमात्र	5.1
ज्ञानस्य परमा	9.9	त्वत्पादपूजासम्भोग	17.27
ज्योतिरस्ति कथयापि	15.17	त्वत्पादसंस्पर्शसुधासरसो	5.12
त		त्वत्प्रकाशवपुषो न विभिन्नं	4.6
तटेष्वेव परिभ्रान्तैः	2.14	त्वत्प्रभुत्वपरि	8.2
तत्किं नाथ भवेन्न यत्र	11.12	त्वत्प्रलापमय	13.18
तत्तदपूर्वामोद	5.19	त्वत्प्राणिताः स्फुरन्तीमे	10.18
तत्तदिन्द्रिय	13.8	त्वदविभेदमतेरपरं तु किं	4.17
तत्र तत्र विषये बहिर्विभा	13.12	त्वदीयानुत्तरसासङ्ग	19.8
तत्त्वतोऽशेषजन्तूनां	9.8	त्वदृते निखिलं विश्वं	10.9
तवेश भक्तेरर्चायां	16.13	त्वदेकनाथो भगवन्निय	5.3
तस्मिन्पदे भवन्तं	7.7	त्वदेकरक्तस्त्व	9.2
ता एव परमर्थ्यन्ते	1.23	त्वद्धाम्नि चिन्मये स्थित्वा	17.11
तावकाङ्घ्रिकमलासनलीना	4.5	त्वद्धाम्नि विश्ववन्द्ये	20.5
तावके वपुषि	13.3	त्वद्ध्यानदर्शनस्पर्शतृषि	17.28
तावकभक्तिरसासव	20.20	त्वन्मयोऽस्मि	11.5
ते जयन्ति मुखमण्डले भ्रमन्	4.14	त्वद्भक्तितपन	7.6
तेनैव दृष्टोऽसि भवद्दर्शना	10.7	त्वद्भक्तिसुधासारै	19.12
त्रिभुवनाधिपति	11.3	त्वद्वपुःस्मृति	19.16
त्रिमलक्षालिनो ग्रन्थाः	15.1	त्वद्विलोकनसमुत्कचेतसो	12.6
त्वं भक्तया प्रीयसे भक्तिः	16.21	त्वत्पादपद्मसंस्पर्शा	5.5
त्वच्चरणभावनामृत	7.5	त्वत्पादसंस्पर्शसुधा	5.12
त्वच्चिदानन्दजलधेश्च्युताः	3.6	त्वमेवात्मेश सर्वस्य	1.7
त्वज्जुषां त्वयि कयापि लीलया	4.12	त्वया निराकृतं सर्वं	12.12

त्वयि न स्तुतिशक्तिरस्ति 18.21
त्वयि रागरसे नाथ 3.7
त्वय्यानन्दसरस्वति 7.1
त्वामगाधमविकल्प 13.20

द

दक्षिणाचारसाराय 2.19
दर्शनपथमुपयातो 12.16
दासधाम्नि विनि 13.10
दासस्य मे 19.15
दुःखागमोऽपि भूयान्मे 16.20
दुःखान्यपि सुखायन्ते 20.12
दुःखापि वेदना भक्तिमतां 16.11
दुर्जयानामनन्तानां 3.13
दृष्टार्थ एव भक्तानां 17.20
देव दुःखान्यशेषाणि 10.16
देवदेव भवद 13.5
देव प्रसीद यावन्मे 19.11
देहभूमिषु तथा 8.4

ध

धर्माधर्मात्मनोरन्तः 15.6
ध्यातमात्रमुदितं 19.7
ध्यातमात्रमुपतिष्ठत 20.19
ध्यानामृतमयं यस्य 20.7
ध्यानायासतिरस्कार 17.4
ध्यायते तदनु 13.6

न

न किल पश्यति सत्यमयं जन 4.19
न कश्चिदेव लोकानां 16.1
न क्वापि गत्वा हित्वापि 20.10
न च विभिन्नमसृज्यत 18.18
न तदा न सदा न चैकदे 12.5
न ध्यायतो न जपतः 1.1
न प्राप्यमस्ति भक्तानां 17.23
नमः सततबद्धाय 2.17
नमः सुकृतसंभार 2.10
नमश्चराचराकार 2.11
नमस्तेभ्यो विभो येषां 17.31
नमो निकृत्तनिःशेष 2.5
नमो मोहमहाध्वान्त 11.15
न योगो न तपो नार्चा 1.18
न विरक्तो न चापीशो 15.4
न सा मतिरुदेति या 12.22
न सोढव्यमवश्यं ते 10.1
नाथं त्रिभुवननाथं भूतिसितं 20.1
नाथ कदा स 9.19
नाथ ते भक्तजनता 15.11
नाथ लोकाभिमाना 9.13
नाथ विद्युदिव भाति विभा ते 4.8
नाथ वेद्यक्षये केन 1.8
नाथ साम्मुख्यमायान्तु 19.10

नान्यद्वेद्यं क्रिया यत्र 3.12
निजनिजेषु पदेषु 8.5
निर्विकल्पभवदीयदर्शन 12.7
निर्विकल्पो महानन्दपूर्णो 6.4
निवसन्परमामृता 18.13
निवेदितमुपादत्स्व 5.13
निःशब्दं निर्विकल्पं च 12.14
नो जानते सुभगमप्यवलेपवन्तो 18.3
नौमि निजतनुविनिस्सरदंशुक 20.2

प

परमामृतकोशाय 2.25
परमामृतसान्द्राय 2.3
परमेश्वरता 16.30
परमेश्वर तेषु 8.12
परानन्दामृतमये दृष्टेऽपि 10.15
परितः प्रसरच्छुद्ध 9.11
परिपूर्णानि शुद्धानि 17.43
परिसमाप्तमिवोग्रमिदं जगद् 4.15
पशुजनसमान 9.17
पादपङ्कजरसं तव केचिद् 4.7
पानाशनप्रसाधन 16.29
पूजां केचन मन्यन्ते 17.37
पूजामयाक्षविक्षेप 17.36
पूजाभृतापानमयो येषां 17.34
पूजारम्भे विभो ध्यात्वा 17.32
पूजोपकरणीभूतविश्वावेशेन 17.35
प्रकटय निजधाम देव यास्मिं 12.15
प्रकटय निजमध्वानं 4.3
प्रकटीभव नान्याभिः 6.11
प्रकाशां शीतलामेकां 3.5
प्रतिवस्तु समस्तजीवतः 18.11
प्रत्याहाराद्यसंस्पृष्टो 1.17
प्रभुणा भवता यस्य 3.8
प्रसीद भगवन् येन 5.9
प्रहर्षाद्वाथ शोकाद्वा 5.10
प्रार्थनाभूमिकातीत 19.1

ब

बत नाथ दृढोऽयमात्मबन्धो 4.24
बलिं यामस्तृतीयाय 10.6
बहिरप्यन्तरपि तत्स्यन्दमानं 5.11
बाह्यं हृदय एवान्तर 15.5
बाह्यतोऽन्तरपि 15.16
बाह्यान्तरान्तरायालीकेवले 10.11
ब्रह्मादीनामपीशास्ते 17.7
ब्रह्मेन्द्रविष्णुनिर्व्यूढ 2.13

भ

भक्तानां नार्तयो नाप्यस्त्याध्यानं 20.15
भक्तानां नास्ति संवेद्यं 16.9
भक्तानां भक्तिसंवेगमहोष्म 17.17

भक्तानां भवदद्वैत	1.15
भक्तानां विषयान्वेषा	17.22
भक्तानां समतासार	17.5
भक्तानामक्षविक्षेपोऽप्येष	17.38
भक्ता निन्दानुकारेऽपि	16.10
भक्तिकण्डूसमुल्लासा	20.8
भक्तिक्षीबोऽपि कुप्येयं	16.7
भक्तिक्षोभवशादीश	17.39
भक्तिमदजनित	7.8
भक्तिर्भक्तिः परे भक्तिर्भक्तिर्नाम	16.25
भक्तिर्भगवति	15.15
भक्तिलक्ष्मीसमृद्धानां	20.11
भक्त्यासवसमृद्धाया	9.15
भगवन्नितरानपेक्षिणा	12.11
भगवन्भवतः पूर्णं	6.6
भगवन्भवदि	12.26
भगवन्भवदीयपादयो	12.8
भवतोऽन्तरचारि-भावजातं	12.13
भर्ता कालान्तको यत्र	10.3
भवत्पादाम्बुजरजोराजि	5.2
भवत्पूजामयासङ्गसम्भोग	17.12
भवत्पूजामृतरसाभोग	17.13
भवत्पूजासुधास्वाद	17.9
भवदङ्गगतं	12.20
भवदङ्गपरिष्वङ्ग	6.10
भवदङ्गपरिस्रवत्सु	18.9
भवदङ्घ्रिसरोरुहोदरे	12.9
भवदमलचरण	19.5
भवदात्मनि विश्वमु	8.13
भवदावेशतः पश्यन्	6.5
भवदीयगभीर	12.23
भवदीयमिहास्तु	18.14
भवद्भक्तिमहाविद्या	1.12
भवद्भक्तिसुधासारस्तैः	1.24
भवद्भक्त्यमृतास्वादा	1.11
भवद्भावः पुरो भावी	15.12
भवन्मयस्वात्मनि	18.4
भावा भावतया	12.28
भृत्या वयं तव विभो	10.14
भ्रान्तास्तीर्थदृशो भिन्ना	16.14
म	
मङ्गलाय पवित्राय	2.16
मत्परं नास्ति तत्रापि	3.17
मनसि मलिने	15.14
मनसि स्वरसेन	12.25
महताममरेश पूज्यमानो	4.25
महादेवाय रुद्राय	2.4
महाप्रकाशवपुषि विस्पष्टे	10.21
महामन्त्रतरुच्छायाशीतले	18.10
महामन्त्रमयं नौमि	2.26
महेश्वरेति यस्यास्ति	10.23

माद्दशैः किं न चर्व्येत 1.22
मानावमानरागादि 16.15
मामकमनोगृहीत 7.9
मायामयजगत्सान्द्र 2.15
मायाविने विशुद्धाय 2.12
मायीयकालनियति 15.2
मा शुष्ककटुकान्येव 19.9
मुक्तिसंज्ञा विपक्वाया 16.19
मुनीनामप्यविज्ञेयं 2.24
मुमुक्षुजनसेव्याय 2.21
मूढोऽस्मि दुःखकलितोऽस्मि 11.8
मूलाय मध्यायाग्राय 2.9
मूले मध्येऽवसाने च 20.13
मोक्षदशायां 19.13

य

यः प्रसादलव 8.1
यतोऽसि सर्वशोभानां 16.26
यत्र तत्रोपरुद्धानां 16.12
यत्र देवीसमेतस्त्व 5.7
यत्र सोऽस्तमयमेति विवस्वाँ 4.22
यत्समस्तसुभगा 13.14
यथा तथापि यः पूज्यो 2.20
यथा त्वमेव जगतः 17.29
यथैवाज्ञातपूर्वोऽयं 16.5
यदि नाथ गुणोष्वात्माभिमानो 10.19
यद्यथास्थित 13.7
यद्यप्यत्र वरप्रदोद्धततमाः 11.13
यन्न किञ्चिदपि 12.29
यस्य दम्भादिव भवत्पूजा 12.10
यस्य भक्तिसुधास्नान 16.17
यस्यानारम्भपर्यन्तौ 17.6
यावन्न लब्धस्त्वत्पूजा 17.21
येन नैव भवतोऽस्ति 11.4
येन मनागपि 11.6
येषां प्रसन्नोऽसि विभो 10.8
ये सदैवानुरागेण 10.2
योऽविकल्पमिदम 13.16
यो विचित्ररससेकवर्धितः 4.13

र

रक्षणीयं वर्धनीयं 15.10
रागद्वेषान्धकारोऽपि 16.16
रागादिमयभवाण्डक 7.4
राज्यलाभादिवोत्फुल्लैः 17.33
रुदन्तो वा हसन्तो वा 15.3

ल

लघुमसृणसिता 8.6
लब्धत्वत्संपदां भक्तिमतां 1.3
लब्धाणिमादि 9.18
लोकवद्भवतु 8.3

व

वन्दे तान् दवैतं येषां 20.3
वन्द्यास्तेऽपि महीयांसः 10.20
वर्तन्ते जन्तवोऽशेषा 20.17
विकसतु स्ववपु 8.7
विचरन्योगदशास्वपि 5.21
वियोगसारे संसारे 6.2
विलीयमानास्त्वय्येव 6.7
विश्वेन्धनमहाक्षारा 2.2
विषमस्थोऽपि स्वस्थोऽपि 16.8
विषमार्तिमुषानेन 19.4
वाचि मनोमतिषु तथा 5.22
वेदागमविरुद्धाय 2.7
व्यवहारपदेऽपि 12.24
व्यापाराः सिद्धिदाः सर्वे 17.2

श

शक्तिपातसमये 13.11
शतशः किल ते 12.21
शम्भो शर्व शशाङ्कशेखर 11.11
शान्तकल्लोलशीताच्छ 1.21
शान्तये न सुखलिप्सुता 18.15
शिलोञ्छपिच्छकशिपु 15.8
शिव इत्येकशब्दस्य 1.20
शिवो भूत्वा यजेतेति 1.14
शिवदासः शिवैकात्मा किं 10.25
शिव-शिव शम्भो शङ्कर 4.4
शिव-शिव शिवेति नामानि 5.23
शुष्ककं मैव सिद्धेय 16.4

स

संग्रहेण सुखदुःख 13.1
संसारसदसो बाह्ये 16.28
संसाराध्वा सुदूरः खरतर 15.19
संसारैकनिमित्ताय 2.8
सकलव्यवहारगोचरे 18.7
सततं त्वत्पदाभ्यर्चासु 17.18
सततफुल्लभवन्मुखापङ्कजो 4.16
सततमेव तवैव 18.8
सततमेव भवच्चरणा 8.10
सतोऽवश्यं परमसत्सच्च 3.18
सतो विनाशसम्बन्धा 20.18
सत्येन भगवन्नान्यः 16.6
सत्त्वं सत्यगुणो शिवे 15.18
सदसच्च भवानेव 10.24
सदसत्त्वेन भावानां 3.1
सदा निरन्तरानन्द 2.22
सदा भवद्देहनिवास 18.5
सदा मूर्त्तादमूर्त्ताद्वा 17.46
सदा सृष्टिविनोदाय 20.9
समस्तलक्षणायोग 2.6
समुत्सुकास्त्वां 12.27

समुदियादपि 8.8
समुल्लासन्तु भगवन् 5.8
सर्व एव भवल्लाभ 1.10
सर्वज्ञे सर्वशक्तौ च 10.17
सर्वतो विलसद्भक्ति 1.19
सर्वदा सर्वभावेषु 17.3
सर्वमस्यपरमस्ति न किंचिद् 4.9
सर्ववस्तुनिचयैक 19.2
सर्वाभासावभासो यो 20.16
सर्वाशङ्काशनिं सर्वा 2.28
सहकारि न किञ्चिदिष्यते 12.1
सहसैवासाद्य 9.10
सहस्रसूर्यकिरणाधिक 3.19
साकारो वा निराकरो 16.22
साक्षात्कृतभवद्रूप 12.4
साक्षाद्भवन्मये नाथ 1.4
सितातपत्रं यस्येन्दुः 3.4
सिद्धिलवलाभ 19.14
सुखप्रधानसंवेद्य 2.23
सुधाद्रार्यां भवद्भक्तौ 15.9
स्फारयस्यखिलमात्मना 13.15
स्फुटमाविश 18.20
स्फुरदनन्तचिदात्मकविष्टपे 5.24
स्मरसि नाथ कदाचिदपीहितं 4.20
स्वप्रभाप्रसरध्वस्ता 6.8
स्वरसोदितयुष्मद 18.6
स्ववपुषि स्फुटभासिनि 5.25
स्वसंवित्सार 9.4
स्वातन्त्र्यामृतपूर्णत्व 2.27
स्वादुभक्तिरसास्वाद 17.42
स्वामिन्महेश्वरस्त्वं साक्षात्सर्वं 11.2
स्वामिसौधमभि 13.13
स्वेच्छयैव भवन्निजमार्गे 4.10

ह

हर्षाणामथ शोकानां 3.9
हस्यते नृत्यते यत्र 5.18
हृदि ते न तु विद्यते 11.7
हृन्नाभ्योरन्तरालस्थः 10.26
हे नाथ प्रणतार्तिनाशनपटो 11.14